The Roman Invasion of Britain

The Roman
Invasion of Britain

Archaeology Versus History

Birgitta Hoffmann

First published in Great Britain in 2013
and reprinted in this format in 2019
by Pen & Sword Archaeology
An imprint of
Pen & Sword Books Limited
Yorkshire – Philadelphia

ISBN 9781526756633

A CIP catalogue record for this book is available from the British Library

Typeset in 11pt Ehrhardt
by Mac Style, Beverly, E. Yorkshire

Printed and bound in the UK
by TJ International, Padstow, Cornwall

Pen & Sword Books Limited incorporates the imprints of Atlas,
Archaeology, Aviation, Discovery, Family History, Fiction, History, Maritime,
Military, Military Classics, Politics, Select, Transport, True Crime, Air World,
Frontline Publishing, Leo Cooper, Remember When, Seaforth Publishing,
The Praetorian Press, Wharncliffe Local History, Wharncliffe Transport,
Wharncliffe True Crime and White Owl.

For a complete list of Pen & Sword titles please contact
PEN & SWORD BOOKS LIMITED
47 Church Street, Barnsley, South Yorkshire S70 2AS, United Kingdom
E-mail: enquiries@pen-and-sword.co.uk
Website: www.pen-and-sword.co.uk

Or
PEN AND SWORD BOOKS
1950 Lawrence Rd, Havertown, PA 19083, USA
E-mail: Uspen-and-sword@casematepublishers.com
Website: www.penandswordbooks.com

Contents

List of Illustrations

Vindolanda, praetorium of Fort II and Severan roundhouses. *Birgitta Hoffmann*

Carpow aerial photograph. *David John Woolliscroft*

London city wall, one example of the increasing use of defences around towns from the late third century onwards. *Birgitta Hoffmann*

Caerwent late Roman defences. *Birgitta Hoffmann*

Richborough: in the foreground the ditches of the third century fortlet around the Claudian monument, in the background the defences of the Saxon Shore fort. *David John Woolliscroft*

Scarborough Yorkshire Coast tower. *Birgitta Hoffmann*

Cardiff Castle, South Wall, with Roman, Medieval and modern walling. *Birgitta Hoffmann*

Burgh Castle. *David John Woolliscroft*

Hen Waliau, Caernarvon, late Roman harbour fort. *Birgitta Hoffmann*

Caer Gybi late Roman fort overlooking Holyhead harbour. *Birgitta Hoffmann*

Preface

This book began its life during a lengthy after dinner discussion with various international scholars at the Roman Army School in Durham in 2007 and was actually finished thanks to the persistence of Philip Sidnell, who proved to be one of the most patient and understanding editors, despite some very unexpected 'curve balls'. My sincere thanks to him and to Karen Selley, his colleague, for their efforts.

Many of the points raised in this book are the result of numerous discussions with friends and colleagues in Britain (especially at the University of Liverpool, the Roman Army School and the Roman Northern Frontier Seminar), and at numerous other occasions with friends and colleagues from Germany, the Netherlands, Ireland (especially at UCD and Trinity College) and the United States. There were so many of you, I fear I can't thank you all in person. But wherever you are many thanks for your time and the ability to find me that last interesting reference, just when I was despairing or thought I was done. Special thanks also to Jo Fenton, who read through earlier drafts of many chapters in search of the numerous grammar and spelling blunders that I tend to leave in my manuscripts.

Particular thanks to David Breeze, James Ellis Jones, Jorit Wintjes, Adam Parker and Eberhard Sauer, who took a lot of time despite being busy, to comment on earlier drafts of this book and helped with suggestions and permissions for pictures and maps. I really enjoyed your help and the ensuing discussions, and I apologize for all the times I kept you awake well beyond everybody else's bedtime. Any mistakes that remain are utterly my own; you did your best.

My thanks go to my family. Who despite numerous family disasters of various kinds, always came through in the end. Thanks for believing in me, when I was ready to pack it all in; especially to you, David.

Introduction

At the beginning of the twentieth century the Camden Professor of Ancient History, Francis Haverfield, was compiling evidence for a history of Roman Britain. As a classicist and ancient historian he was well versed in the Greek and Latin ancient sources; on the other hand the increasing amount of archaeological data from excavations in Scotland, Hadrian's Wall, Wales, but also the numerous finds of Roman material from London or the villa sites in the south of England lacked chronological order beyond the information available through the finds of coins and the few inscriptions naming Emperors recovered at the site.

He decided that the literary sources and their accounts could provide, at the time, the most reliable chronological framework for the study of Roman Britain. Thus a collection of relevant historical texts was created, a handlist. This is the basis even today of our understanding of the history of Roman Britain, and it is small wonder that its current (expanded) reincarnations – such as Stanley Ireland's much reprinted Roman Britain: A Sourcebook (2008) can be found on the shelves of most Romano-British archaeologists.

Many, but by no means all of these sources were written by Romans (or at least holders of Roman citizenship), who came from the Mediterranean world, having grown up in various provinces, before pursuing careers in the centre of power, Rome itself, either as politicians, or as writers patronized by politicians and Emperors. Relatively few of them offer irrefutable evidence for first-hand knowledge of the British Isles, and none have a claim to Britain as their home. Consequently the reason their writings mentioned Britain could be many and various, but frequently were not derived from a need to satisfy ethnographical or topographical curiosity. More commonly Britain was the stage on which events important to the Central Government took place. If the interest of the Central Government shifted, the focus shifted and Britain could drop off the historical radar of the Mediterranean historians for long periods.

It is possible that the above picture is exaggerated. After all the writers that we have available today are not the sum total of the literature accessible at the time, but probably only a small percentage of the accounts and writings that may have been around. A new source, whether epigraphic, literary or even numismatical (not to speak of the archaeological evidence, which has slightly different problems) has the power to completely change our perception of events and as such suggests caution in trusting the statements of any one source too implicitly.

Since the first handlist of historical sources was compiled, Romano-British archaeology has tried to expand its knowledge base in all directions and the material that is today available to scholars is infinitely richer than anything that Haverfield could have hoped to analyze. We have, for most of the island, sequences of pottery that create a historical backbone independent (or nearly so) of the historical sources. These sequences allow us to write an account of the Roman period for areas such as Yorkshire, that received little mention by Roman writers; in fact in the early 1990s Martin Millett argued for the irrelevance of much of the written record for the history of Roman Britain (1990).

In the end, however, a coin is just a coin and a pot sherd is just a pot sherd. To advance from a catalogue of archaeological material found at a site and the dimensions of a building excavated, to an account of what we think it was like to live in Roman Britain at point x in time, is a matter of interpretation, and thus dependent on the context in which the archaeologist/historian operates. Archaeological interpretation reflects our own experiences and expectations, often without us realizing it. This is why students today spend a substantial part of their time at university learning archaeological theory – a frequently little loved, but very important aspect of their skills, which (hopefully) informs them about the origins of some of the interpretations they learn and the various levels of reliability of interpretation, as well as some basic concepts of logical deduction. One of the most valuable lessons they can take away from these courses is the realization that with regard to the past, the use of the term 'truth' as a fixed value may be ultimately unachievable. The amount of material recovered, which is usually considered to be between one per cent and 0.1 per cent of what was originally there, makes it unlikely to ever get to the bottom of what really happened at any given time in Roman Britain – in this respect archaeology and modern forensics have very different expectations. The best any researcher can hope for in reconstructing the past is a 'valid' interpretation. The difference is easy and important. Truth is what computer people call binary – it either is or it isn't. A valid statement by contrast is any statement that takes account of all pieces of evidence as they are known at the time.

To use a case in point: in a typical crime novel a murder victim is found shot in a locked house; none of the other six guests in the house can have come or left since the victim was last seen alive. Without any further information all you can hope to achieve is to produce a list of valid suspects: the number of people in the house with the victim (including the victim itself, as at this point no information has been presented to rule out suicide).

Only with further information can you hope to reduce the number of valid suspects. In our case, if the victim was shot in the back, we can rule out suicide. In a satisfactory crime novel, the outcome will result in the final denouement, that one person who cannot be ruled out and for whom clear evidence exists that links them to the crime.

Roman archaeology (like the archaeology of many other periods), can rarely hope to get beyond the creation of the list of likely suspects, and the most we can do is to present a particularly attractive scenario – but it remains just that, one scenario of many.

What not all archaeologists of today realize, but what was already clear to Haverfield and his colleagues, is that the written sources are equally prone to interpretation. None of the texts that were excerpted by the early scholars of Roman Britain exist in isolation. They are the products of the time in which they were written, formed by the intention, knowledge and experiences of their writers, and their content is limited by what the writer and its audience deemed relevant and/or interesting.

Even the way in which something is phrased may have been decided by consideration of style. It may have been deemed a lot more relevant that the paragraph 'flows well', rather than provide utterly accurate but perhaps boring reading. Latin literature was as much, and probably more than modern prose, governed by considerations of acceptable forms of oratory. We may have rules about avoiding repetition, and not starting sentences with 'and', to name a very few; but to a Roman writer, clearly structured prose, carefully polished and displaying full command of Latin or Greek, often showing that they could imitate styles of other writers or turn a good phrase was a form of defining their identity as a truly cultured human being (hence the use of the term '*humanitas*' for this type of display of education).

A lot of the study of ancient history and classics in the last 100 years has been devoted to better understanding the few bits of ancient literature that we have. Only rarely do we still try and establish the best text in terms of what the Latin or Greek actually says. Much more important to classicists today is what it all means. Any parent of a teenager, or any teenager with a parent, will be able to vouch for the fact that these two statements are not synonyms and that a certain amount of care is needed even today to find out what is being said and what it means.

So why should this outline take up the first two pages on a military history of Roman Britain? Part of it is due to the history of the subject: as more information on Roman Britain became available, it has become more and more common to specialize. Today you can have specialists on Roman pottery, on Roman glass, on Roman villas, as well as on Roman military equipment. Few of us are of necessity true generalists and it can be argued that the level of information is now such, that it is pretty impossible for one person to keep up with everything that is written on all fields of Roman Britain. Perhaps this is one reason why there are now so few detailed general accounts of Roman Britain of similar depth to those written by Sheppard Frere (last updated 1987) or Peter Salway (1981) in the late sixties or early eighties. This is not to say that there aren't numerous accounts of Roman Britain on the market; they are usually addressed to beginners or as a general introduction and some (names have been purposely omitted at this point) clearly believe this to be an excuse to reproduce in an uncritical fashion material culled from books several decades old, as little of importance can have changed.

One of the side effects of this expansion of the subject is an inability (for reasons of time as often as not) to engage with material from a neighbouring sphere of expertise. If the deadline is looming, it is only too tempting to drop the trawl through the literature beyond the must read section (and while a lot of care has been taken with this book, the author is sure that there are important articles she will have overlooked), especially in adjoining fields. What this book hopes to achieve, is to point to some of the studies in neighbouring fields (especially classics) that influence our understanding of Roman Britain and especially its military history. This book will be looking at familiar sources, and then comparing them with data from archaeological reports, but also from studies into classical literature and ancient history as well as some other areas. It will thus try to return to first principles in order to determine how much of what we thought we knew about Roman Britain can really be relied on. The resulting accounts may debunk or at least give us pause for thought over some cherished details, some of which may have been based on little else but the Chinese whispers in a century old discipline: this may bring an almost emotional shock to some. Nevertheless, if successful, it should leave our subject with stronger foundations on which, in future, a more reliable structure can be built.

The point of this exercise is not to discredit one source or the other, but to raise occasionally a note of caution in view of our changed understanding of how and why literature was written and read in Rome, and to occasionally provide alternative scenarios that may on present evidence be equally valid. It is hoped that in future it will be possible to gain more information and limit or refine the scenarios, but for the moment the idea is to underline that there are alternatives or at least problems with some of the existing versions of our established history of Roman Britain, which should offer opportunities for further study.

Even in a book this length and with the limited existing amount of evidence for Roman Britain, it is not possible to cover every aspect of the military of Roman Britain. The material covered was chosen, either for its intrinsic importance, or because it illustrates a particular problem of the historical reconstruction. Hopefully, I should be able to demonstrate the way the argument can develop, when all data is combined and induce somebody to take the argument into areas I have not covered. I have, over the years, tried to make myself familiar with the arguments of my friends and colleagues who specialize in ancient literature, but I am the first to admit that while I spent some time studying Latin and Greek to university level and am still teaching Latin, I am not a philologist in the true sense of the word, or of a calibre approaching some of the experts in the field, who have helped me with my enquiries over the years. I hope I have done justice to their considerable efforts to make me understand the finer points of Roman and Greek literature and apologize for any misrepresentation; it derives not from ill-will, but from a passion for making a wider audience understand the importance of their work.

Chapter 1

A Few Things to Consider,
When Reading Ancient Historians

A s this book is about military history, the written accounts of the Romans about their successes and achievements in Roman Britain are going to of necessity dominate the narrative: this is unavoidable. Archaeology is good at recovering the remains of processes that took a considerable time, if only because the occupation of a Roman fort over 400 years is likely to have generated more discarded archaeological evidence (i.e. rubbish), than the overnight stay of an army on the march to a battle site further north or a naval encounter in the middle of the English Channel. Archaeology is just not good at detecting small scale and short-lived historical events, although admittedly cataclysmic events such as the sacking and burning of Colchester and London, or an entire battlefield as at the site at Kalkriese or Kalefeld in Germany, leave their marks in the archaeological record, even if the relevant historical account may not have survived.

We are thus most of the time at the mercy of the historical accounts as left to us by the Romans in word or more rarely images (the Iron Age has so far failed to produce equally identifiable 'speaking' records for us to recognize). 'At the mercy' might not be too strong a term in this context. With the exception of Julius Caesar's Commentaries, we have no records of Romano-British events from the perspective of an eyewitness. Most of our literary sources were written by Mediterranean residents, living for the most part many years and often generations after the events described. Even the accounts of Tacitus of the governorship of his father-in-law Agricola and Dio's account of Severus' campaigns in Britain were composed more than a decade after the events described. None of these would be considered by historians of more recent periods as primary accounts. Tacitus may have been using eyewitness accounts for some of the events described in the

Histories and perhaps the memories of his father-in-law, and there are several occasions in Cassius Dio, where he claims to have been an eyewitness to events in the first half of the third century. However, with increasing distance from the event (be that chronological or geographical) most of the accounts had to be secondary in nature, using earlier accounts, official documents or possibly even oral traditions, written by authors selecting material of variable quality to compose a historical account of their own choosing.

This leads us to the second problem: none of our surviving records offer a history of Roman Britain. All relevant passages (including Agricola's exploits in Britain) were culled from larger documents, usually providing a much wider context, most commonly an account of the history of the Roman Empire at a certain period or a biography of a series of Emperors/Imperial officers. In some cases we are dealing with speeches in praise of individuals, including the Emperors themselves. In other cases the material comes from a text, prose or poetry to which the historical events are all but coincidental. Some sources focus thematically: e.g. a history of early Christianity. This contextualization is important. Developments in Britain are rarely of vital importance to the wider Empire; usually the British sections are just short chapters within a larger whole.

Anybody who has tried to gain an understanding of the military situation of the Anglo-Scottish/Irish wars under Edward I, or the Stuart kings from any social history of Britain under the Plantagenets/Stuarts/Tudors, will be able to relate how much or rather how little of the information of interest to a military historian gets included in these accounts. A similar case applies to ancient sources – Tacitus does not hide his intention to offer a view different to other historians, who he accuses of falsifying the record for various reasons (Hist. I and Annals I). But in addition to his stated aims in his prooemia, Tacitus' Annals are constructed around the concept of a lost *libertas*, offering first and foremost a social study of Rome and the early Emperors and how Roman society was corrupted by their rule; in the process of which he destroyed the reputations of Tiberius, Caligula and Nero. His account lives through lots of vivid details and characterizations. He makes an excellent point and makes his point in extremely well written language – and he has rightly been named as one of the world's best social historians. After all, his account of life under a reign of terror must be one of the best psychological sketches attempted on the topic.

However, and this is worth keeping in mind, whatever has been expressed above in a positive way, can also be expressed negatively: Tacitus is not good at sustained annalistic narrative of factual events. This may seem boring (which is possibly why he didn't use it), but for a military historian, it is essential for a detailed analysis of the progress of a campaign. So the very features that make Tacitus an excellent social historian, work against him in the military arena.

A similar point can be made for nearly all writings with a historical content. The author's thematic choices influence how and why events are included and how they are treated, or whether they were excluded as irrelevant. None of this should come as a surprise to a modern historian. Selection of material is a very important tool of the trade and thus it is hardly surprising to find that it was already practised in Antiquity. After all, few of us would expect an Argentinian history of the Malvinas to culminate in praise of the British forces in the Falklands, or a sympathetic biography of Winston Churchill to be complimentary of the election outcome of 1945. It is, however, interesting that we credit ancient historians with more universal interests than we would expect of their modern counterparts.

Another point is well worth making, or rather repeating: historical writing in Antiquity was meant to entertain, as well as (morally) educate. This may sound a lot more unusual than people give it credit for, and at the same time a lot less usual than people experience nowadays. There is a tradition in European historical writing of the well-researched academic tome, several inches thick, with lengthy annotations at the bottom of the page or the end of the chapter. It is usually prepared by learned historians based at well-established universities, and is sold at exorbitant prices by the specialist bookshop or bought directly from the academic publisher. It is not a requirement of the genre, but many of these volumes are written in difficult, if not impenetrable prose, that cures insomnia; and with some of the older examples you find that one hundred years after publication the pages after 250 are still not cut.

Many of these works are rightly considered pinnacles of scholarship; their presentation of the period carefully balanced and attempting objectivity of account and presentation throughout. But despite the immense amount of time and skill that has gone into writing these books, they tend to have a very limited readership, and their price and language give the appearance of elitism, whether intended or not.

In the other school of writing history, the books are frequently found to be less than 200 pages long, mostly soft-backed and (lavishly) illustrated. There is little referencing to the origins of the material discussed and instead of a comprehensive bibliography they contain a few pages of suggested 'further reading'. But these books tend to be well written (possibly because often they are written by professional writers such as journalists rather than university based academics), entertaining, reasonably priced and frequently very popular with at least that part of the population that is interested in history, including the writers of the large tomes discussed above.

The two cases illustrate the two extremes within the genre of historical writing. There are many books (including, it is hoped, this volume) that sit somewhere in-between and will satisfy both tastes, of the academic and of the non-university-based lover of history.

It would be easy to deride the second school as a recent development of a 'dumbed down society' dallying in 'education lite'. But most teachers would agree that it is much easier to educate on any subject, if you are simultaneously able to entertain and capture your audience. This realization is centuries old, and thus unsurprisingly, entertaining historical writing is the older of the two schools. While the methodology and technique of the worthy tomes was mainly developed in the late 18th and 19th centuries, the readable and entertaining account has been with us since Herodotos. Few of the ancient writers are particularly good at, or interested in, giving direct references to their sources, but most of the surviving texts know 'how to spin a good yarn' (problems with the translations not withstanding) and tell their story well. It is thus no coincidence that in English (as well as French and German) the words for historical writing and storytelling are closely related.

All historians write history on the basis of their own experiences and the times they live in. This may not be readily apparent when the books are first published, as the readership is likely to share the writers' preconceptions, but if a historical account 'feels funny' or seems 'dated' when read thirty years later, then it is likely that the experiences of the readership have changed from those of the writer and his/her original readers. Ten years ago, it was fashionable to talk about the falsification of the historical record or the use of propaganda on display in historical (and visual) sources. Both terms refer to a wilful selection of material and the order (or way) in which it is presented in a source. It is an old adage; that just because events occasionally happen in a particular order, it does not follow that they were caused in that order or because of each other (this belief is sometimes referred to as '*post hoc ergo propter hoc*'). A black cat crossing the road is not usually the cause of bad luck to the witness, despite all proverbial statements to the contrary.

Consequently if you are trying to give the reasons why certain events happened, it may be better as a historian (or storyteller) to change to a causal rather than a chronological order of events or occasions.

The selection of which material to include is a very personal decision by the writer; this may not be readily apparent at the time of reading. Cassius Dio for example has a tendency to be critical of women in positions of power, especially those who act without proper advice from male relatives. It is possible to blame this on his experience of living through two minority reigns, when the Roman Empire was run by empresses as regents for their small sons (Iulia Maesa and Iulia Soaemias for Elagabalus (218/222) and Iulia Mamaea for Severus Alexander (222/235)). Alternatively it could be due to his cultural background as a Greek from Asia Minor, where this sort of behaviour was not widely approved of (if you think this unlikely, reflect on what Winston Churchill thought of Nancy Astor as an MP, and how Wellington would have reacted to the idea of women in Parliament). However, before we think of these fairly transparent sources of 'inspiration', also consider the option that he may be reacting to his possible childhood experiences (domineering mother, bossy sister – the list of possibilities is endless). In the absence of any autobiographical musings or surviving diaries/personal letters by Cassius Dio, all or none of these scenarios may be correct – but, to pick up on an earlier point, all these scenarios would be valid.

Identifying bias in the written record can be comparatively easy, for example when Eusebius appears unable to identify any positive characteristics in Constantine's opponents. Identifying the problem is, however, different from explaining the reasons for this bias, especially if it is less obvious than Eusebius' hero worship. It is then all the more important to discuss the differences in the varying accounts instead of just brushing over them, or summarily declaring one account superior to the other. By exploring the differences we should be able to find out more about the events and the writers involved.

Every now and then the current readers of ancient sources suspect, or in some cases are able to prove, that source material has been intentionally misconstrued or misrepresented to make a political point. In these cases we need to ask age old questions about motive and opportunity, keeping in mind that it is possible that the material may have been subconsciously influenced by the general climate of the time: no falsification or misleading may have been intended; after all the difference between propaganda and blind belief is bound up with whether the author believes what he says.

On the other hand the motives for misrepresentation might be the need for decisive argument in a political speech at a critical point in Rome's history (Tacitus' Agricola and Cicero's Philippics would probably qualify). Opportunity to use this device to good effect might reflect a chance of writing an account or a laudatory speech (such as the panegyrics of the late Empire) for a particularly important person, who may then reward a flattering description of events.

Whatever their motivation, the ancient writers who told the (hi)stories discussed in the current volume, wanted to impart something that they thought important: they saw their stories as part of a wider context. This may have influenced how the stories were told and how much detail (and more importantly which details) was included. This is important if a classical author thought that military success might be dependent on the moral character of the ruler at the time (as Herodian and Eusebius do), or on the character of the general in charge (as Tacitus suggests in the Agricola). Ancient writers saw parallels in how an Emperor dealt with the assassination of his mother and the partially illegal, but unnecessarily cruel integration of a client kingdom into the Roman province (as Tacitus did with regard to Nero's murder of Agrippina and his treatment of Boudicca).

To underline these parallels, authors like Tacitus or Suetonius used literary 'tricks', citing passages from plays that readers should be familiar with, to suggest to readers how they would like to see a particular event judged. Recasting the entire scene, so that it mirrors or imitates the events of the possible parallel is another. These analogies are often what made these ancient accounts more readable and easier to understand, but to a modern historian they can make them more unreliable as our small sample of surviving ancient literature might make us miss important clues. There are also expectations to fulfil, a case in military history is the imitation of Alexander the Great, thought by many Romans to be the greatest general ever – thus any good general should betray traces of Alexander – Pompey did this by adopting a hair style reminiscent of Alexander and calling himself Magnus ('Great'). Another way is to credit a general with similar experiences to Alexander (the stories told about the birth of Scipio Africanus and Alexander were strikingly similar). But it can also happen, by crediting a general with using the same stratagems as Alexander. All of this can make ancient battle descriptions extremely hard to judge – how much is real, how much is flattery?

In addition, there are standard ways in which a battle can be fought; infantry in the middle, cavalry on the side: the aim is to encircle the other army or make it run away, by breaking through its lines. This might even reflect reality. If this is how battles are supposed to be fought according to the handbooks or 'established wisdom', the majority of generals would probably have done so. It is also possible, if no better information was available, that the writers copied this standard engagement pattern, or just referred to it obliquely, by picking out short scenes, rather than risk boring the audience by giving a blow-by-blow account.

The ultimate literary tool is the battle speech. It is well known that these speeches are unlikely to ever have been the great set pieces of oratory we see in historical writing, if only as without a PA system, very few people would have heard the general and the remainder would have become restless. On the other hand, speeches by the enemy are unlikely to have been available as transcripts after the event. However, battle speeches offer the writer the opportunity to summarize the main differences between the two parties, both in their demands, as well as in their approach to war (discipline vs enthusiasm; righteous need for retribution vs untamed bloodlust). It also gives them the opportunity to portray the moral superiority expected of a Roman general in order to win a battle against Rome's enemies. The enemies' speeches on the other hand give the Roman writers a way to voice the arguments against Rome, in a form that would have been at times borderline treasonous if uttered from the mouth of a Roman ('They create a desert and call it peace' is probably the most striking example (Tacitus: Calgacus' speech in the Agricola)).

The one thing to remember about these speeches is that they are the equivalent to our analysis chapter in a campaign description, but they are not authentic: they present the author's view, not the view of the players.

The problem is that unlike the situation for the history of Rome generally (for most of the history of Roman Britain our sources are so thin) we have problems independently verifying the events mentioned, let alone to actually make more than educated guesses whether a divergent view reflects deliberate falsification of history, a genuine mistake or the personal choice of the author, based on experiences unknown to us.

On the other hand for Roman Britain, unlike the senatorial debates in the city of Rome, we have a further control, the archaeological record. Archaeology, as we have seen, may have its limitations, but occasionally it offers additional insights, such as the dendro-date for Carlisle or the construction dates for the Saxon Shore forts that can change our views of a particular passage or more often broaden our understanding and contextualize events that we would otherwise find ourselves at a loss to interpret.

Chapter 2

Caesar Visits Britain

The military history of Roman Britain starts late in the summer of 55 BC. It is one of the weird coincidences of Romano–British history, that at this early point we have next to no archaeological evidence, but at the same time written sources were of a quality not to be rivalled in the 400 years of Roman occupation, including the eyewitness accounts of the Roman general involved (Caesar, de bello Gallico, Book IV 20–36 from now on cited as BG), written a short time after the events. Caesar, one of the leading politicians of the Late Republic, was at this point roughly halfway through a conquest of what is today France, Belgium and the Netherlands; and was balancing his military success with long distance jockeying for position in Rome. The Commentaries, a report on his exploits in Gaul, were at least partially available in Rome soon after the events, and served not only as a report on his progress, but were meant to further his political career, in a way similar to political biographies published today.

According to his account, Caesar started out by gathering ships in the territory of the Morini, using boats from his Gallic 'allies' as well as the navy built for his campaign against the Veneti the year before. He gathered intelligence by inviting the traders dealing in Britain to his tent to advise him, and backed up their scanty information by sending out Gaius Volusenus with one ship on a reconnaissance mission. While waiting for his fleet of (eventually) 80 ships to assemble and be readied for service, he received delegations from British tribes who wanted to offer surrender and hostages as surety for their good behaviour. His Gallic ally Commius, king of the Atrebates and apparently a person of influence in Britain, was sent with them on the return journey to announce Caesar's impending arrival and encourage the British to seek surrender terms with Caesar. Commius, however, was arrested shortly after landing. Volusenus returned soon after, having restricted his exploration to an observation of the coastline. But despite this professed scanty intelligence (and in view of his experiences during the Veneti campaign the year before this needs to be questioned), and the fact that the transports for the cavalry were not ready, Caesar set out with two legions, the Tenth and the Seventh, to invade Britain.

The fleet arrived mid morning in front of the south coast cliffs, with the British army in position on hilltops. Unable to land, Caesar waited for a change of the wind and tide, and then followed the cliffs to the north for seven miles, until he found a flat and even beach to land on, which unfortunately appeared to stretch out as shallows into the sea, making it hard for the ships to move close to shore.

The landing was heavily opposed by the British troops, who had anticipated Caesar's move and deployed cavalry and charioteers, but eventually the legions managed to form up on the beach and charged the enemy successfully. A beachhead was established, but it was impossible to follow up the charge, as the cavalry had not been able to sail and was still in Gaul.

In the following days the British sent delegations to Caesar to sue for peace and to return Commius, pleading general misunderstandings. The handover of more hostages was delayed, as they needed to be brought from further away.

Four days later the cavalry finally attempted to join Caesar, but a sudden storm broke up the eighteen ships and led to them being dispersed along the British coast as well as driving some of them back to Gaul. At the same time, the storm damaged a large number of the ships in Caesar's camp on the beach, causing concerns about the army being left stranded on the island without adequate supplies to last the winter. Caesar ordered the army to supply itself from the surrounding countryside by foraging, and repaired the ships by cannibalizing the most damaged.

This precarious situation encouraged the British to abandon the peace agreement and renew the attacks on the camp, beginning with attacks on the foraging troops in an ambush from which Caesar himself was only able to rescue them in the nick of time. At this point Caesar adds a small excursus on the British use of chariots in battle (BG IV, 33), but there is little exact detail on how the relief manoeuvre worked, except that Caesar described his own involvement in the safe extraction of the Seventh Legion from the ambush.

After another period of bad weather, which restricted the legions to the camp, but allowed the British to gather more forces, another battle ensued. Caesar fought with only the 30 horsemen of Commius' retinue and the two legions, but managed to gain a victory, although without being able to pursue the enemy, even though the Romans managed to kill 'not a few of them'. As a consequence the British tribes once again sent delegations suing for peace and offered the hostages withheld up to now, which were transported to the Continent. Caesar and the two legions embarked just before the equinox and returned to the Continent.

Caesar's second season
The next year, 54 BC, Caesar decided to return to Britain, and, as before, the most detailed source is his own account (BG V, 1–23, esp. 8–22): his second attempt was clearly better organized, as he used the winter to order the troops to build and repair another fleet to specific designs devized by Caesar himself. Eventually over 800 ships would be available, which he ordered to assemble at Portus Itius. The crossing, initially postponed because of trouble brewing in Gaul, was once again problematic, as the fleet was blown off course, and the Romans were only with great effort returned to best landing ground found in the previous year.

The British, who had been assembling at the site, withdrew when the size of the fleet became apparent. Caesar chose a campsite, of which we are later told, that it was linked with the landing site with a single entrenchment. Leaving the site in the charge of one Quintus Atrius, he proceeded at night and engaged the enemy several miles inland near a river crossing: they having moved their cavalry and chariots from the higher ground to the river. The British troops were driven back by the Roman cavalry and withdrew to a fortified camp in the woods, which the Romans eventually took by building a ramp (*agger*). The pursuit of the enemy was broken off when Caesar received reports of substantial damage to the fleet following a storm. He withdrew to oversee the repairs and ten days later returned to learn that the British had elected a leader called Cassivelaunus, the ruler of a kingdom some 80 miles away across the Thames, at which point Caesar inserts a description of Britain and its inhabitants and resources (BG V, 12–14). When he returns to the subject of the campaign, he describes the fighting encountered on the march, and an attack by the British on a Roman marching camp under construction, during which the tribune Quintus

Laberius Durus was killed. A further excursus on the fighting tactics of the British rounds off this description.

'The next morning' a foraging party was attacked, but the attack was driven off and no further full strength attacks followed. Caesar now divulges that he intended to take the army to the Thames to face Cassivelaunus in his own territory. The only (and difficult) ford was found to be defended by sharpened stakes under the water and on the opposing bank, but again the speed and determination of the Roman forces won through and the British fell back. Cassivelaunus disbanded his troops and changed strategy by withdrawing cattle and humans into the woods and harrying the Roman cavalry sent out to plunder and devastate the area, forcing Caesar to keep his men close together and limit his destruction to the area covered by the legions' march (BG V, 19).

In Caesar's account the action then switched to the Trinovantes, who approached him requesting help against Cassivelaunus. They were linked to Mandubracius, apparently a Trinovantian prince who had already approached Caesar in Gaul seeking help against Cassivelaunus, who had killed his father. In exchange for supplies and hostages, Caesar agreed to make Mandubracius king and protect him against Cassivelaunus. This resulted in visits from other tribes, named as the Cenimagni, Segontiaci, Ancalites, Bibroci and Cassi, who had surrendered to Caesar and revealed to him the position of Cassivelaunus' stronghold, which was consequently attacked and conquered. As a result Cassivelaunus' troops fell back.

According to Caesar, Cassivelaunus had used the interim time to make contact with four of the kings of the Cantii and arranged for them to attack the Roman camp and ships. But the attack was foiled by a Roman sortie. Consequently, Cassivelaunus was forced to start negotiations, with the assistance of Commius the Atrebatian. As time was once again running out for Caesar, who needed to return to Gaul before the autumn equinox made the crossing more hazardous, he stated what hostages and tribute were to be offered and ordered Cassivelaunus to stay away from the Trinovantes and Mandubracius. Foul weather again beset the crossing and in the end Caesar only just made it back to Gaul in time. He then rapidly became embroiled in the Gallic rebellion, which eventually ended with the Siege of Alesia, and this precluded any further plans he may have had for Britain.

Caesar's account is well written (as even his contemporaries admitted) and has been familiar to generations of pupils as one of the first texts to be read in school Latin. Its concise prose and frequent changes between 'heroic adventure' and apparently disinterested 'ethnographic' description, not to mention the device by which Caesar referred to himself in the third person, as if from the perspective of a detached observer, gives the impression of a reliable and objective eyewitness account. But is it?

There are very few fixed points in Caesar's story: he started from the territory of the Morini, in the first season, which was closest to Britain. This suggests the Pas de Calais or West Flanders, but the location of either the principle harbour, or the one further north used by the cavalry, was not stated. In the second year, the campaign started from Portus Itius – which is usually assumed to be Boulogne sur Mer, but could also be Wissant. The only clear indication of where the landing place was on the British side is that it was 7 miles from where Caesar first encountered the cliffs. It appears to have been in Kent, and about 80 miles from the Thames, towards which Caesar's troops moved overland during the advance of the second season. The river Thames is the only other fixed point in the whole story, and acted as a major dividing line in the story of the second campaign. In between we hear of battles involving woods and hills or, north of the Thames, woods, hills and marshes. Most of these references are so generic that they create impressive mental pictures, but do little to help identify progress on a map. But, before we turn to attempts by modern scholars to follow Caesar on the ground, it is probably better to deal with his text and how it fares in comparison to other sources. A few ancient writers also provide accounts of Caesar's activity in Britain. For example, there is material in Cicero's Letters and in Strabo (Geographica 4,5,3), Cassius Dio (Histories), Suetonius (Life of Caesar) and Plutarch (Caesar 23.3). Most of these references are extremely short, and with the possible exception of Cicero (who had at least his brother's account for comparison), at least partially dependent on Caesar's own account. Cicero's evidence takes the form of a number of snippets from letters between his friends and family, two of whom, Gaius Trebatius Testa and Cicero's brother Quintus, were at the time serving with Caesar in Britain and thus in a position to provide him with independent eyewitness information. Unfortunately, what has survived are not their letters to Cicero, but only his replies to his brother and his summary of their information in letters to his friend Pomponius Atticus (Quintus' brother-in-law) (ad. Fam. 7.6.2; 7.7.1 and *epistulae ad Quintum fratrem* 3.1.10 and *Epistulae ad Atticum* 4.15.10, 4.16.7 and 4.18.5). Most of the letters concerning Britain seem to date to the period between the first and second campaigns and illustrate the vacillations of at least one senator, between hopes for wealth and the fears (in the end substantiated) that these expectations might not be fulfilled (Rice Holmes 1907, 328–9).

One of the critical points in this respect is Caesar's motivation for invading Britain. He himself mentioned two: a) that British warriors had interfered in his campaign in Gaul by acting as foreign auxiliaries (and an earlier reference to British warriors can be found during the campaign against the Veneti (BG III, 9)), and b) the need to explore the island. The first seems straightforward from a military perspective, but the second needs more explanation.

Rome's knowledge of Britain in the middle of the first century BC was in a peculiar state. Theoretically, since the fourth century BC, a geographical account of astounding detail existed for the British Isles and North Sea in the form of the description by Pytheas of Massalia (Cunliffe 2008, 8). However, the account was so colourful, that it was dismissed by the likes of Polybius and Strabo (the latter's own account post-dated Caesar's campaigns) as probably fictitious (Clarke 2001, 97–98). In the popular imagination, meanwhile, Britain enjoyed something of a reputation as a semi mythical island at the end of the world, where strange things could happen, in many ways similar to more recent myths about Shangri-La or El Dorado. On the other hand rumours of the economic wealth of the island, beginning with tin and including silver and gold, were current in Rome, to judge from Cicero's disappointment when Caesar (who was looking for it at the wrong end of the island) found no such treasures. Caesar himself mentioned Gallic traders with Britain, who he tried to debrief before the first campaign, but to judge from the results with little success. Archaeologically this pre-Caesarian Continental trade can be identified through finds of Roman material tracing a trade route through Gaul to the coast at Brittany (the area occupied by the Veneti and Osismi according to Caesar and Strabo) and on through southern British harbours, such as Christchurch Bay and centres such as Hengistbury Head or Mount Batten further west (Cunliffe 1995, 59–63; Matthews 1999, 191). However, whilst amphoras reached Britain, Roman traders may not have been directly involved in the trade, and so Caesar's expedition may have seemed attractive to Rome as a way of opening new trade routes, a fact that Brodersen links to the presence of boats built by individuals for their own convenience during the second campaign (Goldsworthy 2006, 280; Brodersen 1998, 22–23). This commercial interest may have been on Caesar's mind too, especially during the second campaign; for he complained that Cassivelaunus removed people and animals out of the way of the advancing Roman army, denying them the chance of plundering at will in the agriculturally rich area he had just described in his excursus (BG V, 19).

This economic warfare angle may sound more like something from the early history of the East India Company, but it receives some support from another episode in the Gallic Wars. A year before the first British invasion, Caesar fought and eventually nearly eradicated the Veneti on the west coast of Gaul. Caesar described them as the most powerful nation along the coast, with purpose-built boats designed to cope with the conditions in the Channel and (thus) controlling the trade with Britain. Caesar was keen to stress the fact that the Veneti initiated the war by imprisoning Roman ambassadors and demanding the return of their own hostages. Strabo (Geog. 4,4,1), however, saw the real motive for this campaign as a war to stop Caesar taking over their trade. If this were so, then one of the outcomes of Caesar's engagement with the Veneti may actually still be visible in the archaeological record, for around the middle of the first century BC the trade pattern along the Atlantic coast changed dramatically. Whilst before, the majority of the trade was conducted via Brittany and the western British harbours, the material associated with the latter part of the century concentrates in the eastern part of Britain and suggests that trade now focused on the ports of the Pas de Calais.

Christian Meier (1995) has added a further dimension to Caesar's motives, bound up with contemporary events in Rome. In 55BC Rome was controlled by the Triumvirate, an informal and unconstitutional agreement, dividing power between Pompey, Caesar and Crassus. In the city Pompey was at the zenith of his influence: Caesar had had a free reign in Gaul for some years, but there were growing voices demanding his recall. The only way to evade this pressure was to outperform the other two Triumvirs, Crassus and Pompey. Unfortunately, Caesar had broken a truce with a Germanic tribe earlier in 55BC, leading to a massacre. The situation was serious, as Rome's Senate could potentially recall Caesar and hand him over to the offended party as redress and as a restitution of good faith. Caesar thus needed to produce some outstanding feats of public relations to improve his standing back home. Bridging the Rhine (earlier in 55 BC) and crossing to Britain were two such adventures, especially as he could exploit Britain's reputation as the semi-mythical island at the end of the world to make it look almost as though he was setting off for an equivalent to El Dorado. Although he was barely able to move inland during the first campaign, he seems to have achieved this aim, so that the censure was deflected and the Senate voted twenty days of public thanksgiving for his achievements that year.

At the same time Pompey dedicated his theatre, the first permanent entertainment venue in Rome, and Caesar began planning two huge public building projects: his forum, and the Diribitorium (a place for the votes of the assemblies to be counted). The spin was that whilst Pompey was wasting money on entertainment, he was providing Rome with necessary administrative and commercial space – to the tune, eventually, of over 100 million sesterces. Moreover Caesar's success in Gaul had managed to parallel Pompey's huge conquests in the East a decade earlier, at least in as much as they took Roman arms to the opposite end of the known world. During the winter of 55/54 BC, Caesar encouraged Crassus' dreams of waging war against the Parthians (which would eventually end in the disaster of Carrhae), but to keep up with Crassus' anticipated victory in the East, he needed to make a similar conquest in the West and Britain remained the only place open to him. The fact that he also had to find large amounts of money for his building projects in Rome suggests that he would have welcomed the chance of putting Britain's reputation as a land of riches to the test. None of this addresses another point, however: what physical evidence do we have for Caesar's presence? The short answer to this is: none. Despite the fact that a camp for two legions in the first year, and another for several legions and 800 ships in the second should have left large collections of pits and probably defences, none has so far come to light. There is no equivalent in Britain to the impressive Roman structures surrounding Alesia, but admittedly, so far, we also have little evidence in Gaul for Caesarian winter camps away from the famous siege sites. This does not mean, however, that researchers have not tried to identify Caesar's line of march to the Thames and beyond, his likely landing ground and/or the sites of the various fortifications he attacked. Such attempts can be traced back at least to the 19th century, with Thomas Lewin's 'The Invasion of Britain by Julius Caesar' (1859/1862). Much of this research was summarized by T. Rice Holmes in 1907 and, although not always acknowledged, this study still underpins much of what we believe today about the progress of the campaign. His material is divided between a narrative account of the campaign and a series of well researched and referenced considerations of particular aspects of it. These include the landings places and various sites that may or may not be connected.

One of the most persistent problems remains the site of the landings. Stukeley appears to have been the first to suggest the shingle beach between Walmer and Deal (Itinerarium Curiosum 2nd edition, 1776, 126–127), but Rice Holmes spent considerable time discussing the question (1907, 519–525) and when reviewing the coastal and geographical evidence then available, he was able to show that the beach is extremely changeable in nature, with alternating periods of erosion and deposition at least since the Tudor period and only regarded the issue as resolved with the location of a Roman cemetery found in 1886 during the construction of the new church at Walmer. According to English Heritage records (Site no. TR 35 SE 13 and 14), the material found consisted of two skeletons associated with Roman pottery found at the bottom of a 50 feet long trench. Iron Age pottery and a lead vessel were found in an adjoining property. These finds, despite being donated to the Deal Corporation can no longer be located, which makes it hard to say anything specific about the age or nature of the cemetery; but the fact that the burial rite was inhumation would suggest a late Roman date, rather than one from the first century BC. Moreover, according to Rice Holmes the erosion or deposition at Deal was, in his mind, a simple question of the shore moving east-west although with frequent changes in intensity. We now know that the erosion and deposition patterns are more complex with elements of longshore drift, erosion and deposition according to storms and the changing sea levels in the area, plus of course any problems caused by eddies and cross currents originating in an open Wantsum Channel. This has led some researchers to wonder how Caesar could have landed at Deal without realizing the anchorage available in the nearby Wantsum Channel, originally a navigable sound that separated the Isle of Thanet from the mainland. The exact shape of the channel at the time is still very much a matter of debate. But our understanding of the historical topography and geography of the area has markedly changed. We have known since the 1950s that the shape and size of the eastern outlet of the Wantsum Channel is very much determined by the Stonar Bank and the extent of the shingle spit at its eastern end. When discussing Caesar's landings Grainge points to the fact that a lot of it hinges on the existence and extent of this shingle spit forming due to the longshore drift (2002, 9–12). As, frankly, we still have little understanding of how the spit appeared in 55 and 54 BC (and Rice Holmes' account makes it clear that it could change considerably even within 100 years) there is little chance of finding the exact landing site. The chances are that it lay somewhere between Kingsdown in the south and Cliff End, near

Ramsgate, in the north, the locations where the cliffs begin again. Caesar described the first year's landing site as *plano et aperto* (even and open). Grainge (2002, 11) interprets this as open to the sea, but given the closeness of the cliffs it can also mean free of rocks. The site of the second season landing is described as the best disembarkation point: *mollis et aperto* (soft and open). Grainge suggests that Caesar meant muddy underfoot here, as opposed to hard sand or shingle and an area again open to the sea. *Mollis*, however, can also mean gentle and pleasant, and in this context might not actually mean anything other than a perfect beach location. In fact Caesar only uses the word two other times in the entire de bello Gallico: at 3,19 he describes the mindset of the Gauls as *mollis* (implying unable to withstand adversity), whilst at 7,46 during the operations at Gergovia, he describes the time and distance needed to attack the Aedui and refers to the extra distance incurred to make the ascent more gentle as *ad molliendum clivum*. On this parallel it seems best to accept *mollis* as meaning gently sloping rather than as referring to the consistency of the actual ground. *Apertus* means open in every way. It can be open as in exposed to the sea, but given the preceding description of the nearby cliffs, it is just as possible to use it to describe a wide beach situation not overlooked or fringed by rocks. As a result it is impossible to identify the original landing place from the text alone – although despite the extent of coastal erosion and deposition, known to have taken place just in the last few centuries, it still remains a possibility that at some point in the future the second campaign beachhead camp, which was occupied for nearly three months and the site of some fighting, might become archaeologically visible, perhaps through a scatter of Roman military finds, and/or coinage of the mid first century BC.

Another site that continues to make it onto maps as a place where a Caesarian presence can be assumed is Bigbury Camp, Harbledown (English Heritage Site No. TR 15 NW 33). The fort was initially suggested by Rice Holmes as the site of the first battle of the second campaign, on the basis of a general consideration of the surrounding terrain, and also because prehistoric remains had been found within it (Rice Holmes 190, 337, and 253). In 1962/1963, excavations by Jenkins in the entrance of this univallate hillfort produced two postholes in the bottom of the ditch along with early Iron Age pottery and an ovoid slingshot 'similar to one from a hillfort in Belgium' (English Heritage HER record for TR 15 NW 33). There is, though, no evidence for late Iron Age activity at the site, contemporary with the Caesarian invasions. Moreover, the find of a 'slingshot' on the site, even if it was of the Roman type, is no evidence for an association with Caesar. It might just as easily represent military activity at any point up to the middle of the second century AD or, just possibly, civilian hunting. Such arguments might appear to be nit-picking, but they are important in raising a more general question that we shall meet again and again: how much real information are we likely to get from Caesar or indeed any other historical text? Most of our classical sources were men whose entire training was designed to create orators, writers and statesmen who could express themselves and their intentions eloquently. This is not to say that in everyday life such Romans never misspoke, but when they composed literature the chances are that if we cannot gain a clear understanding of what they mean, we either possess a flawed manuscript (and such cases will concern us later) or the authors may actually have wanted to be obscure. Caesar's de bello Gallico is not a diary, but a public document by an active politician with axes to grind and a lot to lose.

When reading Caesar, it is easy to forget that he was not operating in a vacuum; he was actually writing numerous letters to influence the political situation in far away Rome. Some of the replies to those letters, or the comments they spawned, are preserved in Cicero's correspondence, and it is possible to cross reference Cicero's letters with Caesar to gain firmer dates as to when, within the second campaign, certain events happened. Rice Holmes (1907, 329ff) spent considerable effort in doing just this and enables us to provide a more detailed framework. On 5 July 54 BC Cicero wrote to Atticus that he expected his brother Quintus to be in Britain by now, but that he had not yet heard anything (Att., iv, 15, § 10; Rice Holmes, 1907, 333). A letter from Cicero to Quintus (Q. fr. Ii, 15 (16), § 4) was sent in the first week of August, acknowledging receipt of a letter detailing his arrival in Britain. A second letter to Quintus (Q.fr., iii, 1, § 10) was written on 1 September in reply to a letter written from Britain before 16 July, saying:

> Caesar wrote me a letter on the 5th of August, which reached me on the 31st, satisfactory enough as regards affairs in Britain, in which, to prevent my wondering at not getting one from you, he tells me that you were not with him when he reached the coast.

> (*Ex Britannia Caesar ad me Kal. Sept. dedit litteras, quas ego accepi A.D. IIII. Kal. Octobr., satis commodas de Britannicis rebus, quibus, ne admirer quod a te nullas acceperim, scribit se sine te fuisse, cum ad mare accesserit. Ib., § 25.*) (Rice Holmes 1907, 349)

The content of both letters is preserved in one of Cicero's letters to Atticus:

> On the 26th of September I received letters from my brother Quintus
> and from Caesar dated from the nearest coasts of Britain on the 29th of
> August. They had settled affairs in Britain, received hostages, and
> imposed tribute, though they had got no booty, and were on the point
> of bringing the army back.

> (*A Quinto fratre et a Caesareaccepi A.D. IX. Kal. Nov. litteras, datas a
> litoribus Britanniae proximis A.D. VI. Kal. Octobr. Confecta Britannia,
> obsidibus acceptis, nulla praeda, imperata tamen pecunia, exercitum e
> Britannia reportabant.* Ad Att., iv, 18, 5.) (Rice Holmes 1907, 350)

Thus Caesar and Quintus were still writing letters from Britain on 29
August 54 BC, three weeks before the equinox, so Caesar's concern of
missing the window for leaving Britain before the autumn storms set in was
genuine. But knowing that the events described happened between the
beginning of July and the end of September and that most of the fighting
appears to have been over by the end of August helps us only so much. Or
does it? For a start, having these dates adds some understanding of how long
certain parts of the campaign took. In Caesar's account, the run up to the
storming of Cassivelaunus' stronghold appears to have taken up a significant
part of the campaign. But, if this is correct, the entire campaign including
the harrying of Cassivelaunus' territory can have taken no more than 4–6
weeks, because Caesar was back at the coast by 5 August (although clearly
not with all of the army as Quintus was still elsewhere). It is tempting to link
back to Caesar's account and suggest that he may have hurried back to the
ships to deal with the threat posed by the kings of Kent. On the other hand
his account of the period in question is beset with problems. By
interspersing the descriptions of British geography and habits between
reports on different parts of the campaign, Caesar created a series of
episodes that are hard to pinpoint geographically and whose chronological
interrelationship becomes obscure. In short he gives a lively account of his
progress, without giving much in the way of hard information.

It is true, however, that until he reached the Thames, Caesar's progress
may seem predictable from our perspective and the Iron Age Britons might
have seen it in the same light. Given adequate indications that his landing
point was somewhere between the South Foreland and the Isle of Thanet,
his progress towards the Thames would have been forced to follow roughly

the route of one of the two modern motorways through Kent, if only because any other approach would have involved major detours in the Downs or the marshes of the Thames Estuary. But geographical problems return, when the vicinity of Greater London is reached. Rice Holmes suggested two possible fords across the Thames. Both may be old, but unfortunately the position of fording points is not necessarily stable and flash floods or storms can change the bed of a tidal river; indeed the status of a ford can be as much determined by the accessibility of the banks as the depth and stability of the riverbed. However, few riverbanks can have changed quite as much in appearance between the Roman period and today as the Thames in the London area. Thus the chance of identifying the Caesarian site depends on pinpointing a cluster of contemporary Roman finds. Sadly, given London's chequered history, Rice Holmes' report of the discovery of some random wooden piles (which could not be dated as the modern dendrology technique had not yet been developed) provided no evidence by itself, as they could represent anything from a ford closure after bad weather, to a Tudor mooring jetty, to a medieval fish trap pile.

Having raised such problems, this may be a good opportunity to review our chances of identifying other Roman battlefields in Britain and elsewhere. By spring 2010, three Roman battlefields had been positively identified through archaeology. One is in Spain and relates to the Republican period, and two are in northern Germany, at Kalkriese and Kalefeld. In addition a number of other siege sites have been located, be they with the Romans as besiegers or besieged, including Alesia, Masada, Amida, Velsen, Vetera and Krefeld-Gellep. Archaeologically these are characterized by the spread of mostly small pieces of military and horse equipment from both sides, with the Roman material easier to identify, simply because the Roman army has been so closely studied. Usually the most common finds are hobnails from Roman shoes, and projectiles such as arrows, bolts, spears and lance heads. Dating tends to be provided by the occasional small denomination coin, while the outcome of the battle can be seen in the provision of mass graves for humans and large pits for animal carcasses such as horses. Experience has, though, shown that identifying battlefields of any era requires large scale coverage of an area by field walking and, increasingly, metal detecting, and thus it is nearly always restricted to open country. Despite Britain being one of the leaders in the field for battlefield archaeology of other historical periods, for Roman times we so far lack concrete evidence. Despite numerous sites having been put forward for a series of historically attested encounters (not least Mons Graupius), none have so far been verified archaeologically. There is better evidence for the sacking of cities or forts (e.g. London, Colchester, and possibly Silchester), but we will deal with this evidence when we deal with the Boudiccan uprising.

In the meantime it is fair to ask about the legacy of Caesar's British campaigns. In fact, this is hard to measure. As the second campaign progressed, events elsewhere were increasingly occupying Caesar's attention. Gaul was rapidly descending into serious revolt under the leadership of Vercingetorix, which would require serious warfare to control, before Rome's final victory at Alesia. Perhaps more importantly for Rome, Caesar's daughter Julia, the wife of Pompey, died in childbirth during the summer. While there is little doubt that Julia was loved by both father and husband, her main political role had been as the guarantor of goodwill between them: the two most powerful politicians in Rome at the time. Her death destabilized a precarious situation, especially as Crassus, third Triumvirate partner had provoked war with the Parthian Empire during the summer of 54 BC, resulting in his death and the destruction of his army at Carrhae in Syria a year later. The Triumvirate was thus in tatters and Caesar must have seen his problems in leaving Britain with increasing misgivings, because this time it was not just a question of keeping his army supplied away from its now well established logistical system in Gaul. He now found himself marooned on an island, at a point in his career where being in speedy and constant contact with the Continental political scene was vital. The summer of 54 BC can be seen as one of the turning points of Caesar's (and in many ways Rome's) fortunes.

As a result of all these events, Caesar rapidly lost interest in Britain. Under the circumstances it is hard to see who stood to benefit more from the rapidly negotiated treaty between Cassivelaunus and Caesar. It is probably fair to say that both were keen to see the episode concluded. It is even tempting to see Caesar's description of the second campaign in the light of such considerations. His episodic treatment is very different in style from either his description of the first campaign or the vivacious accounts of his exploits in Gaul. It still has the battle scenes and feats of derring-do, but the interspersion of geographical data breaks any arc of tension that exists in other parts of the Gallic War. It reads as if he were going through the motions, rather than putting his heart into the tale. History, or at least Roman historiography, dealt with the British campaigns with a certain amount of damnation by faint praise. The campaigns had not brought Rome much wealth; the treasures of gold and silver had not materialized, and in the short to medium term little of benefit had resulted, especially as there is doubt as to when (if ever) the tribute promised by Cassivelaunus to Caesar was paid. Tacitus put a positive gloss on things by saying that Caesar did not so much conquer the island, as showed it to the Romans (Tac.Agr.13), as if this was a conscious reconnaissance in force; or put more bluntly, according to Tacitus, Caesar never meant to do more than 'check the place out'. The most poisonous comment must be Lucan's, who summarized Caesar's exploits in his epic poem Pharsalia (5.572). His quip, like all good sound bites, was often repeated, especially by British writers up to the 18th century, including Geoffrey of Monmouth (History of the Kings of Britain 4.9). Caesar, he said, 'Came looking for the British and then terrified, turned tail.' *(Caesar Territa Quaesitis ostendit terga Britannis).*

Chapter 3

Commius and the Caesarian Aftermath

While the history of Roman Britain is dominated by the Romans, every now and then the British opposition is allowed more than a few lines of generic statements, usually stressing their courage, but lack of discipline; and the Roman sources, especially of the first century introduce the names of individual 'players'. The way the British opposition is usually portrayed, one would expect that they are presented as 'the enemy' and thus the bad guys in the Roman sources, but some of these names acquire enough detail that it is permissible to treat them as characters in a literary sense, instead of bit parts, and one is left with the impression that they were meant to engage the sympathies of the readers, as much as their eventual defeat was seen as inevitable: after all they are the enemies of Rome.

The first example of this dates from the Caesarian invasions, but is not Mandubracius, as one might expect, but Commius of the Atrebates. Caesar first mentioned him on the eve of the first British invasion (BG IV, 21) when he is described as a king of the Gallic Atrebates of Caesar's making, apparently because of his courage and discretion. Caesar sent him as an envoy to the various British tribes, to encourage their surrender in advance of the planned invasion. However this plan did not succeed; after the battle on the beach, Commius is found a captive and released as part of the exchanges of hostages by the defeated British tribes. During the chariot battle (BG IV, 35) at the end of the first season, Commius, or rather his accompanying horsemen prove decisive. As a result, Caesar rewarded him with tax exemption and made another tribe in Gaul tributary to him.

However, during the Gallic uprising under Vercingetorix, we find Commius suddenly on the side of the uprising, acting as the commander of the relief force at Alesia. However, he managed to escape, and in the aftermath of the battle and lost uprising he continued to offer further resistance to the Romans in the north of Gaul, especially amongst the Bellovaci and the Atrebatic territory. After a considerable time as a 'freedom fighter', eventually he surrendered to Mark Anthony on terms, offering hostages for his good behaviour and on condition of him being left alone by the Romans, to the extent that in future he would not have to meet another Roman face to face (Caesar/Aulus Hirtius BG VIII, 47).

The reason for this change of allegiance is never explained by Caesar, who just stated that he changed sides; but his successor as author Aulus Hirtius, who wrote the 8th book of the Gallic Wars, offered very different insights. Throughout the first seven books Labienus, one of Caesar's senior generals is described as a trusted legate of Caesar and frequent excuses, or at least alleviated circumstances, are found for his occasional failures. Aulus Hirtius, writing after Labienus defected to the opposite side in the Roman Civil War, is a lot less charitable about the general's attitudes and abilities. He informed us that Commius changed sides after Labienus ordered Volusenus (the man who reconnoitred the British coast before Caesar's first landings) to assassinate Commius upon hearing that Commius had apparently talked to some of the future leaders of the uprising (Caesar/Aulus Hirtius, BG VIII, 23). The assassination attempt failed, but left Commius seriously wounded (and it seems disenchanted with the Romans). Commius vowed revenge, which he eventually achieved by seriously wounding at least Volusenus. Despite being described only in the 8th book, and thus years after the uprising, Aulus Hirtius made it clear that this event happened at the eve of the Gallic uprising, thus shortly after having been rewarded by Caesar himself and thus provides a context for the unusual lenient treatment of Commius (he appears to be the only one of the leaders of the uprising who is offered terms and survives).

However, c. 100 years later, Frontinus (an experienced Roman general of the Flavian period, about whom we will have to talk more later) wrote a compendium of 'Stratagems in War' and included an episode relating how Commius escaped from Gaul to Britain, by hoisting sail, despite being stranded on a sandbank, thus fooling the pursuing Caesar into thinking that he was already out of reach (Frontinus, Strat 2,13).

There is clearly a story missing between the surrender to Mark Antony and the Frontinus episode, and we are at a loss to explain why Commius would have wanted to escape Gaul. Either way, this incident is the last time we hear of the historical Gallic Commius the Atrebate.

Archaeology, or more exact numismatics provide at the same time a different type of evidence. Here we see a series of coins, which seem to date to after the Caesarian invasion, bearing the name of Commius, and later on several other series of coins, which name Tincomarus, Epillus and Verica, all 'sons of Commius'. As space on coins is restricted most of the names are abbreviated and there are several variations in spelling, but they appear to belong to the same four individuals. Their distribution through Southern Britain varies in detail, but appears to centre on the later Romano-British civitas of the Atrebates, which is why they are frequently named Atrebatic coinage, and the four names are occasionally referred to as the Atrebatic dynasty.

At this point the numismatic evidence ends and interpretation begins: it has until recently become enshrined in Roman military history to see in the Gallic man discussed above, the same Commius who strikes the coins in Britain, and the father of Tincomarus (also sometimes, confusingly, known as Tincommius), Epillus and Verica. He is seen as the founder of one of the two great British dynasties, establishing the British kingdom of the Atrebates (and sometimes also of the Regnii). In older literature, he and his followers were credited with the 'Second Belgic invasion', thus explaining the strong cultural affinities between southern Britain and the Gallic Continent. In more recent years John Creighton (2006, 24) even suggested that Commius may have been made king of the *British* Atrebates on the say-so of Caesar; and that his sons, who Creighton equated with the hostages handed over to Mark Antony, were raised in Rome, as they copied later in life Roman coin types and used coin types similar to friendly kings in other parts of Rome.

So, how sure can we be of this interpretation? As was pointed out in the introduction, there is simply no way of knowing. The poverty of the records for the Roman period precludes even in the best-case scenarios any hope of accurate reconstruction. The best we can hope for are *valid* scenarios, scenarios that fit all the available evidence and information. However, as stated earlier, the big difference between the two is the fact that there is the possibility of more than one valid scenario, especially if there is only limited material available.

So, is the above a valid scenario and is it the only one? What problems would a critical assessment of the current evidence point out? The problems start with the name of the person in question. How common was the name Commius? No medieval European historian would assume that any two Henrys are likely to be the same, unless there is a lot of circumstantial evidence. In fact, Commius is not a unique name; in a period when we probably have fewer than 200 individuals known with Celtic names in Britain, we have at least two 'Commius'; one who is striking coins in the Dobunnic territory and the other in the Atrebatic territory (Van Arsdell 1989, 279 cited via Braund 1996,73).

There is also an issue of chronology: Verica, Commius' son was alive in the reign of Caligula and the beginning of Claudius' (c. 30/40 AD) when he apparently came for help to Rome. His brother Tincomarus/Tincommius came to Rome in the reign of Augustus, probably between 10 BC/10 AD. We have little indication how long their individual reigns lasted, but the Gallic Commius was, in the late 50s BC, a seasoned warrior and even five years earlier a man of great influence, so the assumption that he was in his thirties might not be too far fetched. Assuming that Commius started a new family on arrival in Britain, that would see Verica in his seventies. This is not impossible by modern standards, but would be unusual in view of the much-reduced life expectancies of the later Iron Age. The royal Atrebatic family tree would actually work better if there were another generation interpolated: Commius the Gaul the grandfather, the British Commius, being the father, followed by his three sons.

Russell (2009, 56) actually goes further by suggesting that rather than a blood relationship the expressed filiation might signify adoption (not unknown in other cultures, such as the contemporary Romans across the Channel), thus creating a political stability through the expression of a putative family bond. However, this all still assumes that the Gallic Commius and the British Commius are the same person. A more radical assumption would be that the two are not related, but just two rulers who happen to share the same name.

Creighton (2006) argues that Commius the Gaul was appointed as a 'friendly king', a king that was a close political ally of the Roman; depending on the ruling Emperor at the time, sometimes little more than a puppet, administering his area in Rome's interest at arms length. Again this cannot be ruled out, but there is no evidence to support it either. In fact it could be argued that somebody with the burning hatred ascribed to the Gallic Commius after the assassination attempt (he specifically stipulated to be allowed not ever to see another Roman, and Mark Antony deemed that reasonable), would be a strange choice for a friendly king in a newly acquired territory. It is also more common to appoint friendly kings from within the tribe. In Gaul Caesar appears predominately to choose candidates from inside the ruling families of their own tribes, so the sudden choice of a foreigner, not only not from the same tribe, but not even from the same area, appears to be somewhat far fetched.

But as Creighton points out he is not only Commius, but Commius the Atrebate, thus from the same tribe; and indeed other scholars have credited him with the creation of the Atrebatic kingdom, that eventually becomes the Atrebatic civitas, centred around Silchester. But again, in this case the evidence is actually arguing against it: Caesar (BG V.12) describes the population of Britain thus:

> The interior of Britain is settled by those, who according to their own traditions, say that they are indigenous to the island. The coastal stretches (are settled) by those who came from Belgica for loot and war (and nearly all of those are named after the names of the tribes, from which they came here) and having brought war, they remained here and began to work the fields.

This description described the situation *before* the second Caesarian invasion and recounts facts that appear to have happened some time before the arrival of Caesar, although the timeframe is unclear. What is important is that it is just as likely that the Atrebates were already a recognizable entity (and independent from the Gallic Atrebates) on the British side in 55/54 BC. There would be no need for a foreign founder of a state to explain the existence of a tribe of the same name in Britain. Similar identities of tribal names are not uncommon: within Britain there are the Parisi, which have a parallel in Gaul (as the tribe in the area of modern Paris) and there appears to be a Brigantian tribe both in Ireland and northern Britain (as well as elsewhere in the Empire).

But if the name could occur more than once and there was already an explanation for the existence of British Atrebates, then Creighton's 'irresistible temptation' to equate the name on the coins with the Gallic Commius just does not exist (2006, 22). In fact in many ways it would make for a more coherent argument for the existence of a client kingdom in the south of Britain before the Claudian conquest, if the Gallic resistance leader were just removed from the equation. Then the British Commius becomes an apparently influential but otherwise unknown king, who adopted new minting habits that made it easier for him to deal with the Roman traders.

Creighton proposed for Commius' sons a Roman upbringing, as they are later able to adopt the same coin reverses as other client kings in the Roman Empire (2006, 24). This upbringing was apparently brought about by becoming the hostages demanded by Mark Antony in return for Gallic Commius' good behaviour. Unfortunately, if we trust our historical sources, then the last view of Commius is that of somebody *running away* from the Romans, this does not come under good behaviour and would have seriously risked the life of any hostages that may have been given.

If on the other hand the Commius in question was an unrelated British king, then the hostage scenario would be a much more benign one, of the hostage-giving at whatever point Rome and the British Commius agreed to enter into a treaty, and leaves us without the need to apply special circumstances in the fraught situation of Commius' escape.

Whichever scenario one prefers for the origin of the hostages, it is also the case that it was not beyond the power of Rome to suggest through their messengers and diplomats a suitable expression of loyalty, e.g. the striking of a specific coin type. This would completely remove the need for an expensive education of the British princes in Rome during the height of the Roman Civil War.

In conclusion, after reviewing the evidence it seems it cannot be ruled out that the two Commii may have been identical. But the balance of probabilities and the principle of Occam's razor (which, put in simplified terms, suggests that all other things being equal the easiest explanation is usually the right one), makes the author wonder about the continued insistence on equating the two individuals, when two separate Commii, who happen to share the same name, would make the chronology and the ensuing events much easier to explain.

Chapter 4

The British Forces at the Time of the Invasions – the View from the Other Side?

The Lucan quote given at the end of the Caesar chapter is possibly the most striking compliment for the British fighting power in Caesar's day. Although admittedly Marcus Annaeus Lucanus (39/65 AD), nephew of Seneca, court poet and later opponent to Nero may have had an agenda that far exceeded a description of the Caesarian campaigns (see below). However, it is clear that British Iron Age warriors were seen as a considerable fighting force by Caesar and subsequent generals. It seems thus appropriate to take a closer look at them.

It should be stressed from the beginning that there probably never was a typical Iron Age British warrior. Iron Age studies increasingly point to substantial differences in the material culture and, therefore, we assume in the everyday life of the people inhabiting Iron Age Britain. Thus so far four to six different cultural groupings have been identified in Scotland, and at least two significantly different archaeological groups in Wales, while in England nearly a dozen different groups are known, who can be differentiated by their use (or not) of pottery, their settlement types, their burial rites, their use (or not) of coinage, as well as their art styles. We assume that for the most part they spoke a language derived from the same language family as Welsh and Irish, but whether even in this respect the use of the term 'Celtic' is justified is still debatable. They also differ in their range of contacts with the Continent or the rest of the British Isles, particularly Ireland. During the Late Iron Age the British 'cultures' also appear to have been in a state of rapid development; the world of the Early Iron Age is different from the world Caesar encountered, and for the southern British tribes, things changed before and after Caesar's campaigns.

This is not the place for a complete review of the Iron Age cultures in Britain between 100 BC and 60 AD, and readers are advised to turn to the more general introductions on the topic for further information. What is worth mentioning here is our understanding of Celtic warfare and the result of the Caesarian campaigns on the southern tribes of Roman Britain.

Strikingly, at the time of Caesar's conquest, only the central southern zone of England was still employing hill forts, as well as some parts of Wales. Much has been made of these large southern hill forts being statements of power and/or influence, but they also document a substantial level of military sophistication, especially in the defences. In addition, Cunliffe (1995, 94) has demonstrated that the few Iron Age graves known in this area have clear indications of wounds inflicted by sharp objects, such as long swords. Throughout Southern Britain weapons as well as substantial amounts of horse harness are found in graves and other sacrificial contexts. It seems, therefore, likely that the possession of weapons (and by implication the ability to use them) was part of the self-definition of at least the elite of British tribes. The weapons most commonly encountered are swords, spears and shields as well as possibly slingshot (which can be hard to differentiate from plain small sized pebbles). Cunliffe suggested that some of the high quality of the weaponry, as well as the levels of injury encountered may be linked to periods of warfare or at least raiding, although historical records suggest that in many periods of British history the two are a continuum rather than two distinct phenomena. By drawing on the evidence on the Continent (mainly preserved by the writing of the Romans and Greeks that encountered them), central and western Europe was dominated by power structures that encouraged individuals to be powerful/successful warlords, whose campaigns allowed them to maintain a warband, which was paid/rewarded out of the booty gained. It is possible that the same model applied in Britain. Cunliffe draws attention that from c.120 BC onwards the increased trading in slaves with the Continent may have encouraged further raiding as a way of obtaining slaves as exportable wealth.

It is in this context interesting to note that the area with the most militaristic features, central southern England also appears to be the area with the strongest trade links to the Continent in pre-Caesarian times. Slave trading communities in other parts of the world (e.g. Africa and also parts of North America) frequently display similar features, as the source of their wealth can only be obtained at the price of the higher than usual military force, frequently coupled with substantial investment in defensive features to prevent revenge attacks or hostile takeovers. This analogy, however, while offering an interesting theory is not currently provable from either the historical or the archaeological record for Iron Age Britain.

On the basis of these general ideas suggested by the archaeology, the depiction of the engagements with the British tribes and their fighting technique as described by Caesar are clearly of importance.

This description of the British tribes needs to be taken with some caution. Due to the history of research in this area we understand the Iron Age of central southern England better than the Iron Age of Kent or to a lesser extent the same period north of the Thames, so there are still some question marks as to whether Cunliffe's insights as described above are necessarily relevant to the area Caesar was passing through. In addition to the normal danger of misinterpreting features in a hitherto unfamiliar culture, the Romans had very clear prejudices of what they were likely to encounter north of the Alps and how these people lived.

One of these is the theory that the further away you are from Civilization, i.e. Rome, the more likely you are to encounter strange habits. Some of these are stories that can already be found in Herodotus, the Greek historian of the fifth century BC. Some of these preconceptions are that at the far end of the world live people with their faces on their chests or only one eye. Luckily for our account, the Romans did not believe Britain to be this far removed from Civilization. Caesar was, however, quite prepared to credit people in Britain with sharing wives between different men and expected the Britons not to be able to farm by working fields (i.e. agriculture in the narrow sense) and thus to live on meat and flesh and to clothe themselves in skins, at least further inland than Kent and Cassivelaunus' area north of the Thames, where the opposite was clearly observable, the latter is possibly the reason why Kent is compared to Gaul. (BG V, 14).

Other details, however, cannot be explained by reference to these stereotypes, such as woad and the fact that all Britons are clean-shaven except on their head and upper lip. The problem for the modern reader (and possibly for the ancient Roman too) is to separate the two strands of prejudice/tall story and observed fact in Caesar's account. This is particularly true of the British fighting techniques. The fighting skills of the Gauls, of which the British were apparently considered a subset by Caesar, were proverbial. Rome had had a series of very bad military experiences on the hands of the Gauls, such as the sack of Rome by Brennus in 387 BC and the battles for northern Italy leading up to the eventual Roman victory at

Telamon in 225 BC, both of which had left Rome's communal psyche with nightmares. It, therefore, did not need stressing that the Britons were expected to be equally fierce fighters, although the prejudice ran that they were very aggressive but not very sophisticated in their strategies. However, Caesar provided a series of observations that suggest he came to judge the fighting abilities of the British during the two campaigns very differently. While in the first campaign the British are portrayed as an homogenous group acting together; towards the end of the second campaign, Caesar had begun to differentiate between tribes that appeared to have different agendas (e.g. the Trinovantes vs Cassivelaunus or the Cantii with their multiple sub-kings). This suggests that Caesar was becoming increasingly aware of the complex political situation that he had literally walked into.

Caesar describes three separate kinds of British forces: infantry, cavalry and charioteers (*essedarii*). During the second season he describes the general fighting technique that the British used as the army being deployed into small widely spaced groups. This would theoretically offer a good counterweight to the closed ranks of the legions, who might be induced to follow and break up their closed formation (one of Rome's best assets when fighting) to engage the enemy.

Concurrently the British cavalry appears to have focused on drawing out parts of the Roman forces in pursuit, before turning on them. The *essedarii* or charioteers were clearly the unit that caught Caesar's attention, probably because they were so different from any other form of unit he had encountered to date. He describes them in detail during his first season in Britain (BG IV, 33):

> First of all they drive in all directions and throw missiles and so by the mere terror that the teams inspire and by the noise the wheels generate they throw ranks into confusion. When they have worked their way in between the troops of cavalry, they leap down from the chariots and fight on foot. Meanwhile the charioteers retire gradually from the combat, and dispose the chariots in such a fashion that, if the warriors are hard pressed by the host of the enemy, they may have a ready means of retirement to their own side. Thus they show in action the mobility of cavalry and the stability of infantry; and by daily use and practice they become so accomplished that they are ready to gallop their teams down the steepest of slopes without loss of control, to check and turn them in a moment, to run along the pole, stand on the yoke, and then, quick as lightning, to dart back into the chariot. (trans. H.J. Edwards).

This very vivid description might explain why the *essedarii* eventually became part of the teams of the Roman gladiatorial combat: the colourful account clearly fired the imagination of Caesar's readers in this respect. And Caesar's statement that Cassivelaunus could command 4000 of these charioteers was clearly meant to inspire awe in his readers, especially as Caesar was still victorious.

In many ways what is even more inspiring than their armament and battlefield tactics is the clearly successful strategy and diplomatic solutions employed by the British during the two summers. Even with Caesar controlling the narrative, unlike earlier encounters in Gaul, the impression remains that Caesar in Britain very quickly lost the initiative and rarely managed to reacquire it. In 55 BC the British were clearly anticipating the landing and were ready and waiting for Caesar, having correctly predicted the likely landing site. The British reaction to the storm damage and their successful attacks on the foragers suggests that the British forces were clearly keeping a very close eye on Caesar during his stay, exploiting Caesar's lack of cavalry as much as possible and penning him into a small corner of Kent.

The situation during the second campaign is even more impressive. Instead of meeting Caesar on the beach this time, they prepared a defensive position further inland and let Caesar come to them. When Caesar returned to campaigning after the repairs of the second storm damage, the British appear to have been more than ready for him. Not only have they managed to organize an alliance involving at least two, perhaps more tribes (the Cantii and Cassivelaunus' tribe, which is never actually named), but they are also able to have an overall commander of some experience (judging by his track record of having killed the king of the Trinovantes) to set against Caesar.

What is, however, more striking is the overall level of command and control. During his march to the Thames, Caesar wrote that the Britons had detachments posted along the way to cover each other in turn and provide mutual reinforcements; they also accompanied Caesar along the route and attacked the foraging parties. When Caesar reached the Thames he found the ford blocked with obstacles.

This suggests a considerable amount of foresight and planning on the part of the British. Assuming that, as in the medieval period, more than one ford existed allowing the crossing of the Thames, it can only be assumed that Caesar's route must have been predictable. We have seen earlier that to a certain extent this is so due to the geography, but the resulting corridor is quite wide and to deploy detachments might suggest that Caesar more or less found himself herded towards a particular ford.

On the far side of the ford Cassivelaunus' decision to withdraw livestock and population from the Roman path sounds like an early version of scorched earth tactics used by the Russians during Napoleon's withdrawal from Moscow. The stratagem clearly had some success, as Caesar's comments concerning the confinement of the looting parties to the immediate areas surrounding the legions' march still betrays, 2000 years later, the frustration felt by the commander. The whole campaign appears to have been designed by somebody who was aware that he had little to gain from a head-on confrontation with the Romans. Instead we see a guerrilla campaign using the British superior knowledge of terrain and the advantages of their mobile units (cavalry and chariots), while we hear little about their infantry.

The most daring manoeuvre is, however, the attack on the main Roman supply base by the Kentish kings as orchestrated by Cassivelaunus. Potentially this could have destroyed Caesar's supply chain as well as his escape route. And while it would be easy to suggest that the British warriors were not very likely to succeed in this, it needs to be pointed out that manoeuvres like this are often designed to deflect or disarm an attack elsewhere, in this case the intention may have been to get Caesar to stop taking his advance any further into Cassivelaunus' territory. If Rice Holmes (1907) is right, then Caesar's presence back with the ships at the beginning of August might suggest that this objective at least may have been achieved.

It could be argued that these may have been quite sophisticated stratagems, but that in the end they did not work. Cassivelaunus still lost a stronghold and had to sue for peace. But it is the only one mentioned and the fact that Cassivelaunus was still able to negotiate might suggest that this was not the only power base in his territory. And if viewed from the British side, the fact that Caesar did not come back in the coming years meant that their aims were more successful than those of the Romans (who on this occasion failed to find out where the silver and gold of the island came from).

Whatever view you take on the success of these manoeuvres during the second campaign, there is too much evidence of generalship, of design and planning. The intelligence is too good, too much effort is expended to set traps such as the one at the Thames or the small hill fort on the first night, to suggest that the British warriors of Caesar's period were either unsophisticated or inferior to the Roman army. Caesar's inability to continue his campaigning in Britain allowed both sides to claim a victory; one for scaring off an enemy, the other for beating the opposition in battle and receiving tribute.

Chapter 5

Caligula, Claudius and the Conquest of Britain

After Caesar's withdrawal from Britain, the intervening years of uprising in Gaul and Civil War in Rome, Caesar's dictatorship and death in 44 BC and the ensuing second Roman Civil War, the idea of returning to Britain and (re)establishing Roman control in the South remained just that: an idea. The historian Cassius Dio mentions that in 34 BC (during a lull in the Civil Wars in the aftermath of Caesar's death) Octavian/Augustus had already moved to Gaul to prepare for an invasion of Britain, but had to deal with a Dalmatian revolt instead. (Cass. Dio, Roman History 49, 38, 2). A further attempt was made in 27/26 BC, but again unrest closer to Rome made him change his plans. (Cass. Dio 53, 22 and 25).

In the event the indirect approach of grooming rulers to be supportive of Rome and thus create a system of semi-dependent states (the so-called client kingdoms) on Rome's borders seemed less problematic and/or more cost effective. These diplomatic solutions occasionally resulted in visits by British princes, asking for the support of the Emperor. It might seem strange to find these minor 'princelings' mentioned, but these visits or calls for aid from neighbouring states were valuable bargaining counters for the emerging image of any Emperor as they documented the level of influence he had at his borders, and in the right circumstances could be portrayed as a valuable (political and thus bloodless) victory. This was true for Emperors such as Augustus (27 BC/14 AD) and Tiberius (14/37 AD), whose military expertise did not need reinforcing within the eyes of their population.

The Roman geographer Strabo (c. 64/63 BC–c. 24 AD) once again demonstrates that economic or at least financial considerations played a part, when he discussed whether it would be financially prudent to change the status of Britain, as the cost of the army needed would outrun the revenues currently gained in customs duties, because these would have to be reduced if direct taxation was introduced (Strabo, Geography IV, 5, 3). But while Strabo may not have been convinced about the financial repercussions, others saw this differently, or perhaps had different, non-financial priorities, such as the emulation of Caesar's military successes.

Military experience, especially the ability to successfully lead Roman troops to victory was one of the 'must have' qualifications of Roman Emperors, whose power, while ostensibly based on a carefully choreographed political ballet of consensus with senate and liberality to the people of Rome, was in reality little else but a successfully disguised military dictatorship. The support of the army was the critical element in the creation and continued support of any reign (a fact that allowed Claudius and Vespasian to come to power, while losing the army's support had disastrous effects, as Nero and many of the later emperors learnt to their cost).

Thus the careful game of diplomacy with the British or any other client kings was likely to come to an end with the accession of any Emperor too young or too inexperienced in military matters. The accession of Caligula (aka Gaius Julius (Germanicus) Caesar) in 37 AD and Claudius in 41 AD were such moments.

Not least thanks to Suetonius and Robert Ranke Graves, Caligula must rank as one of the great 'mad men on the throne'. After his death he quickly became a byword for anything that could go wrong in an Emperor, and his surviving Roman biographies, written several generations after his murder were clearly intent on showing him in as bad a light as possible. From a distance of 2000 years it is impossible to say how accurate this image was, and there have been several attempts in his modern biographies to try and see past the 'distortions' to get at the real man as he portrayed himself at the time. There is and can be no guarantee that these results are any more true or accurate than those by ancient historians, thus what follows has once again to be taken with a pinch of salt.

Caligula never set foot in Britain, so much is certain, as is the fact that he was hailed by the army as Britannicus, the victor over Britain. According to Cassius Dio and Suetonius, in 40 AD (from now on all dates are AD, unless otherwise stated) Caligula went to Gaul and after initial preparations engaged in military activities against the Germans across the Rhine, before progressing to the Dutch seashore and ordering his soldiers to collect sea shells as the loot of their victory over the ocean. He then had a lighthouse built, whose location is not specified; Orosius (7, 5, 5), a fifth century historian, says '*deficiente belli materia*' – 'because he lacked the supplies for war'. He also tried to decimate the legions on the Rhine and left precipitately. Upon his arrival in Rome, he held a celebration for his victories over Britain and Germany. While he was on the Rhine he met the Celtic prince Adminius, son of Cunobelinus who surrendered to him, having been banished by his father (Suetonius Caius 44 and Orosius 7, 5, 5 – where the name in the manuscript is garbled into Minocynobelinus). According to the ancient writers the latter was his justification to claim a victory over the entire island of Britain.

In addition to these few historical mentions, there are a number of archaeological/numismatic clues. Recent scholars (Braund 1996, 95; Russell 2009, 88f.) link this Adminius with the AM/AMMINUS coinage in Kent, dated to the 30s and 40s. All his coins appear to imitate Romanized patterns discussed as indications of client king status (see previous Commius chapter). But these coins, while suggesting that somebody of the same name may actually have held power in Kent, add little to our understanding of Caligula's intentions with regard to Britain.

In this respect Balsdon's (1934, 69) and Braund's (1996, 91ff.) analysis of Caligula's actions leading up to the incident with the sea shells offer options: Braund drew attention to the parallels between Caesar's actions (bridge over the Rhine – British invasions) and Caligula's (a ship bridge over the bay at Baiae and then campaigning on the Rhine and against the 'Ocean'). It is worth remembering that Caligula's real name (as opposed to his nickname 'Bootie') was Gaius Julius Caesar, which given this Emperor's character, may have provided more than the usual incitement to follow in the footsteps of one of Rome's greatest generals.

While Braund may have shed some light on the underlying motive, Balsdon (1934, 76–95) provided one possible reconstruction as to the real events of this campaign that may have been hidden by the later distorted historical record. He stressed that according to Cassius Dio, 200,000–250,000 soldiers had been sent to Gaul as part of the expedition force, which would have been a huge army by anybody's standards, but is likely to have far exceeded what would have been possible in Rome at the time, where these numbers represented more than half of Rome's military manpower. But even if one makes allowances for possible exaggerations, Caligula's army was clearly designed to be substantial. According to Balsdon's reconstruction, on his arrival in Gaul, the Emperor first had to deal with a conspiracy by the governor of Upper Germany. This was followed by exercises to re-establish the discipline of the troops on the Rhine in 39 (the military activities against the Germans mentioned above), during which time he received the 'surrender' of Adminius. After a winter spent in Lyons, Caligula continued the next year with his preparations for his invasion of Britain (the original aim of the expedition), which culminated in bringing both the siege equipment and the army for embarkation on the seashore. After a rousing speech and a trumpet signal (for embarkation according to Balsdon), the army refused to move, and in view of this mutiny, Caligula shamed the soldiers, by ordering them to collect mussels or according to Balsdon '*musculi*' sapper huts, i.e. their kit and go home with a minimal donative.

Balsdon suggested that the campaign was basically scuppered by the discovery of the conspiracy and the further discovery of the poor discipline of the Roman army on the Rhine, making an expedition too unlikely to succeed and he suggested that Caligula returned to Rome as the armies would need more time to train before they could be taken on campaign.

While most historians would agree that the record of Caligula's reign may have been altered or at least distorted by later Roman historians, how these events should be reconstructed differs between historians and to illustrate the point the same events are reconstructed by Barrett (1989, 125–139) in a very different manner: He agreed with Balsdon that the raising of an army of 200,000–250,000 soldiers signified the imminent start of a large campaign, but he stressed the series of events that led up to Caligula's departure which included prayers for victory in Germany. He also pointed out that to attempt a British campaign before the successful solution of the military problems on the German frontier would have been very ill-advised. Consequently Barrett stressed the role of the two governors of Germany, P. Sulpicius Galba and P. Gabinius Secundus in reasserting control on the frontier. Different from Balsdon, he interprets the same historical sources, however, to suggest that in addition to the training of the troops, at least Galba definitely conducted some warfare in the area opposite Mainz, allowing Caligula to claim the title Germanicus – victor over the Germans. He also draws attention to the fact that in 41, at the time of Caligula's murder, the German campaigns conducted by governors of the two German provinces were still continuing. Caligula would thus not have had a secure Rhine frontier behind him during any planned British operations.

The British 'campaign' is seen by Barrett to follow immediately on from this German campaigning. He (1989, 136) also mentions a piece of evidence not known, or not cited by Balsdon, relating to the date of return of Caligula to Rome. While Balsdon used 31 August 40 (the date of the ovation) as the return date of Caligula, Barrett mentions a (now missing) fragment of the

Acts of the Arval Brethren, a listing of events and sacrifices performed by a Roman college of priests, that mentioned the Emperor's presence in the vicinity of Rome by the end of May 40. He points out that to travel from the Rhine frontier to Rome would have taken about two months, which would put the events on the seashore at the end of March, perhaps even earlier. The Romans operated a 'closed season' for sailing, during which travelling on the seas was deemed too dangerous. This season ended on 10 March, while any crossing before 27 May was still deemed unsafe by Vegetius (the late Roman author of a treatise on military matters) admittedly several hundred years later, but a look at the channel today during March and April suggests that conditions may not significantly have changed for sailing boats.

He concluded that Caligula must have known this and thus could not have expected to set sail at this point. Instead he argued that the episode was designed to be of political and diplomatic significance, probably connected with the surrender of Adminius. We are left to consider whether this may have been a Roman version of sabre-rattling, and whether the invasion of Britain, from the outset, was planned to start later.

Both scenarios have their attractions. Although 'sober judgement' as suggested by Barrett must have been well beyond the Caligula described by Cassius Dio and Suetonius; after all this is the man who believed himself a god, and more to the point had just constructed a bridge across the bay of Baiae. Surely, the question of sailing too early in the year would not have put him off, unlike the soldiers accompanying him, who would have had more experience of the weather patterns along the North Sea and probably still knew stories about the storms that destroyed Germanicus' army and navy twenty years earlier in the same region. Without further evidence, it will probably never be possible to get to the truth of what really happened in 40 on the Channel coast, and Russell's suggestion (2009, 86f) that there may even have been successful small scale operations against Britain at the time is frankly just as feasible, but equally as unprovable.

There is one more piece of evidence, which has recently come to light and which appears to demonstrate that whatever the events in Rome that led eventually to the murder of Caligula and the accession of his uncle Claudius, the army on the Rhine appear to have been prepared for an invasion for some time before 41.

The Lower Rhine in the Delta area has a very different character to the Rhine frontier in modern Germany. Today, just to the west of the Dutch/German border, the Rhine splits and creates a number of arms, some of a considerable size, which eventually intersect with the branches of the Maas. The river branches are not stable and over the last 2000 years the landscape has changed dramatically; but for our purposes it is important to know that the northernmost of these east/west flowing branches had been fortified since the Augustan period by a series of forts, which stretch nearly as far downstream as the modern town of Utrecht. It seems that originally below Utrecht, no forts existed. The river flowed here between two flanking natural embankments, which provided a fertile albeit narrow ridge between low-lying, mostly waterlogged areas with very little human habitation. Access to the river would have been mainly by boat, following the tributaries coming out of the wetlands. It seems there was originally little interest in expending manpower and importing building material to create a chain of permanent garrisons in this area: it was originally thought that these westernmost forts (which include Alphen aan den Rijn/Albaniana, Woerden/Laurum and Vleuten-De Meern) were eventually constructed in Claudius' reign after the invasion of Britain. However, recent excavations and the analysis of the timber and coins they produced, showed that the timbers in Alphen had been felled in 40, well before the murder of Caligula. In addition, these forts have produced extremely high numbers of Caligulan coinage, which adds to the suggestion for a construction date in the four years of this Emperor's reign. A final test is the comparison of the coin list with those of other forts, which are securely fixed by tree-ring dating to the Claudian reign and which showed substantial differences (Kemmers, 2006). In combination the evidence suggests that the westernmost forts in the Rhine Delta may have been initially constructed under Caligula. Given the Rhine's use as a thoroughfare for bulk goods it is tempting to think of these as part of the logistics chain built up in expectation for an invasion of Britain, but evidence for this last step in the scenario so far eludes us.

Unlike the Caesarian invasion, when we have an eyewitness account (however biased) for the events, which in addition can be checked against other contemporary sources, the historical sources for the Claudian invasion are much poorer, and the sequence of events has to be pieced together from a variety of different accounts. There are five short accounts available in the following larger historical accounts: The Histories of Cassius Dio (third century historian), Tacitus' Agricola (written in the late first century), Suetonius' Life of Claudius and also his Life of Vespasian (both written in the second century), as well as a paragraph each in the fifth century histories of Orosius (7, 5, 9–10) and fourth century history of Eutropius (7, 13, 3).

There are also snippets of information in Josephus (late first century) and Tacitus' Histories (3, 44), which relate mainly to Vespasian's role in the initial conquest. The translations for the passages of Josephus, Orosius and Eutropius can be found in the appendix.

All accounts agree that Claudius only conducted one large campaign, the conquest of Britain, but that the details were not very noteworthy: the army moved in, people surrendered and Vespasian got a chance to display his skills. Claudius himself was back in Rome within six months of leaving, having spent very little time in Britain itself. In addition, both Orosius and Eutropius mention that Claudius included the Orkneys in the Roman Empire; an interesting (and slightly unlikely) fact that we need to revisit.

The motive, or at least the trigger for the campaign is mentioned by Suetonius and Orosius: the island was restless, 'because the refugees had not been returned'. (See Appendix 1)

Suetonius adds the route Claudius travels to get to Britain: from Rome to the Mediterranean coast, where he was nearly shipwrecked, then on to Marseille and hence overland to Gesoriacum/Boulogne, to embark for Britain. (NB: This is the only time in any of the sources that Boulogne is mentioned.)

Claudius' visit is also confirmed by the only contemporary document other than the coins: Claudius' victory monument in Rome. This probably took the form of an arch, which was integrated into the Aqua Virgo and the surviving part of the inscription represents about a quarter to a third of a very formulaic text, with which Claudius commemorated his victory in Rome. The inscription can be reconstructed and translated to read as follows (surviving text is in bold):

To   Tiberius   Claudius   son   of   Drusus   Caesar   **Augustus,** Germanicus

Pontifex Maximus holding Tribunician pow**er for the ninth time, Consul for the Fifth time saluted Imp XXII Censor**, Father of his country. **The Senate and the P**eople of **Rome** (set this up) be**cause 11 (or more) Kings of the Britons** were defeated and without **any losses** he accepted their surrender **and** because he **first** brought the barbarian **tribes** beyond the Ocean under the power of the Roman people. (CIL VI 920 and CIL III.5.7061 = ILS 217)

Clearly like the football results today, the monument concentrated on the most important points: who played (Claudius vs the Britons), who won (Claudius) and what was the score (Claudius 11+, Britons 0). The longest account of how the initial conquest of Britain proceeded came from the third century historian Cassius Dio.

He tells us that Plautius had the troops assembled for the invasion, but that they were reluctant to go 'beyond the known (or civilized) world' and as a result Narcissus, one of Claudius' chief advisers, but significantly a freed slave, had to come and address the troops, who were freeborn. The troops felt offended and joked that the world must be turned on its head, if the slave addressed the Roman soldiers and they agreed to embark.

Once again, as with Caesar, we face a late embarkation. We also hear that the army was split into three parts so as not to hinder each other during the crossing or on landing.

The landings were unopposed and Plautius had some difficulty in finding and engaging the enemy. Eventually they managed to engage and defeat Cunobelinus' sons, Caratacus and Togodumnus after which the Bodunni (sic!) who were occupied by the Catuvellauni surrendered to Rome. The only real fighting appears to be a two day engagement at a river crossing, when we are given the names of three of the four legionary legates, Vespasian, his brother Sabinus and Hosidius Geta, who eventually won the day. The conquest progressed towards the lower Thames; the crossing place is described as close to the estuary, where the river created a lake at high tide. Again the Roman army won, but found themselves in trouble, when they followed the British warriors into swampland.

Shortly after we are told of Togodumnus having been killed, but no details on how this came to pass. Plautius at this point stopped and waited for Claudius to come and reinforce the troops and bring the supplies, equipment and elephants that had been collected for him. Claudius' arrival led to the taking of Colchester, followed by the surrender of some tribes and Claudius' multiple acclamations as Imperator. After sixteen days in Britain, Claudius was able to return to Rome to celebrate his triumph, leaving Plautius with the order to conquer the rest.

The other sources add a few more details on the campaign: in his life of Vespasian, Suetonius tells us that under the command of Aulus Plautius and Claudius, Vespasian fought thirty battles, took twenty oppida (large defended Iron Age settlements), accepted the surrender of two tribes and conquered the Isle of Wight. Of all these achievements, only the Isle of

Wight can be identified on a map. In his Histories the first century historian Tacitus adds that Vespasian had been put in command by Claudius of the *legio II Augusta*.

Other participants of the conquest that are mentioned in the sources include L. Junius Silanus (then engaged to Claudius' daughter Octavia) (mentioned by Suetonius and Cassius Dio), M. Licinius Crassus Frugi, and his son Pompeius Magnus, son-in-law of Claudius (Suetonius and Cassius Dio), T. Plautius Silvanus Aelianus, relative of Aulus Plautius and former in-law of Claudius (CIL XIV 3608= ILS 986), Rufrius Pollio, Claudius' Praetorian Prefect in charge of the Imperial guard during the expedition, Cn. Sentius Saturninus, one of the two consuls, who argued for the reinstatement of the Republic after Caligula's murder (Eutropius 7,13), M. Vinicius (who had been discussed as a possible candidate for Emperor at the same occasion), as well as probably the following: L. Sulpicius Galba, the later Emperor, because of whose illness Claudius apparently postponed the British expedition (Suetonius, Galba 7), D. Valerius Asiaticus, L. Coiedius Candidus, Claudius' *quaestor* (ILS 967= CIL XI 6163) and Julius Planta (CIL V 5050=ILS 206). These names, about whom sometimes little else is known, except that they were awarded the triumphal ornaments by Claudius are listed by Birley (2005, 214–223) as part of Claudius' retinue in 43. An emperor, when travelling was usually not only surrounded by his guards (hence the presence of the head of the guards, the Praetorian Prefect) and officials (hence the personal *quaestor*), but also by any number of *amici* and *comites* (high ranking friends and travel companions). These titles, which became a sought after decoration of the nobility, could cover a large amount of qualifications and duties, either as advisors (Sulpicius Galba's known talent as a disciplinarian and general might have come in useful), as table companions, or just because the Emperor was acting on the age old adage that you should keep your friends close and your enemies closer. Claudius had survived a coup the year before, and including other potential Imperial 'candidates' or members of the Senate with known republican convictions would thus have been wise. Most of these men get mentioned in throwaway lines or not at all in the literary histories, but have been awarded inscriptions and/or statues in various parts of the Empire, commemorating their achievements. With the exception of Claudius' sons-in-law and Sulpicius Galba (who later became Emperor) we have little idea why Cassius, Suetonius, or Eutropius decided to mention them.

In addition we know of a series of reliefs (for example from Aphrodisias in Turkey) and coins that celebrate Claudius' conquest of Britain, but none of these go beyond depicting Claudius as the victorious *imperator*. One of these coins, an issue of the mint of Alexandria (which can usually be very closely dated), is, however, of some importance as it celebrates Claudius as Britannicus, and might therefore provide a date for the Claudian campaign (Barrett 1998). This is unusual, as most of the sources provide hardly any chronological information: the invasion started late in the campaigning season and Claudius spent six months away from Rome, of which only sixteen days were spent in Britain. We have seen in earlier chapters, that the closed season for shipping suggested that little sailing took place before 10 March and that the late Roman author Vegetius recommended not to sail before the end of May in the Channel. On the other hand we know that Caesar was worrying about not being able to get his troops back to the Continent from the end of August onwards. So what does 'late in the season' mean? May or June? More importantly, at which point in the year did Claudius come to Britain? If he had to be fetched all the way from Rome, then a start date in May would suggest that Claudius could not have got to Britain until the latter half of August. So, was his stay of sixteen days determined by the need not to spend the winter in Britain and to leave before the end of September? Unfortunately, there is no fragment of the Arval Acts similar to the one for Caligula to confirm Claudius' presence in Rome for this period. Thus reconstructions of the timeline vary widely in modern studies; suggestions range from arrival dates between the end of July and September, the latter suggesting that Claudius may have spent the winter away from Rome, despite the potential problems of the winter crossing. In addition there appears to be a problem with the consular date provided by Cassius Dio, who claims that Claudius handed the running of affairs over to L. Vitellius, his fellow consul, with whom he had apparently a six month term (Cassius Dio 60.21.2). Other sources for Rome, however, confirm that at least from the beginning of March their successors Pedianus and Pappellius were already in office and that Claudius did not have any six month long consulships, except for his fifth consulate in 51 (Kienast 1990, 91).

On the other hand Cassius Dio claims that Claudius returned to Rome in the consulship of Crispus and Statilius (i.e. 44), while at the same time stating that he had been gone only for six months having left as a consul in 43. Barrett (1990) drew attention to this problem, which can still not be resolved, and throws the entire account of the campaign into a chronological nightmare, as the two fixed points can clearly not be brought to match.

On the other hand in 1998 an Alexandrinian diobol was identified in an American coin collection, that showed on the reverse 'Britannicus Caesar' and gives as a regnal year 'year 3'. Alexandrinian coinage, unlike a lot of other 'provincial coinage' (i.e. coinage not struck in Rome's official mints, especially in Rome) are dated by the regnal years of the ruling Emperor, with the new year beginning on 29 August following Ancient Egyptian tradition. Year 3 ran thus from 29 August 42 to 28 August 43. The importance of this coin lies in the fact that Claudius, as part of his victory celebrations, changed his son's name to Britannicus. If this son appears before 28 August 43 with his new name at the other end of the Empire, then the visit to Britain must have been substantially earlier, possibly in early July, if not earlier (Barrett, 1998). This would, however, require a very short campaigning season for Plautius before the fall of Colchester. In fact, once the average travel times known (about forty-five days in the summer months) between Rome and Alexandria are factored in, the dates once again cause more problems than they appear to solve.

Last striking date in Alexandria	28 August 43
Date of departure from Rome: assuming average travel speed Rome–Alexandria (45 days)	13 July 43
Time to debate in Roman Senate (2 days following Grainge)	11 July 43
Date to depart Boulogne (50 miles/day = 16 days)	25 June 43
Colchester to Boulogne (3 days)	22 June 43

Faster travel speeds have occasionally been recorded between the Northern provinces and Rome, but Claudius is no longer in his twenties, nor is most of his retinue. This does suggest an incredibly tight schedule, and one is left to wonder if perhaps the coin was either backdated or designed in expectation and released late.

This is, however, only the first occasion where our understanding of ancient travel times is causing problems with the reconstruction of the Claudian campaigns in Britain.

Questions of chronological vagueness and the ensuing problems abound throughout the historical account. Cassius Dio's text gives no indication how much time elapses between different events, or whether some of these events might actually happen concurrently. To name just a few issues: How long did Plautius need to locate Caratacus and Togodumnus? How long from the river battle to the Thames?

Similar to what we have seen in Caesar's account, Cassius Dio's style also is episodic, offering momentary glimpses, before the director cuts to the next scene, to borrow from modern film parlance.

In a further parallel to Caesar, geographically we are again left out on a limb: we hear of the Thames as a crossing point, of Camoludunum as a site conquered, of Gesoriacum as the place of embarkation for Claudius. Suetonius adds the Isle of Wight as a place conquered by Vespasian – and Eutropius and Orosius the Orkneys as one of the areas that surrendered to Claudius.

Other desirable topographical information is lacking or abbreviated: the embarkation point(s) of the troops – not named, the landing point(s) in Britain – unknown, the name of the river crossed – not mentioned. The Bodunni are mentioned; if this is a misspelling for the Dobunni, that would place them in Gloucestershire, but we are apparently only dealing with the part ruled by the Catuvellauni, this may imply an exclave, so again we are left without geographical indicators. A tidal pool on the Thames estuary is mentioned, with swamps close by, but there must have been dozens of these before the growth of the Port of London in the medieval and modern period; it cannot be ruled out that we may be talking about some of the deeply cut inlets in Essex, such as the Blackwater.

In addition, it has been argued that we should lose one of the few geographical fixed points: the Orkneys mentioned by Eutropius and Orosius. Most of Orosius' early information appears to have been excerpted from Suetonius, but this section used a different source. Orosius was writing a 'History against the Pagans' at the very end of the fourth or beginning of the fifth century. He can be very well informed – when he deals with events in the Eastern Empire, but Britain is markedly 'out of his comfort zone'. So, where and how would he have heard of the Orkneys? In the aftermath of the wars of Theodosius the Elder (see below) and the accession of his son (Theodosius the Great) in 375 and grandsons (Honorius and Arcadius) in 383 and 393 as Roman Emperors, a number of speeches and poems were written extolling the achievements of Theodosius the Elder in Britain. One of the recurring themes was the exploits of Theodosius the Elder against the barbarians in the Orkneys, Ireland and Thule. We will have to discuss these events in more detail below, but in the context of Claudius' campaigns it is probably sufficient to point to the Orkneys as a familiar geographical term linked to the island in the late fourth century. Orosius might have found the reference in one of the speeches as a laudatory parallel between Theodosius and Claudius and re-used it in his history without quite realizing the exact geographical relationship between the two islands.

Eutropius, however, wrote his 'Breviarium' under the preceding dynasty, and would thus not have been influenced by the Theodosian panegyrics (praise speeches) he may admittedly have heard about the British campaigns under Theodosius the Elder at the time. But before we jettison one of the few sources we have, we should consider a possible alternative: ever since the Caesarian invasions, we hear of British princes coming to surrender to Roman generals or Emperors before any emperor has set foot on the island. Unfortunately, we rarely know where these kings come from, but we have seen that after Caesar's death, Rome probably cultivated client kingdoms in the South and East of Britain. After the conquest we hear of Prasutagus, Cartimandua and Togidumnus who continue this tradition to the north and west of the directly controlled province. Given the extent of the trading networks operating all around the British Isles, an alternative scenario presents itself: an Orcadian 'chief' or trader may have been passing through and felt that in view of the demonstration of military might in progress, making friends early might be a good long-term strategy, if only for the trading opportunities it offered. This scenario would then be similar to the diplomatic boasts found amongst others in the Res Gestae of Augustus. Unlike the close contacts enjoyed by the Southern and Eastern dynasties in England, the archaeological evidence in Orkney suggests, however, that the relationship never amounted to much more than an occasional gift exchange.

Considering the quality of the surviving evidence as a whole, it should at best be described as patchy, contradictory and largely unverifiable by the standards of modern investigative journalism, which likes to see any claim substantiated by multiple sources if possible. If this journalistic standard of reliability is applied, then the only facts that can be trusted are that there was a successful invasion of Britain, that Aulus Plautius was in charge, that Vespasian had a lesser command and that Claudius came for a short period. As demonstrated above some of the other bits of information may or may not be accurate, or may indeed be misleading. Unfortunately, as this book progresses, it will become abundantly clear that most of the so-called facts of the history of Roman Britain cannot be independently confirmed and are thus open to source criticism as well as general doubts as to their veracity.

Using the high standards of journalistic reliability would thus leave the scholar of Roman Britain with very little but the admittedly impressive archaeological evidence found throughout the island. Archaeological evidence is frequently defined as a '*histoire de longue durée*', history that traces long-term trends rather than events, in many ways the direct opposite of what is expected of military history. On the other hand, the unverifiable data that we do have offers enough snippets of information to remind the reader (and the author) that absence of evidence is not evidence of absence and that there clearly were numerous events (many involving the army and thus military in nature) that shaped Roman Britain and its relations with its neighbours. The data that we have clearly does not represent the sum total of the available evidence. The accounts are so vague, written such a long time after the events described and by people who for the most part never came to Britain, that mistakes can happen and also that important facts have been omitted in the account for a variety of reasons. It seems thus doubly important that any reconstruction put forward needs to take account of *all* the available facts.

So, what do we actually know about the army involved? We know it was commanded by Aulus Plautius. A.R. Birley's (2005,17–25) biographical note of Aulus Plautius is able to provide some background to the man: he was given the command to conquer Britain by Claudius as a long-standing friend of the Julio-Claudians, links between his family and the ruling dynasty extend back to at least Livia. According to Birley, he is most likely to have been governor of Pannonia before his appointment to Britain and as such had a vital role to play during the rebellion of Scribonianus in 42 in Dalmatia. He also appears to have brought the *legio IX Hispana* from Pannonia to Britain, as after 43 it no longer appears in the Pannonian records. On the whole he seems thus to have been a safe pair of hands for Claudius, trustworthy of a large command without turning on the Emperor, a characteristic that must have outweighed any perceived shortcomings as a general.

Little is known about the size of the army that accompanied Aulus Plautius. None of the surviving sources offers any figures, so any reconstructions suggesting 20,000 or 40,000 soldiers are snatching figures out of thin air, based on multiplication of the presumed number of legions present and a presumed ratio of auxiliaries and legionaries. Other reconstructions are based on the collections of units found on early gravestones in Britain, such as the Ala Thracum, which are presumed to have arrived with the invading forces. This may be tempting, but as most of these gravestones can only be dated in broad terms, and soldiers do not always settle where they served, occasionally not even in the same province, caution is thus called for. In addition, just because an army unit is present in the province twenty years later is no guarantee that it was there right from the beginning. The more our understanding of the Roman military history of the Roman army in the first century AD grows, the more we begin to appreciate the fluidity of the situation at any one time. Fort sites are sometimes abandoned within a few years of being first occupied, and to assume, therefore, any stability in the manpower deployed might be over optimistic. On the other hand and in defence of generations of archaeologists and historians working on Roman Britain, the quality and quantity of evidence for any given event in Romano–British history tends to be minute and doubtful, and with few exceptions decreasing and depreciating as the history of the Roman province progresses. Thus the only way to create a narrative, i.e. a continuous story, worth telling is to extrapolate from data that may be slightly earlier or later, while wisdom suggests that a regular stocktake/review of what and how much of this narrative is evidence and what is surmise and extrapolation, is highly advisable.

We know the Roman army consisted of legions and auxiliary units. Most Roman military historians operate under the assumption that in general there should be about the same number of auxiliaries as legionaries in a campaigning army. The only legion mentioned by name is the *legio II Augusta* with Vespasian in charge, which had been brought from Upper Germany.

In addition, at the battle of the river crossing, Cassius Dio described Vespasian and his brother Sabinus as *upostrategoi* – the Greek term for a legionary legate. This would give us a second legate in the person of Flavius Sabinus, Vespasian's older brother. The day after Hosidius Geta is ordered to advance from the river, he is the only other Roman mentioned in the account being in a position of command and a senator (Cassius Dio states that he received the *ornamenta triumphalia*, despite not having been a consul); this would make him the third legate and, by analogy, this would require three legions to be present at the conquest. We usually assume that four legions were involved in the invasion; this is based on the presence of four legions in the later province. We also know that all legions that are later stationed in Britain (and which may or may not have been involved in the initial invasion) had been involved in fighting two years before the occupation and while this would make them experienced, it might suggest that they may not have been at full strength. We do know for certain that on the eve of the Boudiccan rebellion in 60 the British garrison consisted of the *legio II Augusta*, *legio IX Hispana*, *legio XIV Gemina* and *legio XX Valeria Victrix*. Only the *legio II Augusta* can be clearly linked to the British expedition, while Birley suggested based on circumstantial evidence that the *legio IX Hispana* had come from the same province as Aulus Plautius. However, in the seventeen years between the invasion and the Boudiccan uprising there are numerous opportunities for a further legion to arrive, or for a legion to be switched; and the possibility that a fourth legion was waiting with the siege equipment and the elephants at Boulogne for Claudius, should not be ruled out.

What do we know about the Roman *auxilia* present? The only units that are singled out for an individual description are a number of troops that can swim in armour through rivers. They are usually identified as Batavi and E. Cary's Loeb translation actually calls them Germans (which is not in the original Latin and is not the only problem with this translation, as he also implies that Sabinus acts as Vespasian's lieutenant during the river battle, when the text implies equal standing).

The Batavians have a special place in the hearts of many admirers of the Roman army, a fact that seems to date back to Roman times. Not only were they an amphibious unit, they had a special recruitment status (the Batavi did not pay taxes, they instead provided enough manpower for several auxiliary units), they were apparently at first always commanded by their own officers and not by Romans, they were always mentioned when the going got tough and finally, they were the only auxiliaries that actually managed to beat the Roman army during the Batavian uprising in 69/71 in Lower Germany. So much for the myth, and as with all myths, it is best taken with a pinch of salt.

However, despite the popularity of the idea of seeing them involved in the invasion of Britain, there is a small, but important problem. Cassius Dio does not mention them: the troops that do the swimming are called Keltoi (Celts), a cultural attribution that is rather doubtful for the Germanic Batavians, but also a name that is not used in the official naming of these units. This suggests that we do not know who these troops are. It is certainly not beyond the realm of possibility that other Celtic units in the Roman army possessed the ability to swim in armour (after all there are several units in the modern British/American forces that possess this ability), but Miles

Russell (2009, 91–114) has recently put forward the suggestion that they may actually have been British troops fighting on the Roman side. There is little to refute the argument, but equally little to support it – our sources are just not good enough to come to a decision, but it remains a valid solution.

Before we discuss where the Romans invaded, it is perhaps necessary to step back from the details of the campaign and look at the larger picture, because the Britain at the eve of the Claudian invasion was a very different place from the one of Caesar's invasion. Most accounts of the invasion of Britain begin with the mysterious island at the edge of the known world, and stress the extraordinary result of Caesar's invasion, proving to the Romans that it existed and was just another part of European real estate.

Roman poets (and to a lesser extent historians) in the first century AD spent a lot of time trading upon this stereotype of 'Britain the Great Unknown' and the place of legend: this image still resonates when Cassius Dio refers to Roman soldiers not wanting to embark for Britain as they did not want to fight beyond the *oikoumene* (the known civilized world). It is possible that this is a literary prejudice (a trope), rather than reality, as Cassius Dio had conveniently forgotten that the same army in the preceding forty years had been fighting deep in the 'swamps and forests' of the Germania libera and had gone with Germanicus' fleet to explore the North Sea (admittedly with disastrous results, when storm struck) and were thus familiar with the problems of life beyond 'Civilization'. However, it makes for a more 'manly' and thus acceptable reason than the otherwise common wish of not wanting to be seasick or drowned during a sea crossing too early in the year in small boats and potentially high seas. Stressing the element of the voyage into the unknown made the achievement of an Emperor in need of a resounding victory a lot more remarkable. 'One small step for a man, one giant leap for mankind' always sounds more impressive than 'we just went and annexed the lands we have been trading with for nearly a hundred years'.

By the time of the Claudian invasion detailed knowledge of the south coast of England was available at least to the Roman traders in the Gallic harbours. Archaeological finds of Roman imports and Continental Celtic coinage in East Kent, the Solent, Hengistbury Head, Portland and Mount Batten identifies a number of sites that were able to obtain Roman goods. Admittedly, it is never easy or wise to jump from the presence of trade goods to the presence of the person whose culture produced them, as the trade goods tend to travel further than their producers; but on the east coast both the Humber Estuary (P. Halkon pers. comm) and Norfolk area (Davies,

2009) appear to have had contact with the Continent, while the west coast of Britain and the Irish Sea had been operating their own trade network from the middle Iron Age onwards (Matthews, 1999). Thus by Augustan times, both the coastal areas, but also the central Midlands were able to acquire Roman goods either directly or indirectly via the South Coast (Cooper & Buckley 2003, 31).

Political and diplomatic exchanges, which may have resulted in silver beakers and an Augustan medallion in the Lexden Tumulus, or in princes like Verica and Adminius turning to Rome for protection, suggest that knowledge about the island had progressed substantially beyond what was available 100 years before.

In addition or perhaps as a result, the Roman approach to conquering the island had changed. Unlike Caesar, who appears to have been genuinely uncertain about the size of the island, Claudius and Aulus Plautius can have had very little doubt about the size of the South of England, especially in view of the 'refugees' in Rome, who would have been able to provide the relevant data. However, Rome had for at least two centuries before Claudius developed strategies for the conquest of large territories: the multiple attack or pincer movement. Whether we are talking about the conquests of Parthia, Armenia, Germany or Spain; Rome regularly split its armies and ordered them to progress independently towards a joint strategic aim. During the Neronian campaign in Armenia, Corbulo as the overall commander would lead one such force, while a second army would progress under Vettius Bolanus from the south, and the list could go on. These pincer movements served not only as a tactical tool to surround the enemy or deal with multiple threats at the same time, but they also made it easier for the army to be supplied. Doubts have been raised whether the Romans would have been able to keep their troops supplied far inland, if they had chosen to land at Fishbourne. However, campaigns in the landlocked area of Hispania, Africa and Armenia, as well as the Julio-Claudian armies in Germany, were regularly operating with much bigger armies much further inland (with admittedly mixed success), and the Roman army had considerable experience in the supply of armies on the march and thus inland operations would not have been a major problem. It is thus not surprising that recently, several suggestions have been made that Aulus Plautius and his legates may have been operating in several columns at least for some of the time (Russell 2009, 108; Black 2000).

On the other hand when discussing the conquest of Britain in the past, it has long been assumed that whoever led the next invasion would either have to, or want to copy Caesar, and repeat his tactics regardless of any improved intelligence. There have been numerous proposals how the Roman invasion of Britain proceeded. They can be divided for the most part into a Richborough and a Fishbourne option; and the frequency with which new modifications of the various theses appear, suggests that we are yet some distance from creating a new 'narrative'. All reconstructions exploit the vagueness of Dio's account. Because of its very episodic nature, it presents a large number of possible scenarios and a recent adult education class in Manchester successfully demonstrated a new theory that used the same geographical detail to support an invasion from the Severn Estuary. I would like it to be understood that I do not endorse this scenario, but it did provide an eye opener to just how vague our 'evidence' is.

One of the problems is that neither the Richborough nor the Fishbourne supporters have so far managed to provide convincing evidence or a 'smoking gun' in support of their theory. Supporters of the Fishbourne theory point to the military structures under Fishbourne palace and its early pottery, i.e. Arretine Samian. Richborough's supporters point to the Claudian double ditches under the later town. Both sides can point to an impressive natural harbour (the Wantsum Channel and the Solent respectively) in their support, although in both cases there remain some interesting navigational problems, neither of which appears to have deterred sailing ships of later periods, both harbours having become successful ports.

Both camps can point to possible sites for the river crossing (be that at Pulborough, at the Medway or any other river proposed), as it is one of the few geographical fixed points. Both end up on the lower Thames and at Colchester.

So why can the two camps not agree? As John Manley has pointed out, there is a lot of emotion and memory and not a small bit of local patriotic feeling attached to the question. Romans do matter to people today, in Kent, in Sussex, and as we are going to see later, in Norfolk, Yorkshire and Perthshire, too, so losing 'your' Romans may be significant for your self-image and in places also to your tourist trade; and at this point, what may have started as an academic debate about the ability to identify a small text reference in the modern landscape may be blown out of all proportion.

Are there solutions to this conundrum? If our dates are right, then within a decade of the invasion we see in Britain a new type of archaeological site, the temporary camp. Temporary camps are not forts and they serve very different purposes. Roman forts are winter quarters, a place where soldiers can relax and recuperate in safe territory, where possessions and family can be left, and where the unit can keep up with the paperwork; they are also essential for coordinating logistics. They tend to be permanent (by comparison) and thus (fairly) well built with permanent buildings. Despite their appearances, they are not meant for fighting in or over (despite some determined efforts on both sides during several civil wars).

Temporary camps are different. According to Hyginus (a surveyor who wrote an essay about how to build a temporary camp in the first two centuries AD), they are where the soldiers sleep on campaign, but the main internal structures are temporary, mostly tents, they should have defences, at least if the soldiers are in enemy territory, although not necessarily ditches, felled trees or just a rampart will do (which is unfortunate, as only the ditched examples tend to be identifiable as crop marks for archaeologists). They are supposed to be built at the end of the march and destroyed the next day when the army moves on (although we are beginning to realize from our excavations that this is a theory, rather than daily practice), they also tend to be a lot bigger than forts, but they can be a lot smaller (we assume the latter were mainly built for practice). The biggest one in England is about 23 ha (Brampton Bryan in Hereford and Worcester), the larger ones in Scotland, which are associated with military campaigning, can be substantially bigger. The ditched examples that have been identified have usually only a single ditch, while the permanent forts tend to have at least two ditches.

The temporary camps are the sort of evidence that we would hope to find for the invasion, but the gazetteer of temporary camps draws a blank for the whole South and South-East of Britain (Welfare and Swan 1995). This may reflect the fact that there is less open country suitable for cropmarks in the South-East or that the Romans did not feel like cutting ditches into chalk every night (although they did cut ditches into granite in some of the camps in Scotland). Either way this most suggestive feature is so far missing from the archaeological record in the South and South-East.

What support can the two sites at Richborough and Fishbourne add to our understanding of the invasion? Both sites are clearly man-made structures and they show clear signs of being Roman structures, especially in the backfill of their ditches, which is full of Roman pottery. There are, however, two problems: in Fishbourne the structures are permanent, the excavated features are substantial and would have taken some time to build, especially the granary. This makes them by the above definition part of a fort – a permanent installation, usually built in friendly territory. They have been discussed in the literature as a supply base, but there is only one, perhaps two granaries, which is what you would expect to find in any Roman fort. Supply bases, such as South Shields on the Tyne, have many more granaries (see page 164) (Manley & Rudkin 2003). In addition, much is made about the fact that Fishbourne features are associated with Arretine Samian and that Arretine ware is by its nature early. There is, however, a question over the 'how early'. If this pottery is so clearly associated with these military buildings, then these buildings are built nearly a generation earlier than the invasion and the question is then: how long did they continue in existence, when were they abandoned? The fact that there is Arretine in the ditches might suggest that the ditches were filled with rubbish when the site was abandoned. This might point to the fact that Fishbourne may no longer have been in existence when the Romans invaded. It is quite possible that at some point the Roman Empire felt the need to establish a base at Fishbourne in support of a client king, but that does not mean that 20 years later the same conditions still applied.

The situation at Richborough is little better. The Claudian ditches are associated with early Claudian material, which suggests that they may be contemporary with the Roman invasion; but they are double ditches, which does not suggest a temporary camp. They are also currently enclosing a triangle of land in a curved outline. The shape is not a problem as Claudian forts on the Continent do not yet necessarily display the normative playing card shape seen later. What is important is that the circuit is not closed. To reconstruct a closed circuit one would have to assume that post-Roman erosion destroyed about three times the current surviving area. However, recent excavations at the bottom of the cliff, which discovered a Roman and medieval harbour suggest that the erosion is nowhere near as dramatic (Millett and Wilmott 2003, 192f.).

This may suggest that the ditches are actually not part of a fort, but an Iron Age site which was backfilled, but no Iron Age material was found at Richborough. Given that Claudian pottery was found in some of the lowest levels of the ditch, it is unlikely to be even earlier.

A second scenario would be that the site was originally open to the water, as it was supposed to provide a safe landing point for ships. Similar sites have been found in Germany, e.g. at Haltern, and it is tempting to associate this with the invasion. However, calculations have suggested that at any one time only 70–80 ships would fit into this landing point and the area enclosed is today only 11 acres (4.45 ha); this may seem large, until you realize that this is the size of the large forts in the north of England, including Stanwix, which are usually predicted to house around 1000 men. By contrast a legionary fortress (for c. 6000 men) would occupy about 16–20 ha. (nearly five times the area). It should be taken into account that whoever is using Richborough, (even using Grainge's scenario (2002, 45–61) the task of embarking in three waves; i.e. approximately a legion and its auxiliaries at a time) needs to have room to disembark and temporarily house 6000 legionaries plus an unknown, but substantial number of auxiliaries and their supplies and equipment. They would also, according to Grainge, come in c. 250–300 ships at a time, not the 70–80 that fit into the site.

Consequently, Richborough's Claudian ditches are just not big enough to be the fortified landing site. They are certainly too small to be the camp of a legion sent ahead to secure the landing place. They are probably even too small to land just Claudius' party which would have involved at least a substantial part (i.e. more than 1000 soldiers) of the Praetorian Guard, as well as elephants and very rich senators (who are unlikely to travel light) and siege equipment. A further point is the question of the number of ships involved. Grainge (2002, 2005) has spent considerable effort to give us a better idea about what would be involved in getting an invasion army to cross the Channel, and thus has considerably changed our perception of what is involved in this event, including having significantly increased the amount of esteem for the skills of the seamen involved in the crossing.

In the course of the discussion he raises a number of interesting points. As to the number of ships, he gauges that Claudius' invasion force may have been bigger than any other invasion force, certainly bigger than Caesar's during his second landing. We know the number of Caesar's ships and Grainge suggests that Caesar would have needed about 30 miles of coast line to bring every ship up to the beach. There are very few beaches on the south coast that are that long, and as a result ships are likely to have been anchored in the bay.

He also draws attention to the fact that this may explain why Cassius Dio tells us that the army was split into three parts. The term used is unusual, '*triche*' is a term that comes from epical and poetical Greek and is certainly not a technical term; thus Cassius' vagueness strikes again. Grainge prefers to see it as meaning split into three consecutive groups, Hind interprets it as an army split between three harbours: both are possible.

If there is one problem with moving in consecutive waves, it is the time involved. Grainge suggests that you could embark the first army during the day, sail during the night and disembark during the morning. Presumably as you are using the same ships, you would sail back during the second night, embark the second wave in the morning, sail again (third night), disembark at day, sail back at night (fourth night), embark the third team, sail again at night (fifth night) and disembark the last group. On the afternoon of the sixth day everybody should be in England. This assumes perfect weather conditions over an entire week (which can happen in the Channel). Also, so that there is some chance of the seamen catching some sleep, we have to predict crews on a watch system, for which we have no evidence, and assume that nothing goes wrong with the ships during landing, disembarkation etc. (a risk that would have been higher with every crossing, if the seamen did not have sufficient time to recuperate). Invasions in waves to avoid congestion on the beaches have been successfully practised on numerous occasions during the twentieth century – with ships powered by oil or coal fired engines. It is hard to underestimate the amount of freedom that these engines give to the planning of journeys, as they free the ships from prevailing wind and currents, while modern instrumentation allows for navigation at night in less than optimum conditions.

Sailing ships are much harder to time, and it is hardly a coincidence that none of the invasions that were studied by Grainge attempted an invasion by waves with their sailing ships. It would indeed be a feat of amazing seamanship if this invasion would have been possible in three such tight waves – and this is without considering the congestion caused in a harbour like Richborough, where only a quarter of the ships arriving can be brought to disembark at the same time within the compound of the Claudian lines – anchoring a ship on the roadstead is not the same as disembarkation, although old pictures of sailing ships in harbours suggest that by lashing ships together more room can be made; but it remains doubtful if this would help with disembarkation. However, in Fishbourne the situation would have been little easier as passing the harbour entrance would have most likely required the ships to be lined up to enter the harbour in single file.

On the other hand landing at three different ports involves three different groups having to navigate independently and the crossings would almost definitely have taken longer than Grainge's preferred Boulogne to

Richborough crossings; there may also be more problems with dangers under and above the water.

At this point the experience gathered by the Roman on past expeditions would probably have paid off. Reading Caesar's account it is clear that if wanted, there were accounts on the possible dangers of both approaches, as in the first season Caesar lost the cavalry, which started from a different harbour; on the other hand at the end of the second campaign, it seems Caesar was evacuating the troops in waves, as not enough ships were available and he found himself worrying as the changing weather situation prevented the ships from returning in time. There would also have been the additional experience of Germanicus' campaigns in the North Sea. As a result it must have been clear to anybody organizing this, that both approaches had their problems that needed to be overcome. These problems are compounded by the fact that we do not know just where the experienced seamen needed for such a crossing were coming from, or at what level within the planning for this campaign local knowledge would have been allowed to be heard. In a worst case (but not unlikely) scenario the crossing may not have been organized by experienced North Sea seamen such as were available to the British or Dutch navies from the late Medieval period onwards, but by a staff of legates, whose military experience would have mainly been gained on land, and who may not have been willing to give the North Sea and the Channel quite the same respect as that of experienced sailors. In this context, the character of the commander-in-chief is likely to play a major role: we know Caesar was a risk taker, we are also told by Suetonius that Claudius liked to play it safe and was easily scared; unfortunately we have no idea what Aulus Plautius' attitude would have been. But without this it is hard to judge what any given general would have deemed an acceptable risk and/or delay.

There is also a valid point to ask: from where is the army sailing? It has already been mentioned that the only known piece of information to the origin of the army is the fact that Claudius and his entourage were sailing from Boulogne. This is not surprising, as Claudius was coming from the south and was ultimately heading to Colchester, or at least to a point north of the Thames close to Colchester. Gesoriacum/Boulogne would have been thus an established harbour on the Gallic coast, far enough north to make it a reasonable target. Unfortunately, we also do not know to where Claudius was sailing. Most people have argued that it must have been Richborough, some that it would be Fishbourne. There appears to be a longstanding consensus that Claudius used the same disembarkation point as the rest of the invasion fleet: only Black (2000) has argued that while the rest of the army would have used Fishbourne, Claudius would have sailed to Richborough, possibly pacifying Kent on the way to Colchester.

There has been substantial criticism that this would not be a likely scenario with an Imperial train. This would, however, misunderstand the nature of a Roman Emperor's role in the provinces. Unlike many modern heads of state, the Roman Emperor and his family, while no doubt well protected, were meant to display *virtus*, 'manliness', a set of characteristics which included courage, especially in military situations. While few (except artists) expected the Emperor to fight at the front of his troops, it was considered reasonable to get involved in the fighting, especially for a member of the Julio-Claudian dynasty, who was brother and son to two of Rome's great generals. The presence in his train of people with military experience suggests that Claudius was well aware of this expectation and had made some preparation for it.

There is, however, a complicating factor: one of the few hard facts mentioned in the sources is that Claudius spent only 16 days in Britain. Grainge (2002) has shown that one day would have been needed to each disembark and embark the troops, which leaves 14 days of possible campaigning. Given that Claudius brought the siege equipment and elephants, their marching speed would be unlikely to have exceeded the normal marching speed of the legions, i.e. 20 miles per day.

A look at a modern Ordnance Survey map of Britain gives the distance from Chichester to Colchester as c. 128 miles, which would be just over 6.5 days' march to Colchester and 6.5 days' back again after the campaign – which would reduce the time available for conquering Colchester, receiving the surrender of the British tribes and inspecting the tribes to a day and a half, two and a half days if the soldiers and senators can be on the march on the same day as disembarkation. The same exercise for Richborough to Colchester, yields a distance of c.134 miles, so again about 6.5 days to and from and again offering no more than a weekend in Colchester.

It is true that Claudius' arch in Rome mentioned the fact that this was an un-bloody campaign and it is probably also true that the visit of Claudius, a man in his early fifties at the time, and according to Suetonius apparently fond of his food and wine, was mainly a public relations exercise. But there has to be some doubt if even this could have been achieved in 48 hours. We should thus consider the option that Claudius was sailing neither to

Richborough nor to Fishbourne, but may have been disembarking closer to Colchester, perhaps in the unknown harbour that had been used to provide the Colchester area with the Roman imports that have been found in its Iron Age contexts.

This also raises the related question of where the other troops under Aulus Plautius started out from. We know that a substantial part of the auxiliaries tended to come from the Rhine army; the legions, with the exception of *legio IX Hispana,* certainly did. We also know that, given a choice, the Roman army did use river transport when available when transporting heavy or bulky items, and we have also seen, as the Dutch have suggested, that the forts on the Oude Rijn west of Utrecht were probably originally built to provide the logistics for an army operating in Britain. Unfortunately, Grainge has completely omitted any discussion of these Northern ports in the Delta, and it is certainly true that it makes very little sense to start from the Rhine to get to Fishbourne. The trade from the Delta to eastern England and Scotland in later periods was substantial and there was even an English 'harbour' at Flushing/Vlissingen, not far from the Roman Nehalennia sanctuary on Walcheren, with its inscriptions of the late first to third century thanking the goddess for safe crossings from the Delta amongst others to London.

On the other hand did the *legio II Augusta* coming from Strasbourg/ Argentorate in Germany use the Rhine route, or did they, the same as Caesar's troops, cross the whole of Gaul to get to Boulogne? Admittedly, this would have been easier than in Caesar's day, as the main road network was, by Claudius' reign, in place; but if that is the case, it would have made just as much sense, and taken about as much time, to march to the Somme or Seine estuary as to Gesoriacum/Boulogne. Once again the vagueness of our sources does not allow for a decision and other sources (e.g. archaeological evidence) are absent. Grainge's study (2002) assumes for the most part Boulogne as the departure harbour; other points of departure are treated much more cursorily.

All these points can be used to raise doubt about either location as a landing point and I am deeply aware that this level of negativity may not be welcomed by many scholars. Both landing sites contain something of merit, but more *hard evidence* is clearly needed at this point. Items such as the Bredgar hoard, which on numismatic grounds must have been deposited between 42 and 47 (Sauer, 2001), are at best circumstantial evidence, as they may just as easily have been hidden by a merchant embarking in

Richborough and hoping to retrieve the money on his return; which never happened. Coin hoards only rarely reveal the reason for their deposition, but without further evidence, neither they nor a helmet fished out of Chichester harbour can prove the issue either way.

Finally, a positive ending to this chapter. The debate focuses at the moment entirely on the first few weeks of the invasions – after Claudius returns, most researchers appear to lose interest, after all Plautius has just been told to deal with the rest. For the moment, it would be good to remember in this context, that wherever the first landfall was, we actually do have extremely good evidence that Richborough very quickly became one of the main supply hubs of Britain. Until it was eclipsed by London and the other *classis Britannica* stations, it was the main port through which goods for the South-East of England appear to have entered the island.

On the other hand it seems highly unlikely that during the first few years of the invasion, Fishbourne or at least the Solent was not the base of a Roman fleet. One of the few incontrovertible facts we are given by Suetonius is that Vespasian took the whole of the Isle of Wight. The Isle of Wight is between two miles and six miles from the mainland: it is impossible to invade it without ships and these had to come from somewhere and be stationed and prepared in the Solent.

So, wherever the personal preference in this debate falls, it is very clear that either site was crucial for the eventual conquest of Britain.

Chapter 6

After the Invasion

Claudius left Britain to celebrate his victory in Rome. In the meantime in Britain Aulus Plautius continued to turn the relatively easy success of one summer's campaigning into a lasting gain of a British province for the Roman Empire. Aulus Plautius, the governor or more accurately the *legatus pro praetore* (literally 'an official with judicial powers in the provinces sent by the Emperor'), had considerable power, but governors were not allowed to just act on their own instinct; on appointment they were given a set of instructions by the Emperor (*mandata*), which contained their mission brief for the term of their office (by this time usually 3/4 years). We know very little of what these *mandata* looked like. But it seems their legality died with the Emperor and most governors waited for new instructions on the accession of a new Emperor. Claudius' instruction, 'Carry on with the rest!' may have been the one line summary of his orders to Plautius; but we hear little in the historical record of what happens next.

We know that various British people surrendered, that oppida (towns, usually fortified) were taken and that the Isle of Wight was conquered, but whether that was before, during or after Claudius came to Britain, Suetonius does not tell us. It is tempting to turn at this point to the next available chronological boundary and proceed with a tale of conquest, but this would be to miss the vital role that the Roman army was playing in the period immediately after the surrender at Colchester.

Unlike almost all modern states, the Roman governors were military commanders within their province as well as civilian administrators. In addition, there would usually be one other high ranking official: the procurator, a salaried official in the direct employ of the Emperor, who would be in charge of the financial aspects of the province and it seems part of the logistics of supplying the army, as well as keeping an eye on the governor, while the governor appears to have on occasion returned the compliment.

The two areas of competence overlapped in the everyday administration by necessity: the money raised by the procurator paid for the army of the governor and the governor's decisions regarding the day-to-day running of the province had repercussions for the finances of the procurator. At the same time the wrong decision on the implementation of taxes or financial administration by the procurator could lead (as we will see) to riots and rebellions.

Romans, or at least Strabo during Augustus' time, expected their provinces to make a profit; a generation later this is not likely to have changed. As a result, the administration was kept small; neither the governor nor the procurator had a large salaried staff, but were encouraged to find a solution to any problems out of their own pockets or with the help of their friends and relatives – and as we have seen from Cicero's comments, the Roman participants expected to profit from this work. Exploitation of positions of power was considered normal, there is not really a term for corruption in provincial administration in Latin, although there is a concept that you should not be *too* greedy. The governor himself could be prosecuted if found to be excessive in the exploitation of the provincials (although there is more than a suggestion in the historical writers that conviction for this extortion did not so much reflect the guilt of the accused, as much as the number of political enemies the man in question had made in Rome).

The only other body that could be drawn upon for the emerging administration of the province was the army. Military personnel could be seconded to work in the office of either the governor or procurator, or be sent on missions to implement their commands.

The army would also have been the only police force available, as at least in the directly administered areas, it would have been illegal to keep free men or slaves under arms or to use violence or to threaten it, unless commissioned to do so by the Emperor.

This is an explosive mix and in a newly conquered province this could and frequently did lead to disturbances, when Roman rule was imposed. (The Varian disaster in Germany in 9 AD was caused by a governor being too keen to impose Roman rule on recently conquered people.) The resulting need was to identify indigenous people who were willing to cooperate with the Romans and administer their own regions or tribes on their behalf. This could be in the form of the *civitas* administration with its own council. How much or little this agreed with the Mediterranean practice remained a matter of negotiation, and the amount of time spent by Aulus Plautius to negotiate these administrative terms should not be underestimated.

An alternative was to use client kings (as before) and let them do the administration. Again this would not have been without problems, as terms needed to be negotiated and probably a team of 'advisers' selected to help with the implementation of some of the requests. We know that by the late 50s we have Togidubnus (sometimes also still known as Cogidubnus; possibly king of the Chichester or Silchester area), Prasutagus of the Iceni and Cartimandua of the Brigantes. These are the three that have for their very different reasons made it into the history books; it is quite likely that others existed, but we lack their names or that of their kingdoms.

In the areas that were under direct control, armed forces were needed to keep the peace. In Modern Britain we tend to differentiate between civilian police forces and the military, although many European states have military bodies conducting policing duties. The same applied in Rome; in addition to any possible *civitas'* watch or royal guards, the army was mostly responsible for the upkeep of the peace. This of necessity demanded a spreading of the available forces over a substantial area. This decision also allowed for a more manageable form of keeping the forces supplied, by dispersing the army closer to their potential food sources and cutting down on the need to guard supply transports, provided the necessary infrastructure was in place.

A Roman army on invasion could be supplied from its area of origin, so initially it is more than likely that the Roman army was supplied from the Rhine and/or Gaul, although we have little evidence for this, except for the rapid speed with which the supply base at Richborough developed. Increasingly it was assumed that the newly conquered area would take over the supply of the army. This would mean that the army needed to have a road/river system that allowed for transport to be brought up to the bases. Britain with its extended coastline and good harbours provided just the conditions for such a system to be put into operations.

The basic underlying pattern of the early road transport system appears to link the major harbours (in Kent, on the Humber, on the Thames and along the south coast) with the major legionary bases (e.g. Colchester, Exeter, Lincoln and Wroxeter) and other large civilian settlements (e.g. Cirencester, Silchester and London). Seven Roman roads criss-crossing the country achieved the links between the river network and these towns: Ermine Street (running from London to the Humber), Watling Street (from

London to Wroxeter), the Fosse Way (from Topsham near Exeter to Lincoln and on to the Humber), as well as the road from Cirencester to Silchester, and then on to London, the road from Silchester to Chichester and the roads from London to Colchester and to Richborough. Research on these roads suggests that some may have had pre-Roman origins (such as in the Wroxeter area), but that the new roads were not all built overnight and the beautifully engineered cambered roads with rammed gravel may have taken several decades to complete (Salway, 1981, 96–97). Nevertheless, the laying out of the routes, rather than the engineering of tracks appears to have happened relatively early and was most likely performed by the army in the first few years after the conquest.

As a result the new province gained an infrastructure which allowed traffic to flow with comparative ease. The fact that many of the forts of the early period were sited along these roads, and the rapidity with which London, which lies at the heart of the eastern part of this road system, had developed, attests to the need for a transport system that allowed for heavy goods, as well as personnel, to safely cross the province.

As stated, the security of the province was mainly in the hands of the military and we know of a number of military sites from the first twenty years after the conquest. In addition further sites have been proposed for various reasons (spacing, strategy, ill defined ditches found during excavations). The Roman army may have been stationed in forts and fortresses at the time, but it also operated within civilian towns and it seems losses of military equipment, especially cavalry equipment may attest to operations, but not necessarily to forts, e.g. at Silchester.

The strategic hubs of the troop deployment at this period are the legions. Some appear to be stationed as a whole in fortresses such as Colchester/Camoludunum, but the majority were accommodated in vexillation fortresses (now often and possibly more accurately termed campaign bases), sizeable military sites of c. 8–12 ha that could accommodate substantial parts of a legion as well as some auxiliary troops. Over a dozen of these bases are known from the first twenty years of the occupation, including Longthorpe, Lake Farm, or Mancetter. In between, we know of a number of auxiliary forts, large enough to take around 500 troops. The large number of these sites suggests a very rapidly changing landscape of troop deployment, something that archaeology (our most important tool in the understanding of this period) has only rarely been able to unravel in the necessary detail (e.g. in two year intervals). Archaeological finds, especially on sites that underlay later Roman towns, can be rare and thus hard to date, and a dozen finds of probable military origin and a few Samian sherds offer little chance of refining the date beyond a general bracket of 'Claudian/Neronian'.

Some sites are exceptions in this context: the finds of gate timbers in the annex of the legionary/vexillation fortress of Alchester which can be dated to 44 together with a gravestone of the *legio II Augusta*, allow us to suggest Alchester as one of the first bases of this legion and thus possible home for a winter or so of Vespasian, its commander and later Emperor (70/79) (Sauer 2005).

In later periods we know that legionary fortresses had access to land that was reserved for their usage. One of the problems of the rapidly changing landscape of the early years is that it is next to impossible to establish whether this was already the case in Claudius' reign. We are also still very badly informed about what units were present at this time, but four legions (*legio XIV Gemina, legio II Augusta, legio IX Hispana* and *legio XX Valeria Victrix*) have left early gravestones of the period in Britain, such as the one of the *centurio* Favonius Facilis of *legio XX* in Colchester. If he died as a serving soldier, it would suggest that *legio XX* was stationed at Colchester, but *centuriones* rarely indicate on their gravestones that they are retired and it is just possible that the stone belongs to one of the first residents of the later colonia. In addition there are auxiliary units such as the *ala I Thracum* of which we also possess a gravestone from Colchester.

In many ways it is not surprising to find this rapidly changing military landscape in Britain, as progress appears to have been rapid; but what is more striking is the uneven spread of military sites throughout the province. While there are numerous military sites in the Midlands and around Exeter and Lincoln, large parts of the country are still empty, in some areas such as west of the Tamar, this may reflect a lower level of research, but apart from Richborough (which may have been military or civilian in character in its early phases), no forts are known in Kent now that Syndale has been disproved (Brit. Arch. no. 77(2004)), and similar sparsely occupied areas exist amongst others in Hertfordshire and south of the Thames. It is a possibility that these territories were not under direct Roman control, but may represent further otherwise unnamed client kingdoms, but there is no further evidence for this theory.

Having established the main administration of the province and a military infrastructure, a further point to organize would have been taxation, revenue and excise. We are told in Tacitus' Agricola (chapter 19) that forty years later there were problems with the grain that the civilians were forced to deliver to the forts, which suggests that some of the taxes were paid in kind to feed the army. But we know little about this early aspect of the province – not even the names of the early procurators.

One of the privileges the Emperor reserved for himself in any province was the right to all valuable ore deposits, especially those containing silver and gold. Silver is rarely found by itself, but more often in combination with other metal ores such as lead. While Caesar after his invasions was still of the opinion that there was little of value on the island, the Claudian invaders would have known better: by 49 lead pigs from the Mendips were in circulation, the accompanying silver no doubt was used for coinage or silver vessels. British ingots of the same period have been recorded in northern France, indicating that lead was being exported to the Continent only six years after the Claudian invasion. It has been suggested that a cistern at Pompeii, buried by the eruption of Vesuvius in 79, was made of British lead. The level to which the army was involved in the exploitation of these deposits seems to differ; according to the inscriptions on the ingots, some deposits were leased and worked by civilian consortia, others are found in close proximity to army installations, suggesting a close relationship.

A final point to consider is the Imperial Cult. While Roman citizens in Rome would agree that the Emperor was anything but a living god, the Roman state since Augustus had found that organized prayers for the guardian spirit of the Emperor (*genius Augusti*) or his *numen* (a hard to define term in English, but close to the divine essence that made him a good Emperor) by the residents of the provinces formed an act of loyalty that should be encouraged. One final duty of the governor (although probably not of the army) was to convince the elite of the province to establish such a cult site for the entire area. We know that by 60, this site was the temple of Divus Claudius in Colchester, but it can only have had this title since 54, when Claudius died. What earlier shape the cult took is so far unknown, and although numerous suggestions have been made that the central seat of the administration of the province must have been either in Colchester or London, there is little convincing evidence to support either suggestion and it is just as possible that during the early years the governor and the procurator found themselves too busy to establish one permanent headquarters, but instead toured the province (Haensch 1997, 120–125).

Given the wide range of duties outlined above, it is perhaps not surprising that little is heard in the written sources about the province under Aulus Plautius' governorship. In many ways, no news must have been good news, as it seems the province was willing to resolve its various teething problems without too many military interventions.

Most of the events described in this chapter come from Tacitus' Annals. Tacitus is a historian who wrote several books, including the Agricola (a short piece dealing with the career of his father-in-law as an example of the successful career of a good governor under a bad Emperor), and two historical works, the Annals, which deal with Roman history from the death of Augustus to the death of Nero (and which have a few books missing including the relevant section on the conquest of Britain), and the Histories, which dealt with the history from the death of Nero onwards, but of which we only have the first few years. Tacitus had been a successful lawyer, orator and politician under the Flavian Emperors at the end of the first century, and appears to have been involved in the coup that brought this dynasty to an end in 96, bringing the Emperors Nerva (96–98) and Trajan (98–117) to power. He has been credited with extremely good insight into the social climate in Rome in the first century and the problems generated by a powerful Emperor operating within a military dictatorship behind a façade of continuing Republican traditions. Tacitus throughout his writing displays wonderfully controlled language and some of his historical scenes, when closely analyzed are full of parallels, linguistic and factual allusions to other events, including occasional moments where phrases or events are duplicated on several occasions. All this makes Tacitean history very powerful literature, but harbours numerous problems for the historian in search of detailed information. On the other hand Tacitus has often been accused of being little interested in military affairs, especially campaign details that do not have consequential political repercussions and generally not thinking much of the army as an institution. He certainly throughout his historical writing has the tendency of focusing on people rather than events or places, and his geographical details, in keeping with historical traditions in Rome, are sketchy, as they were deemed of little interest to the readership (Syme, 1963; Mellor, 1993, 1999; Feldherr, 2009).

The priority of peacefully developing an effective administrative system for the province appears to have changed with the arrival of the second governor Ostorius Scapula. Tacitus (Annals Book XII, 31–40; our only source for the events) devotes several chapters to Britain at this point and the hero is Ostorius Scapula. We know little about him, in the same way that we know little about most Roman senators outside the Imperial families, and those we know mostly from the inscriptions that were dedicated to them, listing their careers or brief sketches in the sources; Tacitus' character sketches of the senators of the first century while vivid, are often also problematic 'sound bites'. Tacitus' heroes follow on the whole one of two types: on the one hand the stoic philosopher who holds to the moral high ground against the wicked Emperor, usually with tragic consequences for himself; the other is the 'old style' Roman general, a straight-laced warrior and strict disciplinarian, with little time for talking/diplomacy, who achieves substantial military successes for the Roman Emperor (and then usually falls into disgrace when an envious/inept Emperor does not know how to make use of such a 'true Roman'). It is hard to say whether the people that are portrayed this way really were as described, or whether this is the image in which Tacitus needed to typecast his protagonists in order to be able to make his wider social points. But it is clear from the description that Ostorius Scapula was one of the Tacitean heroes and that due to his exploits in Britain he had apparently few peers. In the absence of any other sources it is hard to judge if this was really the case.

The transfer of power from one governor to the next in any new Roman province could be tricky, as the Romans knew, and to judge from the description by Tacitus, an unnamed party in Britain was willing to exploit the situation by attacking a friendly tribe. Tacitus describes Scapula's response as swift and to the point: cut down anyone offering resistance, pursue the fleeing, then disarm the suspects to avoid repetition. In addition new forts or camps are built to stop access across the rivers Severn and Avon/Trent (the text of Tacitus is corrupt here and both emendations are in circulation) (Salway 1981, 100–101; Boetticher & Schaefer in: Tacitus 1985, 513).

This intervention, which appears to have focused on the western part of the province (to judge from the mention of the Severn), caused the Iceni to revolt. They came together at a defended site that was hard to access, especially for the cavalry. The auxiliaries under the governor's command stormed the fortification.

Not a lot of this account makes sense. Why would the Iceni in Norfolk care what happened in the West Midlands and in Somerset? Why would they even be concerned with this uprising? If these really were outsiders attacking friends of the Romans, i.e. allies or even client kings, the Iceni can have been neither party – so why would any of the outcomes affect them? It is hard to find any coherent reason for the inclusion of this episode, unless Tacitus either did not know where the Iceni were in relation to the Severn (easily done, if he had never been there), or alternatively it was not that important on the scale of things, especially compared with the final sentence: that this engagement led to the son of Ostorius Scapula being awarded the *corona civica* for rescuing a Roman citizen. Again we are not told why the son was there at all – was he an auxiliary commander, or had he just come along as one of the governor's voluntary staff discussed at the beginning of the chapter? But his appearance is necessary for the flow of Tacitus' account, as he will be mentioned again in the later volumes of the Annals, when Nero forces him into suicide in 66 (Birley 2005, 31), thus making both the Iceni and Scapula victims of Nero.

After the Icenian incident we are told that the province returned to peace and the campaigning is renewed against the Deceangi, who we can place along the north Welsh coast. The area is devastated in hit and run warfare, without a major battle; by the time the Roman army has nearly reached the west coast, another uprising is mentioned by the Brigantes, who appear to have occupied large parts of the North of England, the area north of Manchester and Leeds. A punitive campaign followed.

We know from later descriptions of Tacitus that at the time the Brigantes were ruled by Cartimandua, just as the Iceni were ruled by Prasutagus. It is interesting that Tacitus describes two campaigns against possible client kingdoms in the same year without naming their rulers and without later mentioning these earlier problems. Was he at this point of writing not aware of them? Thanks to Pliny the Younger's letters about Vesuvius, we know that Tacitus contacted eyewitnesses to record their experiences, but the events of the 50s may have been too long ago to still allow this. An alternative interpretation is that the Romans may have decided that it would be easier to return both areas to client control after administering them at first directly, as this would be less likely to cause uprisings. Similar decisions can be seen in the Eastern provinces such as Syria at about the same time, as well as earlier in other provinces – but once again our evidence does not allow us to move beyond hypotheses.

At the end of the first year's campaigning Ostorius appears to have decided to focus on the Silures (in other sources described as living in south eastern Wales and the Welsh Marches). He moved the legion from Colchester and established a new fortress further west at Kingsholm.

Colchester itself was not abandoned, but turned into a *colonia*, a settlement of retired soldiers with their own land grant. We know from elsewhere, that *coloniae* need not have been settlements on completely virgin sites, where only Romans lived. Since the Civil Wars of the first century BC the Romans have been known to create these settlements in established towns such as Pompeii, by confiscating some of the property in and around the town, and allocating it to the retiring soldiers. However, Colchester had been a legionary fortress, built inside the Iron Age oppidum, so the buildings of the legionary fortress could be adapted for civilian use with few problems. We have to assume that some of the land outside it was also assigned to the soldiers, but we know that both the nearby settlements at Sheepen and at Gosbecks, which had begun in the Iron Age, continued in existence. Gosbecks especially must have been home to some fairly wealthy British individuals, who were eventually, and clearly after the conquest, buried in the rich funerals at nearby Stanway.

One of the advantages of a *colonia* was the creation of a settlement that was run on the Mediterranean model and could be used for those wishing to spread Roman culture as a series of model homes. It is unlikely, however, that this was at the forefront of Ostorius Scapula's thinking. He was renewing the conquest within the British province and needed to free up troops from the 'policing duties' outlined above. He could have asked for more troops from the Continent, but with four legions already in the province, it is doubtful if anybody in Rome would have acceded to his wishes. By creating a *colonia*, into which recently retired troops could be moved, he de facto exchanged a unit in full fighting fitness, for an informal unit (similar to later militias or invalid units) that could still be called upon for service in emergencies.

Archaeologically we can identify this redeployment in a series of new bases west of the Fosse Way, close to Siluran territory; including Kingsholm outside Gloucester, which probably became the new legionary base. Further north, along Watling Street, a series of campaign bases have been found at Wall, Kinvaston and a smaller site at Metchley.

There is also a large military site at Wroxeter as there was an *ala* stationed in the nearby auxiliary fort, Webster (in Webster and Chadderton 1988) argues that the military complex could not have been a legionary fortress at this time. This argument, however, is not cogent, especially as we know that several of the Rhine and Danube legions have an *ala* or *cohors* stationed nearby (e.g. Carnuntum, Mainz or Vetera) in the same period, or in the case of Vindonissa possibly stationed within the same fortress. There is thus little reason to delay the arrival of the *legio XIV Gemina* for several years, just because of the presence of an auxiliary unit close-by. In addition, if we assume that the two tombstones from Colchester refer to two soldiers on active service rather than retirees, there would be a similar scenario even within Britain.

We know that at some point the *legio II Augusta* had its base in Exeter (probably from 55 onwards), while there are early tombstones of the *legio IX Hispana* in Lincoln. However, the legionary fortress at Lincoln appears not yet to be occupied at this point and the *legio IX Hispana* may have been split between Longthorpe and one of the other vexillation fortresses or campaign bases (Jones 2002, 32–36).

As the above already suggests, the exact occupation history of these large military sites is problematic. Hassall (2000, 51–67) wrote a comparative article on the various reconstructions and their underlying reasoning: the intervening years have not substantially altered the argument, except by adding Alchester as a new site into the mix, without resolving the issues. What is not in doubt is that from the late 40s onwards we see an increasing amount of military moving towards the West and especially into the Welsh Marches. Archaeologically, we see increasing numbers of marching camps (the temporary accommodation used on campaign or during training) and forts clustering at the mouth of the Severn tributaries, suggesting that while we are still a long way from developing protective Roman frontiers like those seen a century later, we have developed the concept of a springboard site from where campaigns could be organized and to which troops could be withdrawn between campaigning.

Tacitus continued to describe the target of the next campaigns: the Silures and Caratacus, son of Cunobelinus, who appears to have become the general leading the resistance against Rome in the West. He offers no information about Caratacus' career between the battle near the Thames estuary and the last battle in the Welsh mountains; and in the absence of any supporting evidence any proposed biography would be pure fiction.

The Scapulan campaign, about which we hear little, ends in a decisive battle 'in the land of the Ordovices' (which with the help of other sources we can place in north-east Wales, north of Shrewsbury) and once again the only information we are given is a topographical description of the battle site: Caratacus chose a steep mountain, with the easy access blocked by a rough stone obstacle. At the foot flows a river with a tricky ford. Two protruding parts of the hill are manned with armed men.

Suggestions of the location of this battle site once again abound, including the Llanymynech/Abertanat area, proposed by G.D.B. Jones (in Jones and Reynolds 1987). But the description is that of a generic Welsh hillside; selecting the right one amongst hundreds of candidates would have to (once again) depend on the identification of a scatter of military finds, which so far has failed to materialize.

The result of the battle, however, is reported by Tacitus: after heavy fighting the Roman army is finally victorious, and Caratacus' wife and brothers are captured. He himself escaped to the Brigantes and unlike the report of a year earlier, this time Cartimandua is named as the queen of the Brigantes, who handed him over to the Roman authorities in the ninth year after the conquest of Britain (43 + 9 = 51/52). We thus have to assume that the war with the Silures has lasted nearly three years, given that Ostorius Scapula became governor of Britain in the winter of 47/48 and spent the first year dealing with the Iceni, Decangi and Brigantes. It should be stressed that Tacitus' account makes this nowhere clear; we are left with a rapid progression of the narrative between the campaign against the Brigantes, the founding of the *colonia* and the final battle against the Silures and the capture of Caratacus. As a consequence, it is difficult to date the duration of the events described. How long did it take Caratacus to reach the Brigantes? Did Cartimandua hand him over immediately, or are we faced with a protracted hunting down by the Roman army?

The Tacitean account at this point switches from Britain to Rome and the next two and a half chapters (36/38) deal mainly with the confrontation of Caratacus and Claudius in Rome. This offered Tacitus another chance for one of his set piece confrontations of the uncivilized, but morally sound barbarian, against the ruler of the world or his general; civilized, but definitely far from heroic. In nearly all these confrontations, whether face to face as here, or vicarious through opposing speeches, Tacitus managed to make the barbarian appear as the more noble, the more deserving, and the one with the better lines, even if Rome always wins in the end. This goes some way to explain why Rome's enemies always make such good heroes, as they definitely have in Tacitus the better ghost writer. In this particular case, Caratacus refused to be cowed by Rome's grandeur and offered Claudius some philosophical insights into the turns of fate and how his resistance is in many ways a favour to Claudius, as he thus had a more formidable enemy and therefore a greater reputation as a winner due to Caratacus being talked about for the ten year duration of the war. Caratacus then argued that by having him killed, Claudius would just have ended this reputation; while pardoning him would mean that there would be a permanent reminder of Claudius' glory. Claudius (who is depicted by Tacitus as learned, not clever or wise, but easily influenced) did as suggested and pardoned Caratacus and his family. Scapula is awarded the triumphal insignia.

When returning to Britain, Tacitus' account (chapter 38) shows the situation in the province as deteriorating. In the aftermath of the capture of Claudius, Ostorius Scapula faced large amounts of opposition. A prefect of the camp and those legionaries left in Siluran territory to build a fortification were attacked, and despite the success of the rescue mission, the prefect and eight centurions (and we have to assume numerous legionaries) were killed; a further attack on troops gathering fodder led to the Romans fleeing the scene. While the battle could eventually be turned into success, the fighting continued with the Silures being singled out as the most dangerous enemies (which implied that other unnamed tribes were involved as well). The situation appears to have been further aggravated by the undiplomatic suggestion of the governor that the Silures should be treated like the Sugambri, a German tribe, and were either exterminated or resettled in Gaul. Eventually Scapula died during the fighting, but not in battle.

The next governor Didius Gallus appears to have spent considerable time earlier in his career 'campaigning' for the position without success, but seems to have spent the interim gaining substantial military success elsewhere in the Roman Empire. Claudius now appointed him as the successor to Scapula, which according to the sources he did not appear to have appreciated very much (Birley 2005, 35).

Didius Gallus was apparently already an older man, and unwilling to campaign in person, despite the continuously deteriorating situation. Apparently the Silures continued to attack Roman positions, and Tacitus accused both the Britons and the incoming governor of exaggerating the situation, wishing to obtain more glory for eventually resolving the situation: Gallus' exact position. In addition, Didius Gallus and his army were requested to intervene in Brigantian territory, after Venutius and Cartimandua had divorced each other and begun a civil war, which appears to have finally involved an intervention from outside (by whom we are not told), whereby Didius Gallus managed to rescue the queen. Once again we are not given any firm indication as to when this rescue took place. As already discussed, the last event described by date is the capture of Caratacus in the ninth year after the conquest, and Tacitus states clearly that he wished to treat the two governorships together 'so that ripped apart it would not leave too weak an impression'. We know that Didius Gallus' successor died in Britain after less than a year in post in 58. So the above events must fall somewhere between 52 and 57.

The second time Tacitus returned to the events in the province at this time is at the introduction to the circumstances surrounding the Boudiccan rebellion. Setting the scene in a couple of sentences, Didius' career is summarized as having done nothing but retain the ground already won, while his successor Veranius is credited with a few moderate raids against the Silures before he died. The equally short summary in the Agricola (chapter 14) adds that Didius Gallus built a few forts, so that he could claim to have extended the Roman territory. Veranius' successor, Suetonius Paullinus is another of Tacitus' 'men of iron', who was in public esteem a rival to Corbulo, possibly the greatest general of Nero's reign.

Tacitus' language in these passages is clearly designed to create opposing characterizations. Ostorius Scapula and Suetonius Paullinus are great military men; Didius Gallus and Veranius are 'no hopers'. Very little blame attaches to Veranius, due to his early death. Didius Gallus, however, is charged with delegating work to others instead of campaigning himself, because he was old and sluggish and surfeit with honours. He is also accused of exaggerating the successes and dangers, and with portraying consolidation (building forts) as conquest, to artificially inflate his achievements. Tacitus clearly did not get this information from a friend of Didius Gallus. He also appears to have had some problems with the character ascribed to this general. Either the governor was too lazy to seek military glory, or he was exaggerating his achievements; both combined in the same man seems a very unlikely combination. We know from other sources, summarized by Birley (1981, 45–49; 2005, 32–37) that Didius Gallus had substantial military experience: he had been on the German campaign with Germanicus, and as well as being *curator aquarum* (in charge of the water supply of Rome) in the forties, he was in the Crimea during the disturbances caused by the accession of Cotys (Annals 12.15.1). He may also have been involved with the creation of the Danube provinces and the violent integration of the client kingdom of Thrace into the Roman state, although the evidence is thin at this point. In an inscription from Olympia he was described as a legate of Claudius, holding triumphal ornaments (the third governor in a row decorated with the highest military honours available to a Roman senator in this province). All this suggests that Didius Gallus was well qualified for the 'military man' image that Tacitus bestowed on Scapula and later on Suetonius Paullinus.

Jarrett (1964, 32) argued that some of the problems in Britain might have been caused by the death of Claudius in 54, which may have been followed by a rethink and change of direction in British policy in the early years of Nero. Again there is no further evidence to support this scenario, nor is it likely to come to light any time soon. We do not know what happened to Didius Gallus after he left Britain, and there is no explanation for Tacitus' clear animosity.

However, we also have problems with the details of the Welsh campaigns as described by Tacitus. Apparently, the province at the arrival of Didius Gallus is in complete upheaval due mostly to the Silures, but all this vanished when the new governor arrived, but then Veranius had to campaign against the Silures again. The Silures are in the mid 50s a clear and present danger to the province. However, with the arrival of Suetonius Paullinus we hear about him campaigning on Mona/Anglesey, and after two years of success, conquering tribes and establishing strong forts (Agricola, chapter 14). Welsh topography suggests that if you remove the Roman troops from the Gloucester and Wroxeter area to go to Anglesey, it is next to impossible to keep the southern and central Welsh Marches protected. It would also seem risky to campaign at the north-western part of Wales, when the tribes resident in the adjacent areas, the Deceangli on the coast, Ordovices inland and in Snowdonia, are not pacified. Was Suetonius Paullinus an (unnecessary) risk taker, or are we missing substantial parts of the account of the Welsh campaigning due to Tacitus' need to concentrate on the 'highlights', i.e. Caratacus under Scapula and Boudicca under Suetonius Paullinus? As we will see later, Wales was clearly not fully pacified in the late 50s as further campaigns appear to have been conducted later, so what other information can be used to resolve the issue?

We have already briefly touched on the fact that the Welsh Marches are home to a cluster of Roman forts and camps. Davies and Jones (2006) have recently compiled the available evidence for the temporary camps in Wales. This evidence suggests that in addition to the series of pre-Flavian forts in the Welsh Marches, there are a substantial number of camps of sizes between 1.5 ha to over 20 ha that are likely to be associated with the campaigning in Wales. On the whole the marching camps in Wales are between 1.5/20 ha in size, 13–15 are under 5 ha, 11 are between 5/12 ha, while 14 or 15 are between 12/20 ha in size, only 3 camps are larger than 20 ha.

This suggests that the armies operating in Wales are substantially smaller than those used later by the Romans in Scotland. However, despite the fact that these camps can be divided by size into four separate groups there are only a few that appear to form a chain, as you would expect, if they were built by an army progressing at the end of each marching day of 10–15 miles. The standard marching speed of the Roman army on training is 20 miles/day, but as Davies and Jones point out, this is unlikely to be achievable in the inhospitable terrain of Wales. In addition, there are large parts of Wales where marching camps should be present because of the historical evidence (such as Anglesey and the north coast of Wales) and/or because of strategic considerations (such as Herefordshire and Gloucestershire), but have not yet been found.

Early studies of camps sometimes assumed that a Roman army on campaign is likely to produce camps of a uniform size, which can be followed and mapped; but more recent studies have pointed out that there are likely to be substantial fluctuations as the army progresses through its campaigning season. Army sizes are based as a compromise between four main factors: how many troops are available, how many enemies are likely to be encountered, how many men can be kept supplied and how many men can be effectively deployed. The first two require little explanation, but an army that cannot be kept supplied is unlikely to remain in good fighting form for any length of time, while there is also a limit to the amount of men that can be brought to any given site of battle before they start obstructing each other's movement. Thus bringing four complete legions and auxiliaries to deploy on battle sites where there is only room for 3,000 men at most is a waste of supplies and energy. These men could be better deployed elsewhere, either as a separate line of attack during the same campaign or as a reserve force, waiting for their turn in a rotation pattern (for which admittedly we have little evidence in the Roman army away from battle and siege situations). The smaller camps may thus reflect protracted fighting by comparatively small forces in numerous campaigns.

The habit of dividing fighting forces discussed earlier would have meant that camp sizes may have decreased suddenly, before increasing again substantially, when all parts of the army reunite in one particularly large camp, something sometimes called 'gathering grounds' (Maxwell, 1991). As a result, it is not easily possible to identify the course of any one campaign in the archaeological record. However, the surviving camp evidence in combination with the natural routes of traffic through the Welsh mountains can lead to the identification of 'invasion corridors'. Thus the Severn, Teme and Wye valleys appear to have been considered as major invasion routes with large clusters of camps of every size appearing in the Walton Basin, along the Arrow Valley and in the vicinity of Wroxeter on the Severn.

It is also increasingly becoming apparent that there is a difference in marching camps; on the one hand those that may have existed for only one night, and on the other, camps such as Brampton and Kintore in Scotland which to judge from the multiple firings of their ovens, remained in use for several weeks. The latter camps may have been used as a central base of operations during protracted raids and campaigns against 'economic assets' in the area.

But during the course of trying to resolve the question of the campaign routes in Wales, it needs to be mentioned that (while infuriatingly little) there is at least historical data for the conquest by the Romans of this area. In many areas of Britain, we are considerably less well informed. According to the Claudian victory monument, eleven (or more) kings surrendered to Claudius. We can be reasonably certain that this included the Iceni, who are described as coming voluntarily under Roman rule, and the part of the Dobunni/Bodunni that had been under Catuvellaunian rule according to Cassius Dio, and one assumes it also includes the Atrebates and the Brigantes (for whom we have evidence for client kings). The others appear to have no names or known associations.

When the province developed a permanent civilian administration, we hear of other tribes that gave their name to Roman administrative districts or *civitates*: the Parisi, north of the Humber, the Cornovii and the Corieltauvi in the northern Midlands, the Durotriges, 'free' Dobunni and Dumnonii in the South and Southwest as well as the Cantiaci in Kent. The only reference pertaining to their conquest experience is the line from Suetonius on Vespasian's exploits concerning two tribes and multiple towns and oppida. This suggests that our understanding of the Roman takeover in parts of southern England very much depends on the archaeological evidence.

Most of the areas listed have produced little evidence of marching camps, except for a cluster in Nottinghamshire; but the North Midlands have produced substantial evidence for pre-Flavian forts, some of which appear to be very early, while the area of the Dobunni should probably be seen as part of, or at least involved in the Welsh campaigns discussed above. The exploitation of the ore deposits in the Mendips and the deployment of the army at Charterhouse and at other sites such as the coastal site of Sea Mills, suggests a certain level of disruption, while the fort at Cirencester appears to have become, very early on, the focus of development.

Further to the south there is a cluster of forts in Devon, Dorset and Wiltshire north of the Roman legionary base at Exeter (occupied from c. 55 onwards), and recent discoveries have added further forts in Cornwall to the only one known so far at Nanstallon (Hartgroves & Smith, 2008). The evidence from Dorset takes mainly the form of a number of hill forts that were occupied by the Romans. These sites, however, offer the clearest evidence that the Roman takeover in the area was far from uncontested with 'the massacre horizon' in the south-west gate at Cadbury Castle (Barrett et al. 2000, 115f.), Hod Hill and possibly further violent deaths at Maiden Castle. Alternative scenarios such as a possible practice siege site at Hod Hill or a different location of the battle at Maiden Castle have been put forward (Sharples 1991). The exact date of these events cannot be established either; the usual date bracket suggested is 'the middle of the first century AD' (which would cover the period from 43 to c. 60/61 inclusive). It has been argued that the exact date of these events does not matter, just the certainty that the indigenous population at some point stood up to attackers carrying Roman weapons and apparently died in the defence (Woodward in Barrett et al., 2000, 116). However, in the context of the conquest it is surely of interest whether these sites represent resistance to an initial invasion or are a result of a later uprising. The outcome, however, cannot be in question: the hill forts on Britain's south coast saw the establishment of a series of usually very small Roman military installations; some took the form of formal forts, such as Hod Hill, but more appear to have been in the form of possible barracks set within the defences of the Iron Age hill forts, such as Cadbury or Hembury (Todd 2007, 113–117).

At the other end of the Fosse Way, in the area of the Corieltauvi and around the legionary fortress of Lincoln, a similar cluster of early forts has been identified, many associated with finds pointing to the early Neronian period and it has been suggested that they are not designed as an occupation force of the Corieltauvi, but as a 'springboard' similar to the forts around Wroxeter, this time monitoring the situation in the Brigantian territory.

All these sites suggest that the Roman conquest of Britain could be a very different experience for the Roman and indigenous population alike, depending on which part of Britain you were living in at the time. The range appears to have been from little change for the tribe, except in the form of a new 'set of advisors' for the ruling families, to extreme violence in the case of the Silures and in parts of the English south coast.

The literary sources mention that Nero originally considered abandoning Britain and withdrawing his troops: it is not clear at which point in Nero's reign this was considered – two scenarios present themselves; either at the beginning of Nero's reign (as favoured amongst others by Birley (2005, 35) and Jarrett (1964), or after Boudicca's uprising. We do not know what caused these ideas, but given that Nero decided to stay, Rome must have considered the conquest a success and Britain an asset. In 60 things became a lot more complicated.

Chapter 7

Boudicca

oudicca is not just a historical figure – in modern Britain she is an icon, a term sometimes defined as cultural short-hand for a focus of stories dealing in this case with various aspects of British self-definition, whether in the form of statues at Westminster or Cardiff, films and books of various qualities, or a quotation in rock videos or as labels for pubs and ale. She is to some a feminist role model, for others a freedom fighter, or a fighter against governmental injustice.

Most of the stories told about her today have a positive slant, which is surprising, because what they celebrate is after all the perpetrator of an all out massacre of two, perhaps three, towns full of civilians, most of whom had little to do with the injustices she and her tribe the Iceni felt they had suffered. Usually the wholesale slaughter of innocent bystanders causes revulsion in witnesses (even if at third and fourth hand); here it has caused celebrations as a hero. This is not the place for a moralistic essay on the rights or wrongs of this approach, but this chapter is going to look at the evidence for Boudicca's Rebellion, where this heroic celebration comes from, and compare it with the archaeological evidence for the Iceni in Norfolk.

Roman Britain between the Conquest and its client kings

As we have seen the form of administrative integration of a tribe into the Roman Empire could vary, and in addition to direct control, Aulus Plautius and his successors set up at least three, but possibly more client kingdoms. The term 'client kingdom' has sometimes been equated with the modern concept of a satellite state, but the relationship with Rome was more complex. Client status is first and foremost a treaty agreement between the Roman state and a particular foreign ruler, who is called by the Romans '*rex et amicus SPQR*', a king and friend of the Senate and People of Rome.

Technically it is a treaty of mutual support: Rome supports the king's internal claim to power, while the king aids Roman interests in his region. Both offer mutual defence against common enemies. It is worth stressing though, that in practice these treaties were not equal; Rome expected a substantial level of obedience, but on its part could (and frequently did) renege on the deal whenever it suited its political interest, foreign or domestic. This obedience to Rome could be further insured by the provision of hostages, such as the 'offer' of raising some of the client king's family members in Rome. Client kingdoms are furthermore not strictly independent in a military sense, as the Romans could provide military protection for the king and Roman interest in the form of military bases – one of the best known of these military bases is the legionary fortress of the *legio XI Claudia* in Charax in the Bosporanian kingdom on the Black Sea, a longstanding client kingdom of Rome in the Crimea.

As the client treaty was with a particular king, rather than the tribe, the situation was fluid and had to be renegotiated with every change of ruler. This could lead to competition by various sons of a ruling king in gaining the support of the current administration in Rome. We assume that the princes that approached Augustus, Caligula and Claudius at various points before 43 were actually trying to gain Rome's support for becoming the next '*rex et amicus*' within their own tribe.

In the aftermath of the Roman conquest of Britain, we hear of three client kings, the most famous being Togidubnus/Cogidubnus of Chichester/Fishbourne. His client status is mentioned in Tacitus' Agricola (chapter 14), which describes him as follows:

> Certain *civitates* were given to King Cogidubnus, who remained most loyal (to Rome) to within our own memory, following the long established custom of the Roman people of using even kings to make others slaves.

Archaeologically his existence is confirmed by the reading and reconstruction of one inscription from Chichester (RIB 91) which calls him REG MAGN BRIT (*rex magnus Britannorum* – great king of the Britons). His association with Fishbourne palace, while often repeated, is far from secure and more recently he has been associated by some with Silchester; in truth we know very little about him or his actions during his apparently long reign.

Two further client kings are mentioned in the Roman historic sources; one is Queen Cartimandua of the Brigantes, the only *bona fide* woman ruler in her own right that we know of in Roman Britain. The other is Prasutagus of the Iceni. As we have seen in the last chapter, apart from these three client kingdoms, the rest of the South of England, usually assumed to be the area south of the Fosse Way (which in contrast to older research is no longer seen as a Roman frontier by modern scholars) was administered directly by Rome. In addition to the military, which had come from the Continent with the conquest or possibly as later reinforcements, increasingly large numbers of immigrants arrived from other areas of the Roman Empire. They were not necessarily Roman citizens themselves, and they appear to have come from a wide range of cultures within the Empire; but their interests were deeply bound up with the success of Britain as a Roman province. Substantial numbers of incomers settled in the emerging cities. London was at this point an informal trading centre with excellent infrastructure links including the harbour on the Thames, as well as a safe river crossing. The second largest Roman town was the *colonia* at Camoludunum/Colchester, which was set up on the site of the first Roman legionary fortress, which in turn occupied the site of a pre-existing oppidum. This was also the site of the temple to Claudius, and thus most likely the meeting place of the provincial assembly. Provincial assemblies have sometimes been described as early forms of provincial parliaments, but this far exaggerates their power. Their main role was as an assembly of the leading men of the province, who were charged with the proper organization and celebration of the Imperial cult within the province, the cost of which was expected to be born by the members of the assembly. In addition, they could send letters and embassies, usually of a congratulatory character, to the Emperor. We know that elsewhere in the Roman world they voted honorary statues for outgoing governors (and one assumes procurators), as well as occasionally sending letters of complaint about departing officers.

Elsewhere in Britain some Iron Age oppida were slowly changing into Roman *civitas*, capitals with a more Roman character. This process is particularly well understood for Silchester, but can also be seen in operation at Verulamium and Chichester to name but a few. In fact research in Silchester over the last 20 years suggests that it might have rivalled Colchester and London in size. The military units may have changed garrison frequently at this time, but at least the larger forts and fortresses managed to attract civilian settlements around them. On the other hand in many parts of the province rural Iron Age settlement patterns appear to have continued with very little change.

The Iceni

Archaeologically the Iceni are associated with a culturally distinct late pre-Roman and Roman Iron Age group that can be recognized north of the Waveney and Ouse in East Anglia, and which extends westwards into the Fenlands at least as far as Stonea.

While its base metal work, which is dominated by horse harness, is closely associated with what used to be called 'Celtic tradition' and showed some links to the South and the Continent, other characteristics set them apart from their neighbours. Unlike the neighbouring Aylesford-Swarling culture to the south (which has frequently been associated with the Trinovantes and Catuvellauni), this group did not use wheel-made pottery and appears to have had markedly different burial customs, as there are few of the cremation burials that have been found further south.

Like their neighbours to the south and west, however, they struck coins, but they never apparently copied the Roman coinage and its patterns in the manner of the Eastern and Southern Dynasties. In the western half of the group's distribution a series of sanctuaries/areas of ritual deposition have been excavated. Some, such as the one at Fison Way in Thetford, are enclosures with central round houses and shafts for the repeated deposition of carefully selected material. Others like Snettisham appear to be larger areas, where especially gold and silver were deposited in the open.

Within the area, at least four subdivisions can be identified archaeologically with at least four, perhaps five oppida i.e. proto-towns. The most enigmatic is Sedgeford, which appears to cover an area of circa eight square miles including areas of ritual significance and deposition as well as settlement zones. Further south are more traditional enclosed oppida such as Caistor St Edmund, under the later Venta Icenorum, Stonea/Chatteris in the Fenlands, Saham Toney/Ashill and Thetford. The last three are all found in the western part of the area, the so-called Breckland, traditionally the most fertile land, while the eastern districts are even more low-lying and waterlogged over large areas. The fertility of the Breckland might also explain the substantial amount of disposable wealth that can be recognized archaeologically from the Middle Iron Age (c. 200 BC) onwards. In addition to the oppida and sanctuaries, there are a number of smaller sites, both defended (such as the forts at Holkham, Warham, South Creake,

Narborough and Thetford) and open smaller sites, the majority of which appear to have been abandoned shortly after the Boudiccan rebellion.

It seems that by the time of the Claudian conquest the Iceni had merged into a single tribe with multiple centres (e.g. coins were minted at Thetford, Saham Toney and Needham), of which the wealthiest group and thus presumably also the most powerful lived in the western Breckland.

By the time of the conquest coins were struck with the inscription ANTED and slightly later further ones were marked ECEN, both were originally read as abbreviated royal names. John Davies of Norwich Museum, however, considers the ECEN inscription as an indication of the tribal name rather than an individual, making the Iceni one of the few tribes to advertize themselves in that way.

While it is possible that the Cenimagni mentioned by Caesar during his second campaign were predecessors of the later Iceni, the first time we hear about the Iceni themselves is around 48. Aulus Plautius' successor Ostorius Scapula suggested disarming some of the British tribes (including the Iceni), who (or at least some of whom) took offence at this, and started a revolt. Ostorius Scapula sent the army in, the rebels withdrew into a fort with only a single narrow access point and eventually the Roman army stormed the fort, and thus ended the rebellion. There is no archaeological evidence for this rebellion to date, and suggestions that this fort may have been Stonea or Holkham are based on general topographical consideration (large size, difficult access), rather than being based on archaeological confirmation of a battle site. Archaeologically we can identify a number of Claudian military installations in Norfolk, which may represent the initial garrison after the conquest or the response to the uprising. Many of these sites are positioned close to Icenian settlements. Unfortunately, as many of these sites are known from aerial archaeology only, it is not always clear which of these forts are Claudian and which represent the later response to the Boudiccan uprising. One presumably Claudian site, Woodcock Hall, appears to be sited next to the Saham Toney oppidum.

According to J. Davies' chronology (Davies & Robinson 2009, 54f.) at the same time as the first rebellion, silver coins naming Prasutagus began to be struck, which might suggest that the Romans decided that the Iceni may be better administered through a client king, rather than directly. Alternatively Prasutagus may have been chosen at the time of the conquest as the client king. It could then be argued that Prasutagus would have had to face consequences in not keeping his compatriots under better control, but the source (Tacitus' Annals) is too curt to allow us any insights into the context and background of the uprising, thus either scenario remains a possibility. At no point in the historical or numismatic evidence is Boudicca mentioned in any form, let alone as a co-ruler. She differs thus markedly from her neighbour to the west, Cartimandua of the Brigantes, where it appears that Cartimandua is in charge, while Venutius, at least in Tacitus' eyes, is very much the consort. Unfortunately, the Brigantes never struck coins thus depriving us of a possible insight into their view on who the Brigantian ruler really was. We also do not have any evidence for the political preferences of Boudicca; Prasutagus is described as a trusted friend of Rome, but it has been pointed out that just as in the case of Venutius and Cartimandua, the two rulers might have represented opposite ends of the political spectrum.

We hear nothing about the Iceni between this uprising and the events of the Boudiccan rebellion either in Tacitus' accounts or any other literary source. Archaeologically it is possible to point to a number of Roman imports arriving at the Iron Age sites, which demonstrate that there was more than diplomatic contact between the client kingdom and the directly administered part of the province. These included items of considerable value such as the Crownthorpe Hoard, a large collection of copper-alloy vessels, representing a near complete set of vessels needed for a Roman style drinking party (Davies & Robinson 2009, 33).

Reading the uprising

There are four main accounts of the events in the middle of Nero's reign and especially the Boudiccan uprising – one by Tacitus in the Agricola, a much more detailed one in the Annals both written about 40–50 years after the events, and one by Suetonius in his 'Lives of the Caesars', which dates probably to the second quarter of the second century AD. The last one was written by Cassius Dio in the first half of the third century AD.

For reasons which will become apparent, we will start with Suetonius. We know that Suetonius was the *ab epistulis* of Hadrian, the man who controlled Hadrian's Latin correspondence and who was removed from office by Hadrian because Suetonius had behaved to the Empress Sabina 'with greater familiarity than the etiquette of the court required' (SHA Hadrian 11.3). Before this he had been '*a studiis*' and '*a bibliothecis*', two posts which gave Suetonius access to the official archives and libraries in the city, and thus theoretically unrivalled access to the original records – if he had the time or the inclination in his position to actually use them.

Amongst other works, Suetonius has left us a series of biographies on the first twelve Caesars, i.e. the Emperors from Caesar to Trajan. While the biographies can be examined from many different perspectives, and certainly some elements are doubtful in their veracity (for example exactly how would Suetonius know what Tiberius got up to in his bedroom?), there is an underlying subject matter, which is 'what makes a good or bad Emperor?' and one way the twelve biographies can be read is as a series of examples for and against a particular definition of the role of Emperor. To elaborate the issue, the biographies focus on the life of the Emperor himself and his direct actions to reveal his character, less on events that he only indirectly influenced, thus a lot of 'provincial history' is excluded from the biographies.

Suetonius focused his biography very much on Nero's achievements or embarrassments in Rome; his policies with regard to the provinces covers a very short chapter (18): apparently Nero lacked any wish to extend the Empire and even considered withdrawing from Britain.

Suetonius later returns to Britain (chapter 39), when he lists among the disasters that struck during Nero's reign '*a disaster in Britain, where two important towns were sacked.*' By belittling the event, (note that Boudicca doesn't even get mentioned by name) in the middle of detailed accounts of the organisation of games and public performances and the burning of Rome, Suetonius creates the image of an Emperor who had his priorities completely wrong.

The longest account of the uprising is given by Cassius Dio, who wrote a history of the Roman Empire in the first half of the third century. Cassius Dio had been brought up in Asia Minor, modern western Turkey before becoming a member of the Senate following a long career in the service of the Roman Empire, which had taken him mostly to Eastern provinces, but amongst which his northernmost appointment was as governor of Pannonia Superior (modern Hungary) c. 226/8, when his excessive discipline and attitude caused problems with the army of the province. As a result the animosity of the army appears to have led to him not entering Rome for his second consulate in 229; instead he returned to his home province. The Histories appear to have been written over a period of about twenty years from 207 onwards. While Cassius Dio's original accounts appear to have been quite detailed only books 36–60 (dealing with 68/10 BC), 55–60 (dealing with 9 BC/46 AD) and part of books 79–80 (217/c. 220) survive; the rest of his work mostly endures as an abbreviation (epitome) by Johannes

Xiphilinus (and an even shorter version by Johannes Zonaras), both historians of the Byzantine Empire of the eleventh and twelfth century respectively. Xiphilinus is famously not really summarizing the text, but selecting material here and there for reasons that for the most part elude us, omitting substantial sections of the original without trace or reference, which makes it hard to determine whether the choice of material was Xiphilinus' or Cassius Dio's.

The surviving account, whether by Cassius Dio or Xiphilinus, is dominated by two battle speeches, which can be summarized by Suetonius Paullinus' 'Romans win because it is their birth right' and the speech of Boudicca, which suggests that Britain ought to win because the Britons were the more manly warriors and they wanted their freedom back, especially their freedom from taxation. The latter point is important, because in Dio's account the Boudiccan uprising, which is again credited with destroying only two unnamed Roman cities, is depicted as mainly a tax revolt, precipitated by the money-grabbing attitude of the governor, and especially Seneca (who at the time of the event was still the chief advisor to Nero). The description of a tall Boudicca, red-haired, in long loose, multi-coloured clothes with a hoarse voice, holding a spear would have been to Cassius Dio very much the epitome of everything uncivilized, in many ways as shocking as the first punks were to the British establishment of the 1970s.

There is little that is likeable about Cassius Dio's Boudicca; she was wild, uncivilized and needed putting down, a service that Suetonius Paullinus promptly rendered. Any further British attempts at continuing warfare ended with Boudicca, when she died of illness – a very unheroic death indeed.

Overall Cassius Dio's account apportions little blame to the Romans, but when it does, it focuses on Seneca's money lending trickeries, which create an echo to his earlier description of Nero's extravagance and his resulting constant need for money in the aftermath of the murder of his mother Agrippina. For Cassius Dio the uprising is just one of those things the barbarians in the provinces would do, and a proper Emperor would have dealt with it properly and kept his court in better control to avoid this situation arising in the first place. If anything, Boudicca's speech seems to imply that the situation could have been avoided if Nero was a bit less effeminate and less given to entertainment. It is not clear if Cassius Dio is here necessarily commenting only on Nero, or if he was also using the opportunity to pass judgement on the rule of Elagabalus in the early third century, which he witnessed and which would have been fresh on people's minds at the time of writing and whose combination of strong/controlling mother and decadent son provided a good parallel to the events of the first century AD. Either way it is worth noting that neither Cassius Dio nor Suetonius suggested that Boudicca deserved admiration.

This would suggest that the account most likely to have generated the hero worship described at the beginning of the chapter must have been written by Tacitus. Chronologically, the short passage in the Agricola (chapter 14–16) is closest to the events. But it only states that Suetonius Paullinus after two successful years as governor had laid himself open to attack from the rear, when he decided to attack Mona (Anglesey).

The fault for the uprising is seen as general exploitation and mismanagement by the Roman administration, and Boudicca is named as the leader, but in this account only the destruction of the *colonia* – thus most likely Colchester, is mentioned. Earlier in chapter 5 of the Agricola *coloniae* (plural!) are mentioned, but this probably reflects the requirements of a strident punch line '*trucidati veterani, incensae coloniae, intersaepti exercitus*' (veterans cut down, coloniae burned and armies surrounded), which is otherwise all in the plural. An interesting fact is Tacitus' comment that after a single battle order was restored:

> But many retained their weapons. They were influenced by consciousness of their guilt as rebels and by their personal fear of the legate – in case this otherwise excellent man would take high-handed measures against those who surrendered and would punish every offence with undue severity, as if it was a personal affront (Agricola, chapter 16, trans. A.R. Birley).

Here too, Boudicca was just a rebel, who objected to Roman rule and sought freedom, but there is no suggestion that Tacitus saw this as a just cause. Noteworthy for Tacitus was Agricola's involvement; he served as a tribune to Suetonius Paullinus (Agricola, chapter 5) during the rebellion. It was also a crucial part of his concise but strident history of Britain up to the arrival of Agricola as a governor.

The search for the origin of Boudicca as a British hero has thus led us finally to Tacitus' Annals. He (Annals XIV, 29ff) begins his account with a description of Suetonius' governorship, how in competition with Corbulo (a general who was at the time very successfully operating in Armenia, now

Eastern Turkey/Georgia), he had decided to conquer Mona/Anglesey. Tacitus' account suggests that Paullinus was in fact in the mopping-up stages of this operation, when Boudicca's uprising began.

Tacitus saw the origin of the problem in the death of King Prasutagus and his will, in which he named Nero joint heir with his daughters. The resulting military/police operation by the Romans is outlined in a few short shocking phrases: Nero makes himself sole heir to the kingdom, the Icenian kingdom is despoiled by centurions, the king's house by Roman slaves as if he had been conquered. Boudicca, the widow, is flogged, the daughters raped, the leading Icenians are robbed of their possessions and the relatives of the king are treated like slaves.

In response to Boudicca's call for revenge, the Trinovantes and unnamed others join the uprising to regain their freedom. Money problems are mentioned as additional motivation when the priests of the temple of Claudius (which would be the provincial assembly discussed above) are described as being plundered of their funds in the name of religion. The people blamed for these problems are the military and the veterans, who were exacerbating the danger to themselves by leaving the colony without defences.

The *procurator*, Decianus Catus, who as the financial officer must have ordered the ill-judged intervention at the Icenian royal seat, is only mentioned by Tacitus as doing nothing except supplying a mere 200 insufficiently armed men in defence to diffuse the situation.

Consequently Camulodunum was destroyed by the attack; the temple of Claudius which became the refuge for the Roman population held out for two days longer, but eventually was also burnt to the ground. The next attack was on *legio IX Hispana* and its commander Petillius Cerialis, who had tried to come to the rescue of the *colonia*. As a result the infantry was nearly completely destroyed: only the cavalry and the commander managed to escape.

In the meantime Suetonius Paullinus, returning without the army from Anglesey, had reached London, but finding the town undefendable, abandoned the site to its fate. London was destroyed and Verulamium plundered, resulting in c. 70,000 slain Romans, while apparently the military sites were left unmolested or at least unmentioned by Tacitus. In the meantime Suetonius had pulled part of the *legio XIV Gemina* and *legio XX Valeria Victrix* as well as the nearby auxiliaries together and offered Boudicca battle at a site described as follows: a position approached through a kind of corridor, and protected in the rear by a forest, so that the British could not attack from any side but the open plain in the front.

Paullinus deployed his troops in a standard battle line: legions in the centre, flanked by the auxiliaries, while the cavalry is stationed at the ends of both wings. The British are described as disorganized and had even brought their wives as witnesses, who they positioned at the far end of the battlefield. We are given two speeches by the opposing commanders: Boudicca's is given first and focuses briefly on the fact that they are trying to gain liberty from Roman rapaciousness and that the gods were on their side. And thus it was their destiny to conquer now or fall. The speech culminates in the punchline: '*Id mulieri destinatum, viverent viri et servirent.*' – This is the decision of this woman, men might choose to live, but live as slaves. Suetonius by contrast is pragmatic when he exhorted the troops to do their duty and prove their superior fighting skills, despite being in the minority.

The battle was fought and the lack of discipline led to the break of the British battle line and the slaughter of all British warriors, women and horses within reach of the Romans. In a typical Tacitean style we are informed that at the end 80,000 British were dead, while only 400 Romans were killed. Boudicca commits suicide by taking poison. Poenius Postumus, the camp prefect of the *legio II Augusta*, who had refused a direct order and not brought his legion to the battle, committed suicide by an unknown method.

Taken out of context, the way Boudicca is represented does not seem very positive. However, when put into the context of the wider narrative in Book XIV of the Annals, her courage and the portrayal of wronged wife and mother gain force. Book XIV starts with the description of Nero's murder of his own mother Agrippina, which went unpunished and indeed was celebrated by a Senate in fear of the Emperor. The narrative then turns to Nero's behaviour in Rome, and the lavish amusements he indulged in, while Corbulo fought the Emperor's wars in Armenia. The next year's narrative opened with the Boudiccan uprising, before returning to Rome and the descriptions of Nero's reign of terror, first against the Senate and later against the population as a whole, ending with the divorce and murder of his wife Octavia. All three women eventually lose their lives because of Nero's actions, but the way they deal with their fate differs: Agrippina did not control Nero when she could; his wife refused to offer any resistance; even the Roman senators who suffered similar humiliations and who could have done something about it (for example by using the army under their command or attacking the Emperor during a meeting, or by organizing a conspiracy) took the insults quietly and acquiesced; until finally, eight years later the German bodyguards and Vitellius were finally willing to make a stand. In Book XIV, Boudicca is the only one (male or female) who responded to the insults and terror with 'manly courage' by standing up for herself and her cause, a talent for which Tacitus professes admiration throughout the Annals, especially when it was doomed to failure.

As the punchline said: '*Id mulieri destinatum, viverent viri et servirent.*' – This is the decision of this woman, men might choose to live, but live as slaves. Tacitus clearly did intend this line to be a comment on the situation in Rome; but caged in an enemy's battle speech, it gains in power, because an outsider has to show the Romans how to behave. Thus it was not a comment on or probably by Boudicca, but Tacitus' verdict on the behaviour of the elite of Rome under a reign of terror.

The positive view of Boudicca that pervades so many of the modern accounts absorbed this undercurrent consciously or unconsciously. It also fed on a series of historic coincidences. The Boudiccan account in the Annals first becomes available again in Britain in the sixteenth century, first indirectly through the histories of Hector Boece and Ralph Hollinshead and later through the English translation by Henry Savile in 1591. This coincided with the reigns of queens both in England and Scotland and offered numerous opportunities to the contemporaries for some flattering comparisons.

A second era of huge popularity of the Boudicca story was the Victorian period, when Boudicca the wronged wife and mother, was identified with Britannia (and to a lesser extent Victoria). In a period when all over Europe Classical literature was used to find and redefine national heroes, such as Vercingetorix in France, Arminius in Germany and the Batavians in Holland, Boudicca filled a void presenting a heroine who could be interpreted as fighting for British liberty and justice, and who was much less problematic than the Caratacus story, which was intrinsically linked to (the morally questionable) Queen Cartimandua and her surrendering him to the Romans.

So which one of these accounts offers the real Boudicca? David Braund (1996, 145) summarized the problem very strikingly:

To seek the historical reality behind or beneath these images of powerful women in Britain is largely to miss the point. The characterizations of Tacitus and Dio tell us little about Boudicca [...]

but they speak volumes about these authors' attitudes to women in power.

Given how much the account is defining Boudicca through her actions, rather than her words, one has to wonder how far the account has been shaped/distorted to reflect these very different views of her.

Seeing Boudicca in the archaeological record

Having reviewed the different accounts, the second part of this chapter is to fill out the scarce accounts with some more details. Reconstructing a believable military history, which offers times and places in a clear order and makes this campaign reconstructable is beset with difficulties. None of the accounts presented above give us a time scale. We know that the main fighting took place in 61, because of the dates given by Tacitus. But as he starts his account with setting the scene and describing events that fall well before the fighting, it is unclear if the death of Prasutagus fell in the year before and if the disastrous visit by Roman troops is separated by a short or long timespan from the sacking of Colchester. Problems with the timeline continue as there is no indication of the time elapsed between the different events. Are the sacking of London and Colchester weeks apart or just 10 days? How long after the fall of London was the battle fought? In some of these issues, the archaeology can actually add further data, but this may not reduce the level of confusion surrounding the events described.

Boudicca is at her most visible in Colchester and London: the destruction layers in many parts of the towns are thick packets of burnt matter. In addition the excavations in Colchester have provided evidence of methodical looting and breaking up of statues before the town was systematically fired (e.g. Lion Walk and especially St Mary's (Crummy 1997, 80–82; Aldhouse-Greene 2006, 186)). This suggests a substantial amount of time spent in the town. Furthermore, at two locations in East Anglia fragments of the Claudian equestrian statue from Colchester were found, the head in the River Alde and one of the hoofs at Ashill near Saham Toney (Davies 2009, 65), which suggests that at least part of the army had time to return home with its loot. A further fact not mentioned by either Tacitus or Dio is that Colchester had at Gosbecks a nearby auxiliary fort, which could have held c. 500 soldiers; whether these soldiers were actually present at the time, is again impossible to tell.

A further question is the site of the battle of the *legio IX Hispana*. Cerialis was supposedly coming to the rescue of Colchester. There would have been very little chance had he brought the legion from Lincoln; the marching times involved would have made that near impossible. Tacitus suggests in his text that the sack of Colchester came first, but this may be caused by his way of presenting the story in a clearer, more striking way, a literary trick that he has been proven to employ elsewhere. It is hardly surprising then that Aldhouse-Greene suggested that the attack of the *legio IX Hispana* actually happened DURING the British operations against Colchester (2006, 186).

Cerialis may of course have come from Longthorpe, where a vexillation fortress often associated with the *legio IX Hispania* is known. On the other hand as it was during the campaigning season, he may already have been on route to or from campaigning elsewhere. Tacitus suggests in his account of the aftermath of the uprising that Nero sent 2,000 legionaries from the Continent and so made up the losses in the forces. If this is accurate, it does not sound as if the whole of *legio IX Hispana* was involved in the encounter against Boudicca (in which case losing all but the cavalry would have been losses in the region of 4000 soldiers). It raises the next question: how big was Boudicca's army in Colchester?

After Colchester, Boudiccan destruction is also reported from Chelmsford on the road to London (Waite 2007, 101), but these destruction levels are apparently not universal throughout Essex. The Roman small town of Elms Farm, Heybridge, which developed from Iron Age predecessors and contained an indigenous sanctuary, did not apparently sustain any noticeable damage during the uprising (Atkinson & Preston 1998, 92–98, where the earliest phase Late Iron Age to Roman transition is dated 50 BC to 70 AD with no noticeable interruptions).

When we get to London, the evidence is clearer: the destruction horizon is known to cover substantial parts of central London, both sides of the Walbrook, as well as an area in Southwark, as shown by the Jubilee Line excavations in the Southwark area (Bird 2004, 51). But if the rebellion crossed the river, why did they not go south or west to Silchester?

Tacitus mentions three towns by name in the Annals: Colchester, London and Verulamium. Suetonius and Dio clearly state *two* were destroyed. It would be facile to suggest that Cassius Dio has made a mistake; he appears to have got the number from a similar source as Suetonius – and Suetonius is potentially the historian with the best access to the official archives. It may be better to assume that there was some doubt over the third town, i.e. Verulamium. Tacitus only mentions this as being sacked.

Interestingly in her account of the archaeology of Verulamium, Ros Niblett (2001, 67) draws attention to the lack of evidence for the widespread destruction.

> Verulamium has not so far produced evidence for contemporary burning comparable to that found at Colchester. At Verulamium the only buildings that were definitely destroyed at about this time were the workshops in insula XIV; the bathhouse in insula XIX may also have been damaged but it was not totally destroyed. Burnt deposits at low levels in excavations in other parts of the Roman town, most of them found in the 1930s, have since been shown to contain pottery made in kilns in Highgate Wood, north-west of London, and dating from not earlier than c. 80 AD. All this confirms the impression that at the time of the revolt Verulamium was still very much an emerging town where there was, as yet, comparatively little to destroy in terms of 'Roman' buildings. Lack of excavations makes it difficult to gauge the effects on 'native' farmsteads in the immediate area, although on the sites that have seen excavation – Gorhambury, Park Street and Prae Wood – it is difficult to identify destruction layers that can be attributed to Boudicca with any degree of confidence.

On the other hand over the last few years excavations at Silchester continue to encounter evidence for destruction that appears to date to the mid first century and which is extensive enough to relate to Boudicca, rather than any accidental fire (Fulford & Timby 2002, 568–569). This, combined with the confirmed presence of Boudiccan destruction deposits in Putney, Brentford and Staines, all on the route to Silchester, suggests that in addition to the destruction mentioned in the literary sources, there may well have been a further path of destruction aiming west from London rather than north (Fuentes 1983, 216–7).

Furthermore, unless confronted with the excessive remains of burning seen in some parts of London and Colchester, it is difficult to differentiate between an accidental fire (caused for example by oil catching fire in a pan or a lightning strike, or a fire deliberately set to level a site prior to new building) and deliberate enemy destruction. Human remains are a rare find in most destruction deposits, as most people would return and reoccupy the plot and bury the dead, if only to avoid the spread of diseases. Finding a burnt layer is thus not necessarily an indicator of enemy action.

But the question reaches further: which other tribes but the Trinovantes and the Iceni took part in the revolt? Apart from the Claudian statue pieces, there is little evidence of the revolt in the Icenian heartland; in fact, it is much easier to trace its aftermath than the actual revolt. Pottery industries operating in eastern Cambridgeshire before and after the uprising show little sign of interruption (Gibson & Lucas 2002). There appears to be little evidence of destruction further west amongst the Corieltauvi or the Brigantian territories and for the most part the areas south of the Thames appear to be untouched as well.

This leaves the question of the final battle site. Most commentators agree that it should lie somewhere along Watling Street, but in the absence of a clear line of march it is worthwhile calling to mind that this reconstruction is based on the fact that we know Paullinus left in search of more troops, most of which were still coming back from Wales and that the British army was last seen at Verulamium just on Watling Street – thus suggesting that they may have progressed further along it. We again have no indication of how much time extended between these two events or even if the British army really all operated in a single unit – this is at best a good guess – and thus any of the predictions of a battle site, be it at Mancetter as Webster (1978) suggested or the more recently suggested High Cross (Waite 2007, 173–181) depend on this first suggestion being correct. It should perhaps also be mentioned that Nick Fuentes, S. Kaye and David Bird argue that if Suetonius Paullinus hoped to join up with *legio II Augusta* from Exeter, then it would be more reasonable to expect the battle to have taken place close to Staines (where burning is associated with Boudicca) or Silchester, rather than in the Midlands (Fuentes 1983, 314–316; Bird 2004, 26; Kaye 2010, 30–33). The written evidence allows for both scenarios, and in the absence of any firmly identified traces of the uprising or the battle at either location, an open mind may well be a valuable asset for future researchers.

The only time we get a bit of topographical detail is the actual description of the battle site. The site is described as *artis faucibus* (in the style of the entrance corridor to a Roman house). This is usually translated as 'defile', but might just as easily suggest that a plain narrowed before widening out again (perhaps by woodland or slopes) and with a wood behind as cover (and incidentally a serious obstacle in case of flight). A recent computer analysis of this information against a map of southern England suggested 263 possible battle sites covering most of the Midlands and the Thames valley

(Kaye 2010, **32**). This in itself suggests that the information provided in the literary sources is too generic to identify the site itself.

Paullinus' battle lines are arranged as:

cavalry – auxiliary – legions – auxiliary – cavalry

However, the accounts stress that Paullinus kept the army for as long as possible on the narrow protected ground, making sure that the British forces could only attack from the front. Eventually the infantry attacked in wedge formation, while the cavalry rode the heaviest opposition down. It is hard to assess if this is really how things happened, but if it did, then Suetonius Paullinus decided to play this battle exactly by the textbook, taking absolutely no chances, but going for a battle line that had been tried and tested throughout Antiquity. The battle as described in the Annals suggests that it was lost by the British through a lack of discipline rather than any sophisticated tactics employed by either side. The fact that Cassius Dio's description stresses the long duration of the battle indicates that it might not have been as easy a victory as suggested by Tacitus.

The only figures that are given are that about 70,000 or 80,000 (according to Dio) Romans died in the uprising and that Boudicca lost 80,000 warriors in the final battle. Unfortunately, these numbers are not reliable, as very few from ancient battle accounts ever are. There are certain rules to what the expected tally should look like: usually, the winner has to have lost fewer people than the loser. So 80,000 British dead at the final battle means probably little more than 'heavy losses but in total the same as our side lost during the revolt and a few more'. This helps little in our reconstruction of the size of Boudicca's army at the time, nor indeed for Suetonius Paullinus' army which consisted of one and a bit legions (the legion from Exeter had decided not to march and the *legio IX Hispana* had already lost in an earlier battle, leaving two legions, which may have been understrength due to the earlier campaigning in Wales) as well as auxiliaries from the nearby forts – we may be talking about 10,000–12,000 fighting men, but there is just not enough data.

It would be good to be able to discuss this battle in more detail, but the description of the battle is so short and cursory that the points that would really interest a military historian remain once again obscure due to the lack of sources. The accounts differ again as to what happened afterwards. According to Dio, sufficiently large numbers of the British army escaped the battlefield and were preparing to fight again, when Boudicca fell ill and died. Apparently she was awarded a costly burial, before the Britons dispersed to their homes. According to Tacitus Boudicca killed herself by poison (Annals XIV, 37).

Chapter 8

Rebuilding the Province

In many ways it is easier to recognize archaeologically the aftermath of the revolt than recognize it happening. Once again the sources do not agree, but there are several strands that can be made out.

Suetonius (Nero 18) suggests that Nero considered abandoning Britain as a province. As we have already seen there are few indications when this would have become a consideration in his reign; many scholars think it unlikely to have happened before the death of his mother, when most of the real decisions were made by Agrippina, Burrus and Seneca, rather than by Nero (and as we have seen, Seneca had serious business interests in Britain). It is also difficult to place the event in the latter part of Nero's reign, when the annexation of the Brigantian kingdom developed into a rapid push further north. The most likely scenario would place the event in the direct aftermath of the rebellion. Given the constant money problems of Nero's reign, who spent large sums on building and on entertainment and games, finding the money to rebuild the infrastructure of a province, which had lost its two largest cities as well as a substantial part of the population, would have been difficult, especially as the tax revenue would have been depressed for several years to come.

However, the archaeology and historical sources agree that these considerations must have been a moment of doubt which was quickly overcome. Tacitus' account of the rebellion continues with the description of Paullinus leading police operations in the area of the rebellious tribes. The situation was further exacerbated by famine. On the other hand Nero sent reinforcements from the Continent, consisting of 2,000 legionaries, eight cohorts of auxiliaries and 1,000 horsemen (Annals XIV, iv, 38). The mopping up operations appear to have taken some time, and to have been criticized or perhaps even countered by the actions of the new procurator

Julius Classicianus. Tacitus blamed the situation on the private animosity of Classicianus and Paullinus, which resulted eventually in the despatch of an Imperial delegation to Britain, who made a favourable report of Suetonius' actions. Suetonius was later in the year asked to hand over his command to Petronius Turpilianus, who took a more conciliatory part with regard to the province.

Suetonius Paullinus, now in Rome, was suitably rewarded for saving the province: there may have been a donative in his honour and in 66 he, or more likely his son, may have become consul; in 69 he was considered as one of the leading senators and a possible Emperor, and he survived the Civil Wars (Birley 2005, 51).

We know that Classicianus remained in Britain until his death at an unknown point in time: his gravestone was found built into London's Roman Wall and is now on display in the British Museum. The fragmentary inscription reads:

DIS / [M]ANIBUS/[C IUL C F FAB ALPINI CLASSICIANI / … / … / … / PROC PROVINC BRIT[ANNIAE …] / IULIA INDI FILIA PACATA I[…… / UXOR F(ECIT). (Grasby & Tomlin, 2002)

The text suggests that Classicianus was originally from Eastern Gaul/Germany and appears to have been married to the daughter of Julius Indus. There is no way of knowing how common the name of Julius Indus was in the area, but one Julius Indus helped the Romans in 21 to diffuse the Gallic Sacrovir uprising, which had started as a tax revolt and protests against Roman mismanagement. If this were the same man, it might suggest that in the aftermath of the rebellion, it was decided to select as *procurator* a man that may have had a more understanding disposition towards the problems of the provincials. His new partner as governor was an equally interesting choice. Rather than choosing someone with substantial military experience, as had been the case since Ostorius Scapula, P. Petronius Turpilianus became governor, nothing of whom is known, except that he is most likely the nephew of the first governor Aulus Plautius (Birley 2005, 51f.). In 63 he was replaced by M. Trebellius Maximus, who may have had some experience in fighting, but again was not one of the renowned generals we saw before the uprising; Trebellius remains in Britain until 69.

Tacitus' comments in the Agricola (Chapter 16) made it very clear that he disapproved of both governors for not being military minded, although there appeared to be some reluctant admission that in the aftermath of the rebellion a different approach was needed.

We do not know how long Classicianus served in Britain; the next procurator we know from the sources dates to the Flavian period. It seems thus that for the next ten years after the uprising, Rome may have decided on consolidation and rebuilding rather than expansion.

In addition, any attempts at expansion may have been curtailed by the removal of the *legio XIV Gemina* in 66/67 for a planned Eastern campaign by Nero. This may have also involved the removal of eight Batavian cohorts from Britain. The loss of c. 9,000–10,000 soldiers would thus not have left enough men for any significant campaigns.

Archaeologically this picture of careful rebuilding and consolidation can be further refined. The burnt cities were rebuilt on the same site, but in Colchester the area around the fortress itself appears to have changed dramatically: the British site of Sheepen stopped being an industrial settlement and became a sanctuary, while occupation at the Stanway cemetery and at the fringes of Gosbecks appears to have ceased. The biggest change was the reimposition of a stone wall around the refounded *colonia*, which accompanied the refortication of substantial parts of the Iron Age site (Crummy 1997, 85–90). More recent work suggests that this may have been a long drawn-out process, running alongside the piecemeal reconstruction of the town (Crummy 2003, 44–52).

In London the redevelopment was slow; many sites were not redeveloped until the 70s, possibly reflecting the different status of London as an unplanned town as opposed to Colchester, the first *colonia* of the province. However, finds of military equipment in the post-Boudiccan levels show that there is now a military presence in the town, and at Regis House the post-Boudiccan work on the waterfront used scale armour and parts of a leather tent in the infill of the new quay, with a stamp on one of the timbers naming the *coh Thracum* as original owners. In addition, a permanent military installation was deemed necessary: on Cornhill at Plantation Place a ditched enclosure and timber base for a rampart have been identified, most likely associated with a fort (Howe & Lakin 2004, 48f).

The strongest evidence for change comes, unsurprisingly, from Norfolk, where very few of the Iron Age settlements survived into the Flavian period. Saham Toney was abandoned; the sacred area at Fison Way in Thetford was destroyed, although the place itself continued to be used as a place of (ritual?) deposition intermittently into Late Antiquity. There are a number of new forts in Norfolk, most of which are close to the Iron Age sites, such as the one mentioned above near Saham Toney, but also at Threxton and Horstead. According to John Davies, military finds and ditches running parallel to the later town defences might even suggest a short-term legionary fortress or campaign base under Caistor St Edmund. Over the next generation, the focus of the *civitas* moved from the western oppida in the Breckland to the new *civitas* capital at Venta Icenorum/Caistor St Edmund (Davies & Robinson 2009, 73).

Consolidation and rebuilding in the 60s did not, however, equate to no change in the location of forts and fortresses within the province. With the redeployment of troops into Norfolk and other areas north of the Thames, the landscape of Roman occupation was changing, leading to the redeployment of legions. The first new fortress to be occupied appears to have been Lincoln, whose pottery suggests the start of occupation around 60/61 (Jones 2002, 31–36).

Further changes occurred when the *legio XIV Gemina* and the auxiliaries were withdrawn around 67. The removal of such a large part of the garrison forced a rethink of the pattern of occupation. So far one legion and auxiliaries had been concentrated in Lincolnshire and Nottinghamshire, possibly supervizing the situation in the Brigantian territories.

Two more legions and associated auxiliaries were stationed in the Welsh Marches, in Wroxeter and Usk in Wales. The fourth legion was stationed in Exeter supervizing the southwest of the province. All legions except this last one had taken part in the Boudiccan uprising, and while Tacitus lays the blame for this absence at the door of the camp prefect of the *legio XX Valeria Victrix*, it cannot have been missed that the location was more remote than the others and thus harder to reach.

When the *legio XIV Gemina* was withdrawn from Wroxeter, it clearly had to be replaced, as the Welsh situation was not yet resolved, thus the legion was moved from Usk to Wroxeter and the Exeter legion was moved in stages across the Bristol Channel to Gloucester and later to Caerleon. The result was the gradual military evacuation of the Southwest; by the mid 80s very little military remained in the South of England.

This period of comparative quiet ended at the close of the decade. Nero's reign deteriorated into anarchy and eventually the Emperor is helped to commit suicide. Without a male heir the Julio-Claudian dynasty was at an end and the Roman Empire descended rapidly into Civil War, and Britain with it. The fullest account of what happened during the following two years comes from Tacitus' other historical work, the Histories. Written before the Annals, it covered the period from the death of Nero to the death of Domitian, although the surviving parts break off in the middle of Book 5, Chapter 70. As it is difficult to understand the references to Britain by themselves in these years, it is perhaps useful to summarize the events as they develop. Overall Tacitus states that Britain was the province displaying most loyalty during the year 69 (also known as the Year of the Four Emperors) and remaining calmest (Hist. I, 9), but this is clearly only in comparison with other provinces such as the Germanies, which saw rapid political and military changes throughout the year. In fact, Tacitus' more detailed account, which follows the introduction to the Histories, shows clearly that Britain was very much concerned with the events on the Continent. Britain's involvement in the Civil Wars began with the removal of the *legio XIV Gemina* and its associated auxiliaries (probably eight cohorts of Batavians) in 66/67: it was originally meant to accompany Nero on a planned Armenian campaign, but an uprising in Gaul by a certain Vindex led to its redeployment in Gaul. At the beginning of 69 the *legio XIV Gemina* had separated from its Batavian cohorts, which were now stationed in the territory of the Lingones (a large *civitas* based around Langres in France), and were increasingly considered a security risk, as their loyalty was divided between the Roman Empire (their employer) and the Batavian leader Julius Civilis, who had been sentenced to death by the Roman administration. During the oath-taking ceremonies of the Roman army on 1 January 69 the governor of Lower Germany, Vitellius, emerged as the candidate for Emperor of the Rhine armies, in direct opposition to the other declared candidate for the throne: Galba. Following the declarations of the two Germanic provinces for Vitellius, the other north-western provinces followed rapidly: Raetia, Gallia Belgica, Gallia Lugdunensis and Britannia (Tac. Hist. I , 59). This decision appears to have escalated a general deterioration of the relationship between the legionary legates of Britain, led by the legate of *legio XX*, Roscius Coelius on the one side, and Trebellius Maximus, who is accused of greed and 'miserliness' (*sordes*), and leading the legions into poverty (this part is also mentioned in the Agricola, chapter 16) on the other hand. Trebellius accused Roscius Coelius of mutiny, but found himself without support either in the legions, or the auxiliaries, with the result that he had to flee to Vitellius, while the province was administered by a committee of the legionary legates. The support of Britain meant the gain of substantial resources of manpower and finance for Vitellius (Hist. I, 61) allowing him to send three substantial forces against Otho in Italy, who had replaced Galba as the other contender for the throne. On 15/16 April Vitellius' generals defeated Otho's troops in a large battle at Bedriacum, in which *legio XIV Gemina* was involved. Otho committed suicide soon after, leaving Vitellius in sole command of the Empire. Parallel to these events Vitellius had continued to raise troops in Gaul and Britain, including an 8,000 strong force, which was detached from the British army. This is the numerical equivalent of another legion and substantial auxiliary forces, and would have resulted in the size of the Roman army in Britain being nearly halved in comparison to its strength in 65.

Legio XIV, which had fought on Otho's side and was apparently ransacking Northern Italy in the aftermath of the battle, was ordered back to Britain, although without the Batavian cohorts, who remained with Vitellius (Hist. II, 66). Tacitus implies that this happened to rid Northern Italy of the rioting soldiery, and was no doubt an easy solution to removing from the scene a legion which did not support Vitellius, but it might have also been seen as a useful remedy to the understaffed and thus possibly threatened garrison in Britain.

The legion was accompanied on the latter part of its journey by Vettius Bolanus, chosen by Vitellius in Lyon to replace the disgraced Trebellius Maximus as governor (Hist. I, 65). Vettius Bolanus is described by Tacitus as chosen '*e praesentibus*', which can be translated as 'from his entourage'. Unlike his predecessors Vettius Bolanus is a man with considerable military background, and with him we see a return to the appointment of experienced military men as was the case before the Boudiccan uprising. He had been in 62 one of the legates and possibly the second in command of Corbulo during the Armenian campaigns (Tac. Annals 15,3; Statius, Silvae 5.2.31ff), during which he had been in charge of the second arm of the pincer movement that attacked the kingdom; after this in the mid-60s he appears to have been a governor in Macedonia for a year.

We do not know when the legion and the new governor arrived in the province. In the Agricola, Tacitus characterizes his governorship as 'not troubling Britain with enforcing discipline, while the Civil War continued'. Apparently the army continued to be as mutinous as before, but Vettius Bolanus appears to have been more popular with them. The developing situation cannot have been easy for Vettius Bolanus: on 1 July 69 Vespasian (the fourth Emperor within the year, and the same man that had helped to conquer Britain under Aulus Plautius 25 years earlier) had been declared

Emperor in Alexandria, and quickly took steps to improve his situation. With many of the Balkan legions declaring for him, the Civil War had reached its next phase, and Vettius Bolanus was controlling a large province with three understrength legions, one of which was of doubtful loyalty. The latter, *legio XIV Gemina*, appears to have been targeted by Vespasian, as formerly loyal to Otho and thus likely to change its allegiance to him (Hist. II, 86). When Vitellius asked for more auxiliary troops in preparation for the unavoidable battle between the armies of himself and Vespasian, Vettius Bolanus (as well as his colleague in Germany) prevaricated, because 'Britain was never quiet and both men were of doubtful allegiance' (Hist. II, 97).

In the decisive second battle of Bedriacum on 24/25 October 69, the vexillation of the British legions, according to some accounts (which Tacitus appears to doubt) took part in the centre of the battle line on the Vitellian side. The Flavian side eventually won after heavy and confused fighting, and the news of the battle led to a tidal wave of new support for Vespasian, including in Britain, where the *legio II Augusta*, Vespasian's old legion, appears to have led the change in loyalty, although some reluctance made itself felt in the other legions, especially, Tacitus tells us (Hist. III, 44), as Vitellius had been responsible for many promotions.

After the battle the survivors appear to have returned to the province. However, by then the Batavian cohorts had started their own uprising in Germany. In general the situation in the autumn and winter months of 69/70 appears to have been troublesome and confused in many western provinces. In the chapters following the second battle at Bedriacum in the Histories (III, 45–48), Tacitus reviews the various provincial uprisings that had their origin in the Civil War and the fact that the legions were elsewhere employed. Moving from East to West he quickly gives the origin and history to date of uprisings in Britain, Germany, Dacia and Pontus. Only for Dacia and Pontus are we given any indication on the resolution of the problem, as this was addressed by Mucian and Vespasian personally. In fact, in the city of Rome rumours circulated that the legions in Moesia and Pannonia were surrounded by the enemy; similar rumours abounded also about Britain (Hist. IV, 54).

However during the suppression of the Batavian uprising in 70, Britain was able to send a legion (the much-travelled *legio XIV*) to help Petillius Cerialis; and we hear next of this legion and the *legio II Adiutrix* fighting together against the Batavians near Castra Vetera in Lower Germany. After this battle the *legio XIV Gemina* was moved to Upper Germany and at some unknown time later the *legio II Adiutrix* arrived in Britain, bringing the garrison once again up to four legions.

Cartimandua

In the meantime the Roman army in Britain was contending with their own unrest in the province (Hist. III, 45): Venutius, husband of Cartimandua apparently induced the Britons to exploit the situation of the Civil War to their own advantage. His motivating factor was seemingly his hatred of all things Roman as well as personal hatred of his former queen and wife Cartimandua. The latter had great influence and wealth, not least because of her handing over of Caratacus to the Romans. At this point she seems to have rejected her husband Venutius in favour of his armour bearer Vellocatus. The result was major unrest in their household, which escalated when Venutius involved support from outside the kingdom, and thus started a civil war among the Brigantes. In the end the Romans had to rescue Cartimandua. Tacitus ends with the terse statement: '*regnum Venutio, bellum nobis relictum*'. (Venutius was left with the kingdom, we with war).

The passage is highly problematic as it duplicates one from the Annals, which appears to refer to the governorship of Didius Gallus in the late 50s, already mentioned in previous chapters. Both passages include details that are unique. Thus, in the Annals, Cartimandua takes the family of Venutius hostage; in the Histories we hear the name of the new husband, Vellocatus, armour bearer of Venutius. On the other hand both accounts mention the marital strife escalating into civil war and the eventual rescue of the queen by the Roman army.

Without any further independent information, it is impossible to resolve the relationship between these two accounts. Depending which reconstruction or reading of the sources is preferred, interpretations vary: some, especially older accounts prefer to think of the two events as separate, and thus include a possible remarriage between Venutius and Cartimandua, which is not mentioned in the sources. This has the advantage of not having to criticize Tacitus' account, but on the other hand, creates a very improbable scenario, where the Roman Empire have had to extricate the queen once and then allowed the same scenario to repeat itself on its own doorstep, a fact that many scholars deem unlikely.

Other theories suggest that one is a duplicate of the other and that for some reason Tacitus accidentally misplaced the Cartimandua story. In this scenario the account of 51/57 is in the wrong place, and should really only be discussed in the context of the Histories in 69. A third theory suggests that both accounts are correct and refer to the same incident, but the Annals' account which provides more detail, was put in the wrong place. In both cases, there would only be one intervention by the Romans, and in both cases probably in 69. But equally the questions remain, why would you have the earlier account, and why was Didius Gallus so clearly associated with the events?

The final scenario is sometimes referred to as the 'flashback' theory and suggests that we have indeed two Roman interventions, one in the governorship of Didius Gallus, while the second intervention is the long-term result of events nearly twenty years earlier. The main problem with this theory is that it has to be decided at which point the flashback ends. Did the couple fall out and was Cartimandua rescued and propped up for the next seventeen years by Roman power, until Venutius decided to attack again? Alternatively, did Cartimandua need 'extracting' in the late 50s and did Rome decide to leave Venutius in command of the kingdom, while its forces were committed elsewhere? This would thus explain Tacitus' punch line of 'Venutius was left with the kingdom, we with war'.

The problem is further aggravated by the fact that we possibly do not have the whole account of this intervention. As it stands, Hist. III, 45 deals with the state of play of the Roman Empire directly after the Second Battle of Cremona, and we know that Tacitus committed a considerable amount of space in books 4 and 5 to the resolution of the Germanic War (better known as the Batavian uprising) that he described next. This might suggest that further details about Venutius were meant to be forthcoming at a later stage, but are now lost, together with the rest of the Histories.

As it stands the situation is not resolvable by interpreting historical sources, as not enough detail exists in these two short passages. Can archaeology contribute to the solution of this problem? It has long ago been claimed that the Iron Age site Stanwick near Scotch Corner may have been the site of Venutius' last stand (Wheeler 1954). However, while modern excavations have confirmed that Stanwick was a high status site with numerous Roman imports in the Late Pre Roman Iron Age, there is little to suggest that the site was subjected to a siege (Haselgrove et al 1990) and it should be kept in mind that neither of the two Tacitean references mentions the storming of a settlement.

Thus while it is possible that Stanwick formed at some point (one of?) the power centre(s) of the Brigantes, there is no direct link with the rescue missions described in the Tacitean accounts. Furthermore, there are a number of camps known both in Nottinghamshire and Lincolnshire, i.e. at the south-eastern border of the Brigantes territory as well as in North Yorkshire and Cumbria that have in the past been cited as possible evidence for the involvement of the Roman army in Brigantia. However, Roman camps in northern England (as elsewhere) rarely produce finds in any quantity and the small amount of dateable material led the RCHME in their volume on the Roman camps to refrain from associating any camps to any historical events (Welfare & Swan 1995, 24f.). On the other hand we have seen that earlier campaigns in the South, especially during the conquest period have next to no marching camps associated with them at all. So the absence of camps dateable either to the late 50s or 69/70 is not necessarily a proof that no rescue mission was undertaken in either period. Once again, absence of evidence is not evidence of absence.

It should also be noted that neither of the sources mentions explicitly the integration of Brigantian territory into the Roman province, thus perhaps adding in the past to the perception that the entire area north of Chester and the Humber only became part of the Roman Empire a decade later. Here, however, we do now have a series of archaeological sites that argue against so late a date. The best known is no doubt Carlisle, where dendro-dates from the first timber fort date the felling of the trees to 72, thus documenting that by this point at the latest, the area was considered under Roman control. On the east side of the Pennines, Peter Wilson (2009) has recently reviewed the evidence of new discoveries and singled out a series of sites with possible military occupation evidence of the pre-Flavian period, including possibly York fortress, as well as a number of forts including Roecliffe near Aldborough, the later Brigantian *civitas* capital. If this interpretation can be further substantiated, it may point to a period of consolidation on the eastern flank of the Brigantes that predates any military intervention in 69. Forts, unlike camps, as we have discussed before, suggest areas under Roman control, rather than areas of active campaigning, but if the Romans were able to push their military installations that far into Brigantian territory before 69, it might suggest interesting possibilities, including that Venutius had been perceived as a threat long before the trouble in 69 and that the Romans may have been preparing for the eventual intervention for some time. It has to be admitted that the latter sentence is at the moment a hypothesis that needs confirming or refuting through future work and should in no way be considered a proposition for a new orthodoxy.

Dover lighthouse. *Birgitta Hoffmann*

Wroxeter fortress baths. *Birgitta Hoffmann*

Interior of the Lunt, one of the many pre-Flavian forts in the Midlands, in the background the reconstructed granaries. *Birgitta Hoffmann*

Reconstructed fort defences at the Lunt. *Birgitta Hoffmann*

Silchester defences. *David John Woolliscroft*

Caerleon Prysg Field, corner of the fortress. *Birgitta Hoffmann*

Stanwick defences. *Birgitta Hoffmann*

Chester, corner tower of Roman fortress. *Birgitta Hoffmann*

Dere Street, in a typically straight stretch in County Durham. *David John Woolliscroft*

Caerleon Prysg Field, legionary barracks. *Birgitta Hoffmann*

Inchtuthil fortress. *David John Woolliscroft*

Cawthorne Camps, Yorkshire. *Birgitta Hoffmann*

Hadrian's Wall on the Whin Sill Crags of the central sector. *Birgitta Hoffmann*

Risingham Roman fort. *Birgitta Hoffmann*

Roman road at Roundlaw, Perthshire. *David John Woolliscroft*

Aerial photograph of Chester fort. *David John Woollicroft*

Aerial photograph of Housesteads. *David John Woolliscroft*

Milecastle 39 on Hadrian's Wall. *David John Woolliscroft*

Milecastle 49 to Birdoswald. *David John Woolliscroft*

The gate at High Rochester fort. *Birgitta Hoffmann*

Aerial photograph of Bewcastle fort. *David John Woolliscroft*

Antonine Wall base in Bearsden cemetery. *Birgitta Hoffmann*

Roman road cutting at Innerpeffray, Perthshire. *David John Woolliscroft*

York, Multangular tower. *Birgitta Hoffmann*

Aerial view of Vindolanda; the praetorium of the Severan fort is on the right hand (western) end of the Vicus. *David John Woolliscroft*

Vindolanda, praetorium of Fort II and Severan roundhouses. *Birgitta Hoffmann*

Carpow aerial photograph. *David John Woolliscroft*

London city wall, one example of the increasing use of defences around towns from the late third century onwards. *Birgitta Hoffmann*

Caerwent late Roman defences. *Birgitta Hoffmann*

Richborough: in the foreground the ditches of the third century fortlet around the Claudian monument, in the background the defences of the Saxon Shore fort. *David John Woolliscroft*

Scarborough Yorkshire Coast tower. *Birgitta Hoffmann*

Cardiff Castle, South Wall, with Roman, Medieval and modern walling. *Birgitta Hoffmann*

Burgh Castle. *David John Woolliscroft*

Hen Waliau, Caernarvon, late Roman harbour fort. *Birgitta Hoffmann*

Caer Gybi late Roman fort overlooking Holyhead harbour. *Birgitta Hoffmann*

Chapter 9

Moving Beyond Brigantia…

With the end of the Annals and the beginning of the Flavian dynasty the military history of Roman Britain reaches a significant milestone. Up to this point the accounts of military events have been based for the most part on Roman histories and biographies or autobiographies. The evidence may not always have offered the detail wished for by an archaeologist or military historian, but the sources encountered use familiar genres, despite the different stylistic requirements of Roman and modern historical writing; not least of which, is a claim to the veracity of the facts described, to which most students of ancient historiography would subscribe. We have seen that this can be problematic, when truth becomes subjective, even if Tacitus claimed that he wrote his history *sine ira et studio* (frequently translated as without anger or bias). As with many modern historical accounts, truth is a matter of standpoint and given everybody's subjective views on the world, staying aloof of personal opinions is more difficult the closer to the events the author feels.

Beyond 70 the only major history that remains with us is Cassius Dio. Unfortunately, between the events of 46 to the death of Caracalla, the history of Cassius Dio actually only survives in the versions abridged by the monk Johannes Xiphilinus, of the Byzantine period, who seems to excerpt the original text, but omits passages which he deems of no interest. The result can be very detailed, as in the account of Boudicca, who appears to have grabbed his attention, or deeply frustrating, when stories are abbreviated and sometimes garbled into a very short precis.

An even more abbreviated version is found in the twelfth century historian Zonaras, who used Cassius Dio as one of several sources, but whose abbreviated sections are more likely to make sense (Millar 2.1999, 2–3). As a result there are problems with the text, but before Dio/Xiphilinus are completely vilified, it should be remembered that even in the small section of Tacitus relevant to Roman Britain there are textual problems, and as far as we are aware, these are not due to abbreviation, but stem from Tacitus' own stylus.

Dio preferred his history in large brushstrokes: he does not seem to have an agenda or subplot like Tacitus' in his Annals with his description of Imperial rule as anathema to freedom. Millar also characterizes Dio as likely to omit any detail that is not relevant to the story in hand (Millar 2.1999, 43–45). The overall result is that Dio's history is not as good a read as Tacitus, a fact which shows in the esteem he is held in comparison with other Roman historians. Most importantly, however, Dio's history was written in the first half of the third century, over 200 years after the establishment of the Principate. His views are very much influenced by his experience of an Empire that has settled down to Imperial rule, in which the military was accepted as a major source of power. Dio's recurring topic, if one can be easily identified, appears to have been the abuse of power by those unable to wield it (not a lot of change there from Tacitus) and the way that this could lead to the weakening of internal and external security. Restoring the Republic was, however, no longer an option for Dio; maintaining a strong Principate to ensure a safe Empire was.

Away from Cassius Dio, the majority of evidence for the Flavian period comes from a very different set of sources: in addition to a number of short lines in Pliny the Elder's 'Natural History' and Plutarch's 'Discourses', there are a series of poems (Valerius Flaccus and Silius Italicus), who mention the Flavian achievements in Caledonia and occasionally Thule, written for approval by the ruling family, the Flavians. Another poem praises the achievements of Vettius Bolanus to his son (Statius, Silvae). Finally there is Tacitus' 'Agricola', which is purportedly a belated eulogy by a son-in-law in praise of his deceased father-in-law. The latter has in the last century increasingly been treated as an historical account, bound by the same claims to veracity of Roman historiography, but this is far from the case: Syme described it as a *laudatio* developed into a biography (Syme 1963, 125). Others have detected within the text the elements of parables on the nature of the good ruler (Braund 1996, 158), as well as elements of other genres. What everybody appears to be happy to agree on is that it is NOT a history.

Laudationes or eulogies, and panegyrics, laudatory speeches praising Emperors and deceased fathers have one thing in common: Romans did not expect them to be utterly truthful; plausibility is more desirable. This is in many ways derived from Roman political culture. Unlike nowadays it was deemed acceptable, at least since the late Republic, to accuse a political opponent in a very direct and scurrilous form, including suggestions of sexual deviancy. At the same time it was understood that a client looking for support by his patron (such as a poet writing a poem) or a relative praising a deceased man (*'de mortuis nihil nisi bene'* – nothing but good things about the dead), was expected to exaggerate his positive achievements.

In such a world of mutual praise and belittlement of each other's achievements, distortions of the truth were acceptable, the extent of which appeared to have depended on context and person addressed. We have already seen that the accounts of the early governors of Britain given in the Agricola can be a lot more dismissive than their description in other sources, including Tacitus' other works. The problem of the modern historian writing about the Roman period is often having to guess their way through the conflicting claims and counterclaims. If only one side of the exchange exists, the problem becomes even harder to solve.

Several scholars have in the past suggested that when Dio and Tacitus cover the same material, Tacitus should always be treated as the superior source. This statement is deemed so universally true that it is frequently reproduced without references and is applied as justification to resolve a difference in date between Tacitus' 'Agricola' (83) and Cassius Dio (79) on the circumnavigation of Britain in favour of Tacitus. This assessment is, as far as the author could ascertain, ultimately based on Ronald Syme, who was however, a lot less absolute in his dismissal of Cassius Dio's writings and restricted his examples to comparisons between the Annals and Histories on the one hand, and Dio on the other (Syme 1963, 388–389). Research has since moved on, and many historians would today argue that differences in portrayal by the two more often reflect a difference in world view and cultural background, rather than a right and wrong portrayal of the same fact (e.g. Woodman, Mellor). A good example of this contrast is the marked difference between the two in the portrayal of Boudicca that we discussed earlier. Much more importantly in this case is, however, the fact that when comparing Tacitus' 'Agricola' with Dio, we are not comparing two historical writings, but a laudatory speech with clear political overtones (Braund, 1996; Woolliscroft & Hoffmann, 2006) with a history written decades later in a much more detached manner.

Entering Caledonia

If Britannia as a remote island had been a recurring theme for the Julio-Claudians, the accession of the Flavians saw the emergence of a new 'buzz-word': Caledonia. As Flaccus and Silius Italicus stress, the conquest of Caledonia was to be the lasting achievement of the early Flavian dynasty (Vespasian and Titus), only to be trumped by the even more dramatic achievements of Domitian in Germany (the official line taken by the palace, whatever the truth). Braund and others have pointed out that as with many good slogans, the truth was probably more complex (including the fact that according to Tacitus the final conquest of Caledonia came under Domitian with Agricola, and that Wales still needed more campaigning). However, each Emperor needed to stress his military success and being able to point to the extension of the edges of the known world by claiming the conquest of the north of Britain and even Thule, was a feat worth shouting or more literally writing about. The imagery established of these areas being the edge of the world became so powerful that Thule, and to a lesser extent Caledonia, continued for generations in the Roman imagination as the furthest you could go, holding apparently a similar emotional value to the way we might talk about the North Pole or the Moon.

The problems begin when a geographical definition is attempted. Stan Wolfson (2008) has recently published a thorough philological study of the surviving evidence in support of identifying Thule with the Shetland Islands and the suggestion that Agricola's conquest of the whole of Caledonia was exactly that, the whole of the island; suggesting that the final season and the battle of Mons Graupius must have happened somewhere in Caithness. While his philological studies appear to be hard to fault, it has to be stressed that once again, as in nearly all cases so far studied, neither Agricola's army nor navy of the final year of campaigning, nor the battlefield, can be identified in the archaeological record. But this does not distract from the fact that the Flavian poets were celebrating the generals as the achievers of complete conquest. Caledonia is not a clearly defined term: it lay to the north of Brigantia, but to judge from how it is used by the poets, it must have meant something equivalent to 'up north somewhere', and that was probably as close or as detailed as they wanted to be, especially when writing from the comfortable distance of Rome or the Bay of Naples.

We have, however, two writers that differ in this respect and qualify their description of Caledonia further. One is Statius (a poet of Domitian's reign (81–96)), who apart from celebrating the opening of the Colosseum wrote a

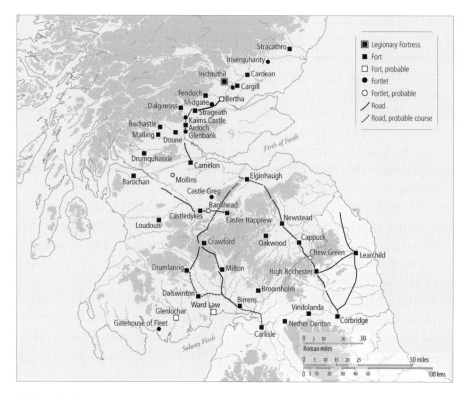

Flavian Scotland. *Frontiers of the Roman Empire project / David John Breeze / RGZM*

wide ranging series of poems to friends and fellow members of Domitian's court. In one of these poems he celebrated Crispinus' incipient career by comparing him to his deceased father Vettius Bolanus. In the middle of celebrating Bolanus' British achievements, Statius mentions the Caledonian plains. This cannot be brushed aside as a stereotype, quite the opposite: nobody else appears to use the term in this way – and it thus probably conveys some genuine geographical information – and given the general topography of Scotland, limits the area it could have covered to some of the Lowlands, especially the central belt, the Straths on the east coast or the coastal area of Moray and Aberdeenshire. There is, however, not enough data to be more specific.

The other reference comes from Pliny the Elder, who died in 79 in the Plinian eruption of Vesuvius. Pliny was a prolific writer, although only his 'Naturalis Historia' has survived. As the preface states, it was finished before the death of Vespasian (70/79), as it is dedicated to Titus Caesar (Emperor

79/81). The text is a kind of encyclopedia of the then known world and while Pliny includes some fantastic stories, most of these are qualified by 'I have heard', to express doubts as to their reliability. He mentions not as a rumour, but as a fact, that thirty years since the Roman conquest the knowledge of the island had not progressed beyond the fringes of the Caledonia *Silva*.

Silva's first meaning, most commonly used in translations is 'forest', but it can also mean 'mountain range', as in *Hercynia Silva*, the Black Forest. Either term suggests that Pliny may have been referring to the Highland fringe. But it would also allude to the fact that despite everything, within ten years of the Flavians coming to power, campaigning at least was progressing well into the Scottish central belt.

Three governors are known from this period: Vettius Bolanus, Petillius Cerialis and Julius Frontinus. The first, Vettius Bolanus has already been discussed in the context of the Civil Wars and Cartimandua. Statius (Silvae V, 2, 142–149) mentions in a poem for his son that he campaigned in Caledonia and that he built watchtowers and forts and captured the breastplate of a king. There is no doubt exaggeration in this poem, and the reference to the breastplate, which is an allusion to the old republican practice of *spolia opima*, the practice of a general dedicating the breastplate of an enemy leader who had been slain in single combat, is probably one of them.

There are substantial differences as to how to interpret this activity. Most scholars are now agreed that Vettius Bolanus campaigned against the Brigantes and possibly beyond. Identifying the watchtowers is a more problematic issue, as so far we know of two areas where timber watchtowers have been assigned first century dates (despite the notorious absence of any dateable finds within them) in Britain: in the Stainmore Pass (hardly in an area that can be described as a plain, with site elevations above 1,100 feet), and on the Gask Ridge (where at least the southern and northernmost towers can be described as being in a plain, although admittedly the central sector is on higher ground, overlooking Strathearn at about 300 feet above sea level). It is of course possible that we are missing other watchtowers.

A further, more striking problem is the marked difference in the assessment of Vettius Bolanus' activity between Statius and Tacitus in the Agricola. One claims great military successes, the other credits him patronizingly with having been popular, but not very active. This is a typical case of the exaggeration and denigration discussed above in action, especially as Tacitus (writing in 98) quotes other lines from the same Statius poem (written in c. 95) nearly word for word. He describes the general's activities on campaign, including exploring the area, selecting sites for camps etc. Statius uses the phrases as descriptions of Bolanus' campaign experience in Armenia; Tacitus applies the same wording to Agricola (chapter 20). It is hard to avoid the conclusion that this either was a sophisticated literary joke (the kind that most people fail to see the funny side of) or there may have been scores to settle, either of a literary or personal nature.

The importance of this passage has to be stressed, in view of the fact that for the next two governors Petillius Cerialis and Julius Frontinus, we only have Tacitus' account in the Agricola.

> But when, together with the rest of the world, Vespasian recovered Britain as well, there came great generals and outstanding armies, and the enemies' hope dwindled. Petillius Cerialis at once struck them with terror by attacking the state of the Brigantes, which is said to be the most populous in the whole province. There were many battles, some not without bloodshed; and he embraced a great part of the Brigantes within the range of victory or of war. Cerialis, indeed would have eclipsed the efforts of any other successor. Julius Frontinus, a great man, in so far as it was then possible to be great, took up and sustained the burden; and he subjugated the strong and warlike people of the Silures, overcoming not merely the courage of the enemy but the difficulty of the terrain (Agricola 17 transl. A.R. Birley).

Compared to Vettius Bolanus, both are being clearly complimented on their achievements in Britain, and it is worthwhile to look into the different backgrounds of these two governors. It is noteworthy, that unlike Bolanus, who was Vitellius' candidate in origin, the latter two were closely linked to the Flavian dynasty. Petillius Cerialis appears to have been married at one point to Vespasian's only daughter Flavia Domitilla, although she appears to have died before her father became Emperor. If Birley's reconstruction is correct, he would have also been the father of Vespasian's only granddaughter: in short, he was very much a member of the new Imperial dynasty (Birley 2005, 65f.).

Cerialis was already mentioned as the legate of the *legio IX Hispana*, who tried in vain to stop Boudicca's advance. During the Civil War he raised a cavalry force against the Vitellians to rescue Vespasian's brother, but failed again. In both cases Tacitus blames his rashness for the defeats.

Nevertheless, Cerialis was given by Vespasian the role of pacifying the Batavians after their uprising during the Civil War. Tacitus' descriptions in the Histories suggest that he was an inspired and very lucky general, although at times his own worst enemy, especially if women were involved. Nevertheless, despite the lack of final detail, as Tacitus' account stops in mid-sentence, we know that he managed to resolve the situation in Lower Germany and was then sent to Britain, possibly to resolve the Brigantian situation. He arrived, bringing the *legio II Adiutrix*, which had been under his command in Germany, to replace the *legio XIV Gemina*. He is credited by Tacitus with the largest military success in Britain, but then protocol demanded as much from a prince of the Imperial house.

Archaeologically, we know a number of forts that are built all over the Brigantian territory during his governorship: the most closely dateable one is Carlisle with its dendro-date of 72; other sites that are traditionally associated with him include the legionary fortress of York (home to the *legio II Adiutrix*), but as we have seen in the last chapter there is some debate over its date. In addition, it is usually assumed that the legionary base at Caerleon was occupied during his governorship. The move might have been in preparation for further campaigning in Wales, although this is not mentioned in any of the surviving records. Further forts in the north of England almost definitely belong with these key sites: Hodgson (2009, 8–10) has recently suggested a list, but further research is likely to add to them.

Cerialis appears to have been not just consolidating the situation, but campaigning as well. If Tacitus' Agricola is to be believed, his achievements, as we have seen, are mentioned in the summary of governors, as well as probably obliquely in the description of Agricola's second and third season (Agr. 20, 3 and 22, 3), where tribes that had previously been involved in warfare are described as surrendering and giving hostages or being faced with continuous warfare summer and winter alike.

Cerialis left most likely late in 73, in time to return to Rome for his second consulship in 74. We do not know what happened to him later, but it is generally assumed that he was dead by the time Tacitus wrote the Agricola in 98.

His successor Sex Julius Frontinus clearly was still alive in 98 and as we understand it, was one of the most powerful men in Rome, an Emperor-maker and the power behind the throne of the Emperor Nerva (96/98). We know little of his early career, but he was *praetor urbanus* in 70, and thus on 1 Jan 70 the highest ranking official in town, able to call together the Senate and co-ordinate the handover of power to Domitian, Vespasian's son and representative in the city in the aftermath of the execution of Vitellius a week earlier. Later in the same year, he was also, as one of the generals of Cerialis, involved in the pacification of Gaul and Germany, and apparently received the surrender of the Lingones.

He succeeded Cerialis in 73 as governor of Britain and remained there until summer 77, when he returned to Rome. We know from his later career that he accompanied Domitian on his German campaigns, and c. 84/85 he was proconsul of Asia. Afterwards he turned to writing, with interests ranging from surveying to two titles on military matters, of which the *stratagemata*, a handbook on military tactics, survives.

During the events of 96/97 Frontinus appears to have been one of the leading statesmen behind the coup that deposed Domitian (Grainger 2003) and thus possibly one of the people who encouraged Tacitus to write the Agricola. Frontinus afterwards became *curator aquarum* (the man in charge of the water supply in Rome, a job that resulted in another book) as well as being involved in other roles in the governments of Nerva and Trajan.

He has been singled out by Tacitus as the person who finally defeated the Silures, which as Davies and Jones (2006, 53) have argued may be shorthand for the whole of the south of Wales. In addition the two passages in the Agricola (20, 3 and 22, 3), cited in connection to Petillius Cerialis, may apply just as much to him as to his predecessor. Similarly the fort building in northern England discussed above, apart from Carlisle, cannot be separated between these two governors on the basis of archaeological finds. Nor is it currently possible to date the early Flavian network of over forty forts in Wales to the individual governorships. The largest of these new sites is the legionary fortress in Chester (which replaced Wroxeter), which must have been started either by Frontinus or very early in his governorship by Agricola.

Gnaeus Julius Agricola, the next governor had a very different background. He shares with his two immediate predecessors a close connection to the Flavian cause: while mourning his mother, who had been killed by Otho's soldiers in northern Italy in 69, he became one of the earliest supporters of Vespasian in the area. Up to this point his mainly civilian career had been somewhat lacklustre, but did involve a military tribuneship during the Boudiccan uprising. Having levied troops during the Civil War for the Flavians in Italy, his career took a turn for the better he became legate of *legio XX Valeria Victrix*, the legion that had been the leaders in the mutiny against Trebellius. It is possible that he saw action as legate under Petillius Cerialis, but the references are rather vague. After his legateship he was made governor of Aquitania, a peaceful province, and after his consulate was given the governorship of Britain by Vespasian.

In the summer of 77 Agricola arrived in Britain. The description of his activities in his son-in-law's account takes up twenty-one chapters, thus instead of offering a retelling, the following summary of his activities needs to suffice:

77: Agricola arrives late in the season and immediately starts campaigning against the Ordovices in north Wales, followed by an attack on Anglesey.
78: Consolidation of earlier achievements, Romanization policy discussed by Tacitus.
79: Agricola's army advances '*usque ad Taum*', possibly the Tay in Scotland; fort building.
80: Consolidation of what is won so far. Tacitus states that a frontier could have been found between Forth and Clyde, *if* the honour of the Roman people had permitted it.
81: Crossing in the leading ship to discover people hitherto unknown. Agricola considers conquering Ireland.
82: War on people beyond Bodotria (Forth estuary) by land and sea. Night attack on the *legio IX Hispana*. Revolt of the Usipi and their accidental circumnavigation of Britain.
83: Final advance, Battle of Mons Graupius. Official circumnavigation of Britain.

In addition to the campaigning activities the archaeological record shows that Agricola was involved in the construction of forts and fortresses. The best evidence comes from Chester, where the construction of the fortress probably started just before his arrival. However, the find of inscribed water pipes naming the governor, which is in itself an unusual feature seen otherwise mainly in the city of Rome, suggests that he took a very strong interest in the construction of the fortress, and especially in the unusual features such as the Elliptical Building, which remains unparalleled (Mason 2000, 66–95; Mason 2000, 110–119).

There have been over the years substantial arguments on how reliable this account is and views range from utterly reliable (Ogilvie and Richmond 1967) to problematic (Hanson 1978; Woolliscroft & Hoffmann 2006) and many shades in between. At the heart of it is once again the question of genre. If we are to accept that the Agricola is a laudatory speech as well as a biography and a parable, then its level of reliability is no higher than celebratory poems like the Statius discussed earlier. The level of geographical detail presented is certainly no higher than the information we have discussed in Tacitus' or Cassius Dio's historical works, and thus reconstructing detailed routes of advance is problematic, to say the least. This is, however, not the place to review the entire argument, which has been discussed several times elsewhere; except to correct a misunderstanding that appears to have crept into some of the literature: neither Woolliscroft (2002) nor Woolliscroft & Hoffmann (2006) have stated that all of Scotland was conquered by Petillius Cerialis instead of by Agricola (*contra* Hodgson 2009, 13), but they have always suggested that all four Flavian governors are equally likely to have participated in the conquest of the north and that not enough evidence exists to date to offer a more detailed scenario.

Mons Graupius
The account of the governorship of Agricola culminated in a now famous set-piece battle: Mons Graupius. The battlefield is (once again) presented in the Agricola in the most cursory terms: the site lies on a slope, the Britons occupied the high ground, the Romans approached from lower ground, with a river dividing them from their enemies. A description that differs mainly from the battlefield of Caratacus in the provision of the two ridges that were used by Caratacus as elevated fighting platforms; while Paullinus' battlefield is equally on the high ground, this time with no river, but sufficient obstacles that he could not be surrounded. One has to ask: does Roman Britain in the first century only offer one type of battlefield, or is what Tacitus describes as 'the perfect battleground' in Roman (or at least Tacitus') eyes, chosen by every general worth his salt?

Due to the vague description there are numerous slopes that have been put forward as Mons Graupius, covering most of Scotland north of the Forth-Clyde isthmus, but concentrating on the east coast. Wolfson (2008) has recently proposed Caithness as another possible site of the battle (although the current author has so far failed to identify a battlefield site in the area that would fit even Tacitus' limited description, given Caithness' propensity for comparatively flat, but very waterlogged countryside). Many of these make tactical sense and can be fitted with the Tacitean account – in some cases they have also been associated with the evidence from marching camps – but none has so far produced the sort of evidence that we now

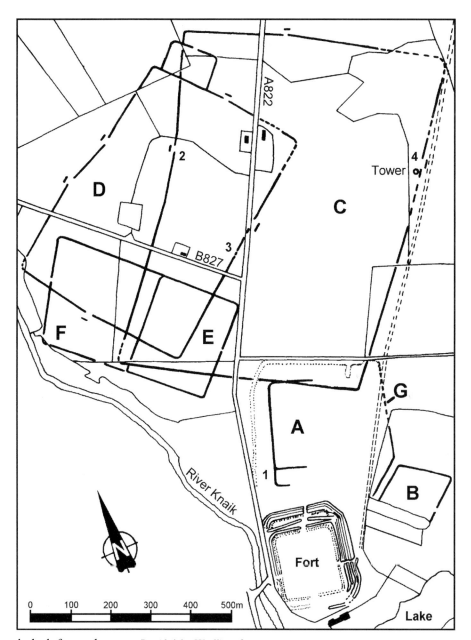

Ardoch fort and camps. *David John Woolliscroft*

associate with Roman battle sites: scatters of broken military equipment, not least hobnailed boots or possible graves, such as those found in Kalkriese and Harzhorn in Germany; and as we have seen in the case of Boudicca, the fact that the description could fit so many possible sites may suggest that we do not have sufficient information to locate the site from the historical account alone.

Thus so far we are still no closer to understanding the strategic function of the battle, while its literary function within the Agricola is clear enough – it is the final victory, the crowning glory to a seven year governorship, nicely topped off by naval achievements by the fleet. The perfect culmination to a long career, worthy of a noble governor, even if the bad Emperor Domitian did not appear willing to agree with Tacitus once Agricola returned to Rome. There is a substantial difference between the literary function and a strategic reason for the battle. Ending a war with a decisive event makes good narrative sense; but as we have seen in the Caesar, Caratacus and Boudicca chapters, the Iron Age peoples in the south of Britain may have defined their objectives differently. Their defeat in a large battle appears not to have been a reason to offer universal surrender, but seems to have been a moment of reconsidering tactics. Neither Caratacus nor Boudicca appear to have considered surrendering after their lost battles (at least if you follow Dio's account, rather than Tacitus as we have seen). Interestingly, a look at the history of Republican Rome shows that the Romans took a very similar view of their wars. The historical accounts of the third and second century BC are full of instances where even after a crushing defeat like Cannae, the Romans just 'dug their heels in' and raised another army to continue the fight.

After a hundred years of experience of fighting in Britain, it is interesting to note that Roman historians (and possibly generals) appear to have been unwilling or unable to recognize the same determination in other Iron Age societies. Did Agricola really believe that the Battle of Mons Graupius was the final step towards the conquest of Scotland, as well as the last battle during the governorship, or are we just led to believe this to be so, as it suited the narrative of Tacitus at this point?

One further major problem persists: according to Tacitus the circumnavigation of Britain, a feat ranked as being as important as the military success of Agricola, happened at the same time as the final battle at Mons Graupius, making Agricola's final year in Britain a double success. This may be surprising, but proving beyond doubt that Britain was an island and thus not linked to the Continent also meant establishing the size of the island, and as such added substantially to Rome's knowledge and ability in a military sphere to predict future threats and upcoming military commitments. Islands, because of the problems of landing more armies from outside, intrinsically lend themselves to total conquest and the development of a comprehensive defence in a way rarely offered by areas on larger landmasses. In addition, it should also be remembered that until recently, the discovery of major new territories was considered an important achievement in most European nations. Agricola's circumnavigation is also mentioned in other sources: a minor essay by Plutarch (De defectu oraculorum) and in Cassius Dio. In Plutarch the reference is oblique; Agricola is never mentioned: but one of the participants of the discussion, the Grammatikos Demetrius, has just returned from an expedition to Britain. The date of this probably fictitious dialogue is given in Olympiads, a Greek form of time keeping that counts the Olympic games since their inception. When resolved into modern dates it translates most likely into 82, which would mean Demetrius would have to have returned from the voyage before it actually took place according to Tacitus. It could be argued that as this is a fictitious dialogue, the dates are irrelevant, but the conventions of this genre suggest that use of historical characters and dates was supposed to give the piece credibility, inferring that it was advisable for the authors to get the dates right. The second source, Cassius Dio mentions the circumnavigation outright; in fact he links the award of the triumphal ornaments with the circumnavigation rather than any military success. In Dio's account, however, the circumnavigation is dated to the reign of Titus. It has been argued that this just means that Dio is wrong, because Tacitus is the better historian. But as we have seen, the Agricola is not a historical work, and thus Dio's claim should be looked at on its own merit. The date of the circumnavigation in Tacitus is designed to create a point of resolution in a carefully constructed narrative; that would not have been achieved if the triumphal ornaments had already been awarded three years earlier (compare the feeling of deflation in the Annals, between the early years of Ostorius Scapula, which culminates in the capture of Caratacus and the later years, where he is bogged down in unrewarding fighting in Wales). For Cassius Dio or rather Xiphilinus the award of the circumnavigation was one of the lesser pieces of news in the context of the major crisis of Titus' reign, worth mentioning in passing, but little more. On the whole, events in this category are rarely distorted: why bother, if they are just 'background noise'? It would thus seem that Cassius Dio, unlike Tacitus, had little reason to change the date of the circumnavigation.

With the return of Agricola to Rome, the literary sources for Roman Britain become scarcer; instead inscriptions from Britain and elsewhere replace historical accounts. A brief reference in Suetonius' Life of Domitian says that Domitian killed a governor of Britain called Lucullus for naming a new design of lance after himself (Suet. Domitian 10, 2–3); this is symptomatic of the new style of evidence. But in the absence of any other records of further conquests or discoveries, it is probably correct to assume that with Agricola the conquest of Britain achieved its maximum extent. The remainder of the story, which is one first of consolidation and then increasingly of defence of the status quo, has a very different character.

The aftermath of conquest: the Flavian camps and forts in Scotland
The archaeological evidence for the conquest and occupation of Scotland is substantial. As well as a large series of marching camps there are numerous forts in Flavian Scotland, in addition to those which were rapidly developing all over northern England. Given the substantial number of forts (they were often larger than normal), it has been convincingly argued that it is unlikely that these forts all existed at the same time, as the garrison of Roman Britain is unlikely to have been large enough. It is thus more likely that the Flavian period saw rapidly changing garrisoning patterns, with forts established and then quickly moved when the situation changed. Disentangling this history on a fort by fort level is likely to take decades and is very much dependent on large scale excavations to separate individual phases and establish their full extent. At the moment there are forts, such as Cargill, Cardean and Strageath (Woolliscroft & Hoffmann 2006 with further literature), where areas within the fort see rebuilding, while at others (e.g. Fendoch and Elginhaugh), no major repairs were postulated by the excavators (Richmond and MacIntyre 1939; Hanson 2007).

There are also substantial differences of opinion as to the earliest dates of these forts, and as a result, differences of opinion exist between scholars as to how the conquest and occupation of Scotland is viewed. The two supposed fixed points for this debate are Carlisle, with its dendro-dates of 72 on the western side, and Elginhaugh on the outskirts of Edinburgh, for which the excavator proposes a date of construction on the basis of a dispersed coin hoard to 79 (Hanson 2007).

Hanson's assumption is that the Roman advance progressed on both sides of the island at the same speed and thus that no fort further north could be earlier than Elginhaugh, for which he postulates an important strategic position along Dere Street. This view, however, is not as uncontroversial as Hanson and others (Hodgson 2009) make it out to be. The crucial coin hoard of 79 was 'dispersed': some of the coins were found together, other coins

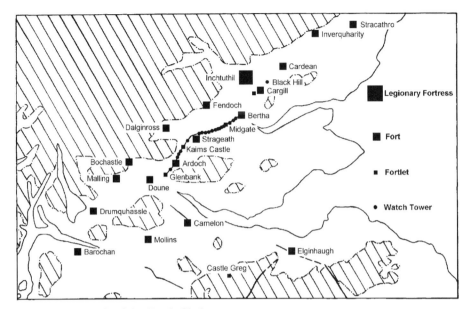

Flavian sites north of the Forth Clyde. *David John Woolliscroft*

including the one that has been claimed to date the hoard to 79, were found spread on the Roman surface, thus raising doubts about its original context. Also as presented in the final report, there is little information on the crucial way in which the hoard relates to the different layers of construction, repair and demolition within the *principia* where it was found. No sections or detailed plans were published which would establish beyond doubt these important relationships. In addition, recent rescue excavations in the fort's annex produced a coin of the Emperor Trajan (97/117) (DES 2009, 120) in the backfill of an enclosure ditch. This particular find, which is most likely to have been lost during the second century, possibly the Antonine period, suggests that in addition to the Flavian period, later activity took place in the fort, thus querying its status as a single period site abandoned for good in 86/87.

A much wider problem is, however, the question of how far dates from Elginhaugh can be transferred to other forts and how deeply connected it is with the role of Carlisle, built in 72. This early date for the latter fort was first proposed nearly a hundred years ago by Bushe-Fox (1913) on the basis of early Samian found at the site, and while it did not find acceptance then, the point was taken up again by E. Birley (1951), who saw in Carlisle a fort that separated the Brigantes in the South from their Scottish supporters in the North. He proposed at the time a very different scenario for the Roman invasion of Scotland, which is worth quoting in full:

> It seems a reasonable inference, that before Dere Street was built, to carry the main Roman trunk line from York into Scotland, the principal northwards road followed by early man was over Stainmore, across the Cumberland plain and so into Dumfriesshire; and that is the line of the Roman road from York to Carlisle, Birrens and beyond. We may be justified, I suspect, in supposing that the Votadini of Northumberland and the eastern Lowlands were either pro-Roman or neutral, and that the main force of Venutius's supporters was found among the Selgovae and Novantae in the centre and west; and it would be logical, in that case, for Cerialis to aim first at securing Carlisle, and then perhaps to mop up all the centres of Venutian resistance to the South of it. But we can hardly exclude the possibility that his campaigns continued northwards into Scotland; for when we turn to examine what Tacitus has to say about the governorship of Agricola, it is most remarkable, that for all the superficial impression of active operations in his narrative, it is not until the fifth season of his governorship that Tacitus is able to credit Agricola with meeting tribes previously unknown. (E. Birley 1951, 57)

This passage would suggest a very different scenario from Hanson, with the Roman advance mainly progressing on the western side of the Cheviots and bypassing the Votadinian territory (on the East coast of Scotland, Southeast of Edinburgh) for the most part by following roughly the course of the modern M6/74 and A74. This scenario has again recently been proposed by Jones (2009). If this were the case, then Elginhaugh's position would not be looking North, but South, guarding an exit from Votadinian territory in a similar fashion to the Nottinghamshire and Lincolnshire forts and camps in the 50s and 60s.

Wolfson (2008) suggests that the conquest of Scotland probably saw ebbs and flows, with advances and regroupments, but also with conquest in different parts of Scotland progressing at different speeds and by different methods, resulting in similar scenarios to those we have seen in the South, with parts of the province apparently free of military occupation, while neighbouring districts may show substantial evidence for intervention.

As we have seen the literary sources are once again unable to lend support to any of the theories on the Roman advance into Scotland for lack of detail.

In this particular case and as we will see for most of the remainder of Romano-British history the evidence is mainly to be found in the archaeological record, in the form of inscriptions or structures. These, as we have seen, usually document the consolidation phases of any military action, while the conquest phase again remains invisible.

For Scotland this conquest phase has, however, left further evidence in the form of frequently large marching camps, a substantial number of which form series, and in addition often cluster at specific sites, leading to groups

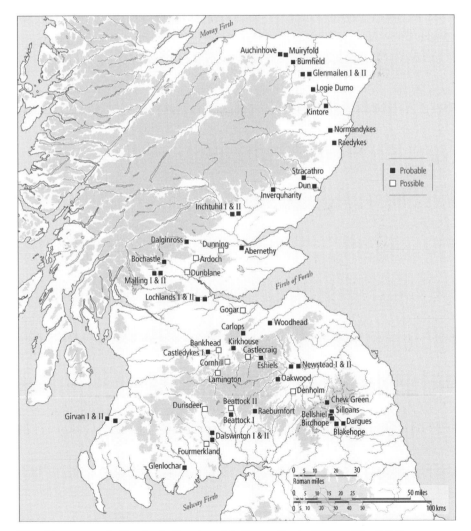

Marching camps in Scotland. *Frontiers of the Roman Empire / RGZM / David J. Breeze*

of intersecting marching camps which thus provide a chronological sequence between camps of different design (see plan of Ardoch page 127).

Following the long standing research of Prof. J.K. St. Joseph from 1951 onwards (inter alia 1951), many of the 220 camps known from Scotland have traditionally been grouped into series on the basis of the available historical evidence associated with campaigning in Scotland. In the case of the camps north of the Forth-Clyde isthmus these were usually associated with either the campaigns of Agricola or the campaigns of Septimius Severus (see below).

In addition to these there are a number of camps in the Scottish Lowlands, which currently form independent series, which cannot be ascribed to any campaign known from the historical accounts.

The most common way of cataloguing these camps is by size, but further features are the gate types: particularly the so called 'Stracathro' gate type, a very characteristic form of gate construction, where one side curves outwards,

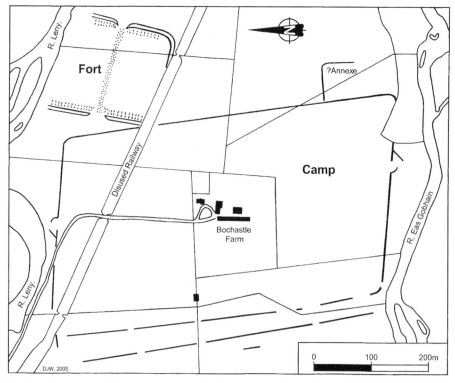

Bochastle camp and fort, note the Stracathro gates in the camp. *David John Woolliscroft*

while the other approaches at an oblique angle. It has been identified so far at sixteen sites. However, although these camps are traditionally associated with the Flavian period; they appear to be no longer common in the mid second century and are frequently found close to (later?) Flavian forts, their sizes vary from 1.5 to 24.5 ha. They thus do not represent a series of campaign camps (Jones 2009, 75–6). In addition the high level of occupation in the Scottish Central belt makes it much harder to link the patterns observed in the Scottish Lowlands with the camps north of the Forth Clyde isthmus.

Most camps have seen only small scale excavations over their ditches to confirm their existence; large scale excavations in the interior are rare, with Kintore being the most extensive. The large scale excavations of this 110 acre camp in Moray produced substantial evidence for internal structures, especially in the form of ovens. The radiocarbon dating of these ovens suggests that the main phase of occupation dates to the late first century, thus probably coinciding with the period of Flavian campaigning.

However, the excavations also underlined that this camp was not just used for one night, but that some of the ovens were repaired, suggesting re-use of the camp at a later point. The evidence for re-use has now been recognized at other sites too, although more commonly this evidence is in the form of

Rock-cut marching camp ditch at Raedykes. *David John Woolliscroft*

ditches that have been allowed to silt up (as at Bochastle), before being recut, or a camp being re-used by inserting a smaller installation inside the earlier ditches (as in Dunning) (Jones 2009b, 23). All this is likely to complicate the building history of the camps as well as our understanding of their use.

At the moment we are reasonably confident that the 110 acre camps belong to the Flavian period, while the 63 acre and 130 acre series might belong to the second or third century (see the chapter on Severus for a discussion of these). The general distribution of the camps of Roman Scotland suggests that on the whole they tended to follow the later Roman roads: a line of camps follows Dere Street in the East, while another series follows several Roman roads out of Carlisle heading North or into Dumfries.

The extent of Roman control in Scotland is also still a matter for debate. The 110 acre series which reaches furthest north, starts at Normandykes to the south of Aberdeen, and continues via Kintore to Ythan Wells I/Glenmailen and Muiryfold into Moray. There are so far no camps detected further north, despite extensive flying programmes in the Highland area. As there are also so far no 110 acre camps south of this area, these four are unlikely to represent a full campaign. In addition, in the middle of these camps lies the 144 acre camp (58 ha) of Durno. Although the latter is frequently associated with the Flavian campaigns and has sometimes been associated with the final battle of Mons Graupius, it needs to be stressed that it is unique in its size, but only 9 ha smaller than a series of 165 acre (c. 67 ha) camps in the Scottish Lowlands north of the Newstead that are more commonly associated with the Severan campaigns.

It is thus apparent that currently despite significant research time being invested over the last 100 years and more, our understanding of the conquest of Flavian Scotland is far from complete. It is clear, however, that the Flavian Emperors were initially willing to invest substantial amounts of men and material in the conquest and retention of Northern Britain, especially of Caledonia. The return, in addition to the taxable agricultural produce and population, consisted of the discovery and exploitation of substantial mineral deposits, many of which appear to have been (at least initially) capitalized by an army. The conquest of Wales brought, in addition to copper and iron, which for the most part remained in private hands (or so the archaeological records appear to suggest), silver and lead (galena) (e.g. in Flintshire) and in Southwest Wales small amounts of gold at Dolaucothi near Pumpsaint fort.

In the North of England and Scotland, galena deposits included those in Derbyshire and in the Northern Pennines near Whitley Castle, possible deposits in the Lake District as well as the silver mines in the Scottish Lowlands in Drumlanrig, all of which can now be shown to have been exploited by the Romans within a short time of their arrival in the area.

In addition to the large number of auxiliary forts built, the Flavians eventually even moved one of the legions north to a new base at the foot of the Highlands at Inchtuthil near Dunkeld. This suggested that the occupation was considered permanent. Unfortunately, both for the Roman Empire and the Roman legions involved, the early eighties saw the middle Danube erupt into full scale warfare with the Dacians attacking across the river. A series of commanders were sent to stabilize the situation, usually with little success and sometimes with catastrophic losses, which may have included some of the legions. As the Danube frontier was essential for the security of Italy and thus Rome, Domitian was forced to redeploy troops from other provinces to stabilize the situation. This included the removal of one of the British legions and probably its associated auxiliaries. The result was an extended province that now had to be held with a reduced level of manpower; an amount that had proved barely adequate in a smaller province in the late 60s the last time a legion had been withdrawn. As a consequence, we see throughout the North of Britain and Wales a re-organization of the army. This redeployment is particularly striking in Scotland, where all of the forts north of the Forth-Clyde isthmus, including the legionary fortress, were abandoned early in 87. There appear to have been some attempts to forestall the withdrawal south of the Forth-Clyde line, but over the next decade more and more forts were abandoned and eventually the Roman military occupation withdrew to a line between Carlisle and Newcastle. *Britannia omnia capta, statim missa* – Britannia was completely conquered and immediately let go, as Tacitus (Hist. I.2) summarized the Flavian involvement.

Chapter 10

The Second Century in Roman Britain – A Time with Little History?

T he decades after the collapse of the Flavian dynasty are sometimes called the period of the adoptive Emperors, a time of great prosperity for the Roman Empire, when warfare (still present) takes second place to great building activity and the Emperors appear to be more interested in philosophy than madcap exploits in the dining or bed room. While it is hard to deny that the archaeological record in Rome and the provinces suggests a period of increased prosperity, our perception of a very 'grown up' Roman Empire is probably also due to the fact that for better or for worse we are missing critical details. Until the death of Hadrian (138), the epitome of Cassius Dio is still available, but the beginning of the reign of Antoninus Pius (138–161) starts with the stark statement: 'It should be noted that the account of Antoninus Pius is not found in the copies of Dio, probably because the books have met with some accident, so that the history of his reign is almost wholly unknown.' (Cassius Dio, Epitome of book LXX, 1)

Even when Britain does get a mention in the historical or biographical writings, such as in the Scriptores Historiae Augustae (SHA), a fourth century series of biographies with numerous question marks over its authorship, date, intention and origin, or in the letters of Fronto (the Latin professor and close friend of the later Emperors M. Aurelius (161–180) and Lucius Verus (161–169)), the material is often without clear dates and context. As a result, scholars rely mostly on the archaeological records, inscriptions and sometimes coins to reconstruct the history of the second century in Britain. As already mentioned archaeology's strength is in detecting long term processes rather than short term events, so it is hardly surprising that we are able to document the long-term military developments in Britain, but short intervals of warfare may escape us.

One, and possibly the best documented, example of this is the War of Hadrian in Britain. We have two very short mentions of this war.

In the SHA we are told that *'Britanni teneri sub Romana dicione non poterant'* – The Britons could not be kept under Roman control (SHA Hadrian 5, 2). The statement comes as part of a list of 'subject' people that caused uprisings during Hadrian's rule: the Mauri (in Africa), the Sarmatians on the Danube, as well as trouble in Britain, Egypt, Libya (probably the Cyrenaica) and finally Judaea.

From what we can tell from other sources covering these events, the sequence appears to be roughly chronological: the Mauri uprising in western North Africa dates to Hadrian's accession, the Danube war was resolved by Hadrian on his way from the East to Rome (so before 119/120), Egypt and Libya refer to what we know as the Jewish uprising, which also dates to the beginning of his reign, and finally Judaea can be linked to the Second Jewish War in the 130s. This would suggest that the British War may have also been part of the uprisings at the beginning of his reign.

However, it is possible that there is also a geographical sequence from the furthest southwest (Mauri) to the north (Sarmatians), even further north (Britain), to the south (Libya and Egypt) and finally the east (Judaea). The pattern is not fully correct and modern writers would probably have put Britain before the Sarmatians and progressed from west to east, so there is some debate as to which of the two criteria might have been the more important.

The British War is also mentioned in Fronto's letters to Marcus Aurelius during the Parthian War in 162: *'Quid? Avo vestro Hadriano imperium obtinente quantum militum ab Iudaeis, quantum ab Britannis caesum?'* – What? Under the rule of your grandfather Hadrian, how many soldiers were killed by the Jews, how many by the Britons? (Fronto, P.218, Loeb transl. vol. II, 23) Fronto was Marcus Aurelius' Rhetoric and Latin teacher, but at the time of writing, M. Aurelius had long since finished being a student, but the exchange of letters continued, often creating little impromptu gems with considerations of style more than once trumping content. Unfortunately, this letter is very fragmentary and so we know nothing more on the subject, nor do we learn more about the losses under Antoninus Pius, apparently the subject of the next sentence. Again there is no chronology implied, but as in English, Latin cadences work better when you finish with the longest phrase, thus the three syllable 'Britannis' has to come second for stylistic reasons.

In addition to these two throw away sentences, there is also an inscription from Vindolanda, found reused in the praetorium (the commanding officer's residence) in 1998, which was reconstructed by Tony Birley as follows:

D(is) [M(anibus)]
T(itus). Ann[ius ...f ...]
Centur[io.leg......praepositus. coh. I]
Tungr[orum Ann.........stipend]
Diorum [......cecidi]
T. in bell[o Britt? ab hostibus. inter]
Fectus [T. Annius (or Annia)...)
Fil et Arc[......]
H(eres) e[x testatmeno fec(erunt)].

To the spirits of the departed: *Titus Annius...centurion* of legion...acting commander of the 1st Cohort of *Tungrians*, a thousand strong, aged...with... years of service] *died in the... War, killed by* the enemy. Titus Annius... *His son and Arc...his heirs* had this set up, in accordance with his testament (the italicized text marks the translation of the surviving parts of the inscription (Birley 1998a and 1998b)).

Birley argues that the fighting must have taken place in the vicinity of the later Wall, but this does not follow, as the inscription comes from a gravestone, not a battlefield memorial. Graves could be built as cenotaphs, as the Caelius stone shows, set up twice, in the Roman province of Germania Inferior and outside the city of Rome, to commemorate the death of a *centurio* of one of Varus' legions, although no body was available for burial.

Scholars over the last hundred years have linked the two texts with coins struck early in Hadrian's reign (117/118) suggesting an early date for the above war and more recently for the inscription (in itself undated).

The coinage of Hadrian's reign has attracted some attention from Romano-British archaeologists. There is frequent reference to issues regarding the mentioning of Victoria on the coinage of 119/120, as well as Mars the Avenger and Jupiter Victor, and also the now famous Britannia *aes* issues (RIC 577a and 577b = BMCRE 1175 and RIC II 845), which show Britannia seated on a rock, facing the viewers, holding a long sceptre (or spear) with a large shield visible to the right. The inscription in the exergue reads: BRITANNIA. In addition the mint of Alexandria issued a NIKE (Victory) issue to Hadrian in the year beginning August 119.

Much has been written about these coin issues in the context of Romano-British archaeology, suggesting that they may show Britannia defeated and thus in combination with the victory issues, a military victory over Britain. Birley (1997, 104) has raised some doubts about this reading. Problems arise on several levels.

Firstly, the Alexandrian issue commemorates a victory of the Emperor, not the Roman army, implying active participation of Hadrian, which could not be possible for a British campaign. However, Hadrian had just won a victory by resolving the Sarmatian problems in Moesia in person, it may thus be easier to ascribe the Alexandrinian issue to the Sarmatian war.

Secondly, the question of the Roman victory issues: first of all, it needs to be stated that none of the Hadrianic coins of that period appear to celebrate victories in the same way as the 'Judaea Capta' issues of the Flavian period, or the 'Nemausus' series celebrating the victory over Egypt with a crocodile chained to a palm tree. This means that either Hadrian had developed a new visual language or preferred not to commemorate the various victories in coinage.

A third problem is the context of the coin within the other coin issues of Hadrian in the period 119/122. This consists of two thematic series of coins, in addition to several special commemorative one-off issues. The first is a series of deities: Hercules, Minerva, Jupiter, Neptunus, Oceanus, Mars and Roma. The second series presents a catalogue of virtues, which includes Victoria, but also Fortuna (fate), Genius Aug/Bonus Eventus (the guardian spirit of the Emperor/the spirit of good endings), Felicitas (luck), Aeternitas (eternity), Concordia (harmony), Pax (peace), Pietas (duty), Salus (wellbeing), Spes (hope), Providentia Deorum (divine providence), Securitas (security), Libertas (freedom) and Virtus Augusti (the courage of the Emperor).

In combination these coin issues appear to present a generic catalogue of Imperial virtues/principles of the reign and Rome's protecting deities rather than commemorating a specific victory. It certainly differs little from similar series of coins known from earlier Emperors. The only unusual feature on these coins is the frequency with which Oceanus and Neptunus occur, as well as the fact that the Felicitas Augusta coins tend to display a galley.

With regard to the Britannia coins, two features stand out: unlike other Roman issues commemorating defeated people, Britannia is not bound; quite the opposite, the long implement suggests that she is armed. By the early second century the Romans have developed a clearly defined iconography on how to portray defeated enemies, usually bound, often tied to trees or victory trophies; the Hadrianic Britannia just does not comply with any of these expectations. Furthermore, very similar designs (including the armour) appear in the provincial series at the end of Hadrian's reign, when he honoured most of the provinces he visited with a special coin issue (this series incidentally includes another issue with a 'dejected' Britannia, holding her face in her right hand – still with the weapons next to her (RIC 845 = BMCRE 1723) and discussed by Jarrett (1976)). Most of the frontier provinces feature armed allegories and many of the island provinces are shown sitting on a rock, possibly to differentiate them from their landlocked counterparts. There is, in fact, a very similar coin issue for Germania (RIC 302), which shows Germania standing frontal, head turned right, holding a spear and balancing a shield with the left hand. As far as the author is aware this coin has never been claimed as evidence for a Hadrianic war in Germany; but it should be remembered that the Romans thought the only way to distinguish between the two heavily armed border provinces was to portray one standing (Germany), and the other sitting on a rock (Britain). In addition to the late series of provincial issues of the 130s, there are also a number of coins with provincial allegories that were struck contemporary to the Imperial visits to the provinces, usually accompanying coins showing Hadrian meeting the provincial armies or being greeted by the province on her knees. Seen in this context it looks more likely that instead of a victory issue, these Britannia coins were actually part of the coins issued in the context of Hadrian's visit to Britain.

This image of Britain as seated and armed remained in use for some time beyond the reign of Hadrian. In 154 a similar design is chosen for Antoninus Pius' Britannia issues. In this context the conclusions of D.R. Walker, on studying the coins from the Sacred Spring in Bath, are important, as he points out that while the late Hadrianic provincial series (those struck between134/138) can be found evenly distributed in all parts of the Empire, the early Britannia issues (119) (RIC 577) are near exclusively found on British sites, suggesting that they represent a special batch of small change, created for circulation in the province. This unusual distribution pattern can also be seen in the near identical Britannia *asses* of Antoninus Pius (Walker 1988, 290 and 294). The suggestion that a potential Hadrianic victory issue should only be available in the 'defeated province', where people would have known of the war anyway, seems highly unlikely and certainly without parallels in the Imperial mints. But without these coins, there is no compelling evidence for a war in Britain in 117/118, leaving us with the undated wars mentioned in the SHA and Fronto.

In addition to this early war, other scholars have suggested that a further war may have been fought in Britain in the 130s, this time citing the second Britannia issue of the 130s as evidence, and quoting in support the fact that Britain at this point was run by Julius Severus, according to the SHA, Rome's best general at the time, although as Jarrett has pointed out, just because somebody was a good general, it did not even in Rome imply that there had to be a war wherever he went . The second argument adduced for a war in the 130s is the second 'dejected' Britannia issue, which as we have already seen above forms part of a wider series commemorating the Imperial travels to the various provinces earlier in the reign, and which as Jarrett pointed out, is accompanied by other issues celebrating the British army (EXERC BRIT) and his arrival in the island (ADVENTUI AUG BRITANNIAE) (RIC882) (Jarrett 1976, 145–152).

Further evidence usually quoted in support that the situation in Britain was apparently far from peaceful comes from two inscriptions by two different officers, T. Pontius Sabinus and M. Maenius Agrippa mentioning an '*expeditio Britannica*' by Hadrian, as part of their careers. The former is sent to Britain after having been *primus pilus* (senior centurion) in the *legio III Augusta* in Africa, the latter was sent to take a force of 3,000 legionaries from Spain and Germany to Britain by the Emperor.

Maenius Agrippa, according to the inscription, was 'chosen by Hadrian and sent on the *expeditio Britannica*' (CIL XI 5632 = ILS 2735). The same Maenius Agrippa, who later became *praefect* of the *classis Britannica* and then *procurator* of the province, is also known from a series of inscriptions from the Roman fort of Maryport in Cumbria, where he commanded the local auxiliary unit (Birley 2005, 307–309). Unfortunately, once again none of these altars can be independently dated, so they offer no help with the reconstruction of when this *expeditio Britannica* may have taken place. Various reconstructions have tried to fit these inscriptions into the period of the apparently non-existent war of 117/118, with critics pointing out that Pontius Sabinus' earlier jobs would have left him with an extremely crowded career. Frere (2000) has argued that this expedition should be moved to the governorship of Julius Severus in the 130s, to allow for the career to progress at a more manageable pace, perhaps unaware that Jarrett (1976) had already argued against the historical reality of this event.

Frere's main argument for such a late date is that it would be impossible to call Hadrian's visit to Britain in 122 an *expeditio* as this particular word has overtly military connotations of active campaigning, which would be inappropriate for an Imperial visit in the British context. He also points out that the inscription mentioned the term *missus* (sent) instead of using a term that implied he had accompanied Hadrian (Frere 2000, 25). Frere gives no parallels for somebody as junior as Maenius Agrippa being described as a companion (*comes*) of an Emperor. The term *missus*, which according to Lewis and Short's Latin Dictionary can mean 'sent', also has two more appropriate connotations: in phrases such as *ad cenam missus*, it can mean 'invited' (in this case to dinner), while it has in other contexts the meaning of 'guarding' and 'escorting' – both meanings would be only too appropriate in the context of an Imperial visit.

More importantly, while Frere is probably right in most cases about the meaning of the term *expeditio*, in this particular case, the Emperor Hadrian appears to disagree with him. In 122 during his visit to Britain a series of coins are struck in Rome, showing the Emperor in armour on horseback with the legend: EXPED(ITIO) AUG(USTA) (RIC 613a and 613b =BMCRE 1261). As we know where Hadrian was during 122, first on the German frontier, then in Britain, and then in Gaul, it can be assumed that the term *expeditio* was indeed used by Hadrian for his trip to Britain, and thus copied by his military men. This may not have been approved by Latinists, but as Favorinus said, after being faced with a very similar misuse of Latin by Hadrian: 'You are urging the wrong course, my friends, when you do not suffer me to regard as the most learned of men the one who has thirty legions.' (SHA, Hadrian XV, 12–13)

It, therefore, appears that the two officers and the accompanying legionaries could have arrived at the same time as Hadrian in 122, but this still does not help to establish when the 'war in Britain' occurred. It has been argued that bringing 3,000 soldiers suggests the existing army had been depleted and that the legionaries were used to bring the other legions up to strength. However, most *vexillationes* of the first and second centuries are expected to return to their original units sooner or later and it may be just as likely that Hadrian brought the extra troops to have a sizeable field army for possible campaigning.

On the other hand Hadrian stayed only a few weeks, making it unlikely that he could have inaugurated or inspected Hadrian's Wall in addition to leading a significant campaign. We have, however, in addition to the

Alexandrian coin issue of 119, another Nike issue in the years 124/125 and 125/126 and John Casey (1987, 65–72) has argued that the likeliest, and in many ways the most convincing, candidate for these victory celebrations would be the War in Britain.

David Breeze (2003, 13–16) has drawn further attention to a series of construction changes in the building of Hadrian's Wall, including a layer of soil which accumulated over the foundations of the fort of Birdoswald, a change in the standards of workmanship in the construction of the Housesteads fort and a narrowing of the Wall when work eventually resumed. Breeze's proposition has not received universal acclaim, especially as the time span envisaged seems very short (Hodgson 2009, 16f). If it were to be accepted, it would provide a new scenario, where Hadrian decided to visit Britain in 122, and which he chose to have described as an *expeditio* on his coinage. We are not sure what prompted this visit, but there is no evidence that there was warfare in 117/118. There may have been military concerns though, as he was accompanied by a substantial number of additional troops, as well as spending some time inspecting or initiating the building of Hadrian's Wall. It is not clear whether warfare was undertaken in advance of the Wall construction or as the building progressed, or alternatively if the building of the Wall itself destabilized the situation dramatically, leading to further campaigns in 124 and 125, which eventually required drawing more troops from the Wall itself, thus interrupting construction. Two successive victory issues in Alexandria in 124/125 may suggest protracted fighting and the casualties from the campaign, which might have included T. Ann(ius) from Vindolanda, were clearly remembered by Fronto, who would have been a very young man then, as one of the defining moments of Hadrian's reign.

While the above might be valid and may even appear to be a convincing (one hates to use the term attractive in this context) argument to some, it should be stressed that other scenarios over the last sixty years describing Hadrian's British War have been deemed equally compelling, only to be taken apart within a very short time. The evidence for any reconstruction of this and similarly badly recorded events of the second century is just too thin to allow for substantial confidence in any proposed scenario.

Designing a Frontier

While trying to place a war within the reign of Hadrian, Hadrian's Wall has been mentioned several times. The Wall is without doubt the military structure with which Hadrian is most associated, both in Britain and beyond. It is certainly Rome's most architecturally elaborate land frontier and it is hard not to be impressed by its remains. In its current form, it represents the result of strategic repositioning by the Roman Empire, as well as the result of a long series of tactical decisions of how these new ideas were to be implemented.

When we first reviewed the deployment of troops in the province, two main considerations dominated the decision-making process for the Romans; policing of the conquered areas and positioning the army in a suitable spring board position for the next conquest. We have seen how this could lead to forts being placed close to former power centres (such as Colchester, Saham Toney or Hod Hill) or at the end of valleys suitable as routes of march into enemy territory, but well connected to the hinterland to

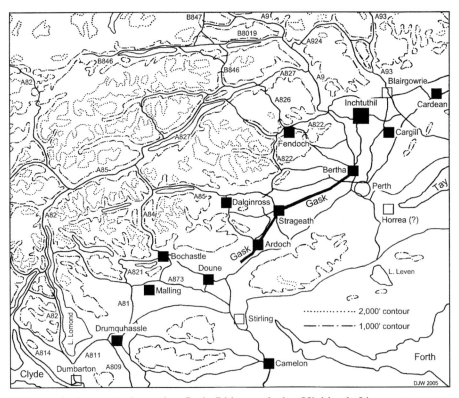

Military deployment along the Gask Ridge and the Highland fringe. *David John Woolliscroft*

allow for ease of supply (the so-called spring board sites such as Gloucester, Wroxeter, or the vexillation fortresses of the 50s in Lincolnshire).

None of these structures was inherently designed to defend a marked out area or pre-defined territory: the spirit of the Julio-Claudian age (to avoid a problematic term such as propaganda) was to see the world as an area which was there for the taking. Drawing a line between what is Rome, and what is not Rome, is unlikely to have occurred to anybody. This does not mean that there were no parts of Britain where Rome's control did not reach, but we have seen that client kingdoms were not necessarily deemed to be independent and other border territories could be perceived as 'not yet Roman', especially in view of the rapid growth of Rome in the hundred and fifty years between the fall of Carthage and death of Augustus. By the end of the first century, a different, and to modern readers, probably more realistic sense of Rome's relationship with its neighbours had begun to develop. Conquest may still be preferable, but for example in Sala in Mauretania (modern Morocco) and also in the Delta area of Holland, towers were added that allowed forts to keep an eye on areas where access needed to be controlled, if only to prevent raiding of local livestock by populations on the opposite side. In Britain this is the state of play seen in Rome's occupation of Scotland, south of the Highland fringe. Access in and out of the area was mainly along the wide valleys of Strathearn, Strathalmond and Strathmore, which provided fertile ground for agriculture. All the forts are carefully placed to allow control over river crossings or exits from a series of narrower interlocking valleys leaving the Highlands.

The backbone of the system was a road that came from the south. In its current form this is a carefully engineered all-weather road with cuttings and substantial underpinning to allow for the use of wheeled traffic. Recent work at Innerpeffray has, however, suggested that this road may not have been constructed in the Flavian period, but is a later addition, probably of the mid second century. If that is the case, then we are probably looking in the Flavian period, with a series of patrol tracks, suitable for mules and horses but not for heavy wagons, and road stubs leading out of the forts, which were 'in the process of being upgraded' when the order for the withdrawal came.

The main track along the central sector of this system crosses a small ridge, which kept traffic out of the waterlogged valley bottom, but also obstructed the view for the forts across from the Highlands on the north and the Ochills on the south side. At this point an additional feature is added in the form of a series of towers, which line the road. All of these towers have excellent views, either north or south, but in some cases both (although much of these are today obstructed by dense woodland). As they are also visible from the forts, it is possible to keep control over any traffic passing out of the Highlands or the Ochills. Further north, two towers are so far known, and they too are placed in such a way as to link the forts of Cargill, Cardean and the fortress of Inchtuthil.

The result is an area of tight control for the Romans, where they can police any disturbance with relative ease, while keeping the province further to the south and east free of problems. What it lacks is an artificial boundary, perhaps because the Highland fringe is used like an over-dimensional wall with limited exit and entrance points.

There is some discussion as to whether this represents an early Roman frontier. In some respects, particularly its depth, it differs from later Roman frontiers. Later frontier systems are often very narrow; all necessary installations are concentrated in a thin strip of land, with only the occasional outpost fort to document that Roman control was not meant to end at the barrier, while the back up of the nearest legion could be more than a day's march away.

At the Gask and the Highland fringe, there are no outpost forts, and no hinterland legions; instead the military is deployed in almost a twenty mile

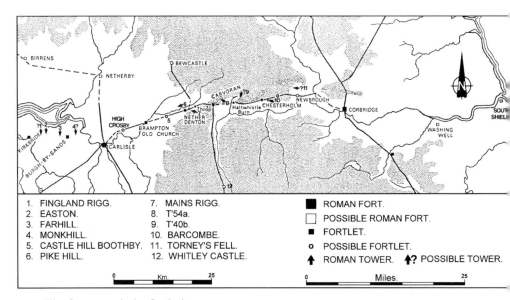

The Stanegate in its final phase. *David John Woolliscroft*

wide corridor with a forward screen of forts on the exits of the Highland and a second line of forts along the tower line in the central sector. The legion at Inchtuthil is thus integrated into the frontier zone proper. All elements are clearly designed to work together. Woolliscroft and Hoffmann (2006, 234) called these elements 'frontels', elements that together make the frontier: the geographical barrier of the Highland fringe, towers that provide a supervized area, a supply road that keeps the forts supplied while being simultaneously guarded by forts and fortlets; some forts such as Bertha that are close enough to navigable rivers to have additional logistical functions. None of these 'frontels' are designed to work on their own. There is currently no evidence that there may have been a phase one with the Highland forts and a phase two with the forts along the road, but at the moment the evidence suggests that when the order to withdraw came in 86, the entire system was envisaged to operate together as a unified whole.

As described, this is clearly not a Roman frontier like the ones that can be dated to the second century. It still has some of the elements of the spring board deployment that we have seen in the mid first century AD in Wales, with one legion moved as far as possible to the front of the line and good logistical support for the forts in the form of supervized tracks, although the logistical roads in the Midlands were never guarded by towers as far as we can tell. However, the troop concentration is higher than before, and all later frontier elements are already there: road, barrier, tower, and fortlets. The system is then a hybrid, in-between the two types: this is the first time we see the Romans deploying a spring board for the armies and combining it with the development of a guarded zone at the margins of the province, and thus probably creating Rome's first frontier.

In the years following the withdrawal from Scotland the military situation appears never to have stabilized to such an extent that another frontier line could develop. By 105, twenty years after the heyday of the Gask system, the forts had been withdrawn to the Stanegate. The debate continues whether there is another frontier system operating on the Stanegate before Hadrian's Wall is built in 122. It is becoming increasingly clear that the earliest forts between the Tyne and the Eden were not designed or built to be a frontier line, but instead to have been deployed to facilitate the usual policing duties. By 105, when the area became the northernmost line of deployment of Roman troops, this situation appears to have changed. The withdrawal appears to have resulted in a much higher number of Roman forts to the west of the Pennines, and it is possible that after 105 we can see the building of some fortlets between the forts, as well as isolated towers, that extend the

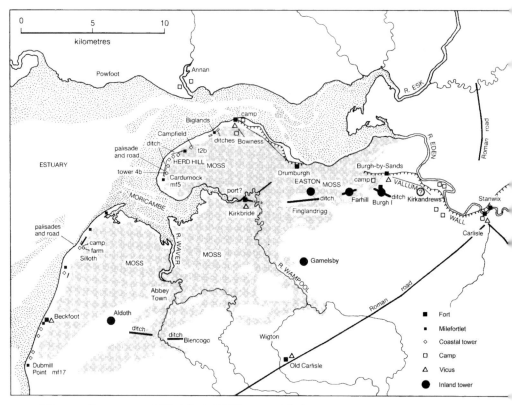

Western Stanegate and Hadrian's Wall's coastal defences. *David Woolliscroft on the basis of a drawing by GDB Jones*

field of vision of the forts north beyond the high ground of the Whin Sill. However, there seems little evidence that this incipient system continued east of Corbridge, although Barri Jones first raised the possibility that it may have stretched westward beyond Carlisle to Kirkbride on the Cumbrian Coast (see Breeze & Woolliscroft 2009, 70–71 for a recent review of the evidence). If so, this system would again be a frontier without a continuous artificial barrier, but appears to be using the natural barriers of the Whin Sill and the Eden and Cumbrian coastal wetlands. Barri Jones believed that he could detect short stretches of palisade ditch along the route to Kirkbride, linking the low-lying areas and thus closing the areas to north-south traffic. If one accepts his findings, it would suggest that by the Trajanic period the Romans in Britain were already experimenting with artificial frontier obstacles. In the end the early phases of Hadrian's Wall appear to have overtaken and replaced this system.

In 122, around the time of Hadrian's visit to Britain, a new frontier system was being constructed along the Tyne-Solway line. Originally starting at Newcastle in the west and running into the east as far as Bowness-on-Solway, it provided at its heart an 80 mile long wall (built of turf in the west and of stone east of the Irthing) which featured every mile a milecastle and two towers. In addition there were two major gateways: the Portgate in the East took Dere Street through the Wall to the North, the other must have been in Carlisle, but has not yet been identified. As originally designed, the wall and the towers along it were built to be visible to the forts along the Stanegate, such as Vindolanda and Haltwhistle Burn.

This system suggests a major change from the Gask: now the forts are kept along the road, while the towers are moved ahead, usually as far north as the field of vision allows. The result, however, is the same; the forts, fortlets and towers together create a large zone of supervision with controlled entrances at the gates and milecastles. The major differences are the advance line of forts at the feet of the hills and the proximity of the legion at Inchtuthil, in comparison to their location at Chester and York, well in the rear of the Wall. Finally, the controlled zone (nearly 20 miles in Scotland) is initially narrower in the first phase of Hadrian's Wall; in some parts it is under a mile and a half. As a result, the first phase of Hadrian's Wall in many ways appears to be a slimmed down version of the situation at the Highland fringe; and without the close proximity of the legion, a system that does not have the ability to be turned into an offensive spring board.

Plans for Hadrian's Wall were, however, not static. Within a very short time, perhaps as little as a year, a new chain of forts were built up to the line of the Wall. They appear to be in many cases in addition to those on the Stanegate, many of which like Vindolanda and Corbridge stay in use. A further addition was the creation of the Vallum; a misnomer, as this is not a city wall, but the name appears to date back to the Venerable Bede and is hallowed by long usage. It consists of a deep flat-bottomed ditch which was flanked on both sides by substantial mounds set back from the lip of the ditch, as well as smaller, but contemporary mounds close to its edge. The whole obstacle is up to 30 metres in width and even in its current dilapidated state forms an impressive obstacle over substantial parts of the Central Sector of the Wall. Discussions about the function of this feature abound, and while it certainly presented an obstacle to the traffic across the area, both animals and, as Wilmott stresses, people, it is not clear if this was its main intended function. We have already seen above that David Breeze has mentioned the disruption of the wall building by the possible war in the reign of Hadrian, and it is possible that the Vallum may have been provided as an obstacle, precisely because Hadrian's Wall itself at this point was barely higher than foundation level in many places; but there are problems linking this scenario with some of the stratigraphic evidence from the Wall itself, and the search for a possible function will be occupying researchers for many years to come.

When Hadrian died in 138, Hadrian's Wall had on paper become a formidable obstacle: a central wall wide enough to take a wall walk, fortified with a chain of alternating milecastles and two towers, with fourteen forts along its line, which had by now been extended to Wallsend on the Tyne. Behind the Wall ran the Vallum with crossing points at the forts and the gates. In the East the system was augmented by a series of free-standing towers and milefortlets along the Cumbrian coast from Bowness-on-Solway to Maryport. The strategic reserves in case of attack were probably the two closest legions at Chester and York, a substantial distance to the south, but in between, a series of auxiliary forts to the south of the Wall continued to be occupied. There were also a series of forts in advance of the Wall along the main roads leaving the line. These outpost forts were Netherby and Birrens in the West, and High Rochester in the East; a further fort at Learchild may have had a similar function as well, as did the later additions of Bewcastle and Risingham. The wall line itself was in many areas still not finished, but in advance of the Wall there was in most areas a ditch (sensibly dispensed with along the Whin Sill crags in the Central sector), as well as a series of further approach obstacles between the ditch and the Wall itself.

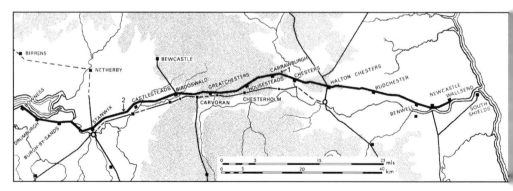

Hadrian's Wall. *David John Breeze*

However, with the death of Hadrian the political landscape changed once again. A new Emperor, Antoninus Pius, had to prove his credentials as a military leader and it appears that Britain was chosen as a convenient location. Hadrian's Wall was abandoned, and a new wall, the Antonine Wall was built between the Clyde and Forth.

For most of its course, the new wall ran along the southern edge of the central valley of Scotland, often overlooking both the rivers Kelvin and Carron and their surrounding wetlands. There are, however, a number of differences, beginning with the geography. While Hadrian's Wall stayed south of the Solway estuary, the narrower upper end of the Clyde was taken in by the Antonine Wall, which ends at Old Kilpatrick on the north side of the Clyde bridge, 37.5 miles in length from the other (possible) end at Carriden: it is thus substantially shorter than Hadrian's Wall and lacks the elaborate defences on its western flank. To date there are only a number of small fortlets known, such as Lurg Moor, despite the fact that the Clyde is much narrower than the Solway estuary and more easily crossed by boat. In the east there were a number of forts along the southern shore of the Forth such as Cramond and Inveresk.

The biggest difference is, however, the Wall itself, which is throughout built of turf, usually on a stone base. Again we can detect a change in plan while construction was still in progress. Initially, in the first phase, six large forts and fortlets had been planned along its length, to which at a later stage a number of smaller forts were added. While Hadrian's Wall forts on the whole were large enough to house entire units, this is demonstrably impossible with many of the Antonine Wall forts, which are much closer together than the Hadrian's Wall forts.

There is also so far no indication of the same dense cordon of milecastles and towers that we see on Hadrian's Wall. There certainly are a number of fortlets known from the Antonine Wall, and over the years several series of possible mile fortlets have been proposed, but very little work has been undertaken to confirm or rule out their existence. The most remarkable absence is, however, the lack of integrated towers. While these clearly have been identified in the Turf Wall sections on Hadrian's Wall, their absence further north is striking, so much so, that over the years other features have been proposed, such as expansions, of which seven are known, some of which have produced evidence of burning. The other candidates are small enclosures, but without any remains of structures within their ramparts their function remains problematic.

A further candidate along the line of the wall is a free-standing tower with an unfinished ditch at Garnhall near Castle Cary (Woolliscroft 2009). Stratigraphically the structure is earlier than the Turf Wall, but the only finds were two unstratified glass bangles, which do not allow a decision as to whether this is 'earlier' during the construction process (in which case the Wall may only be later by a year or so) or 'much earlier' (such as the Flavian period).

Two further differences are the additional approach obstacles. While the Antonine Wall, at least east of Garnhall appears to have *cippi* (pits probably obscured by brushwood and possibly central stakes), similar to the ones

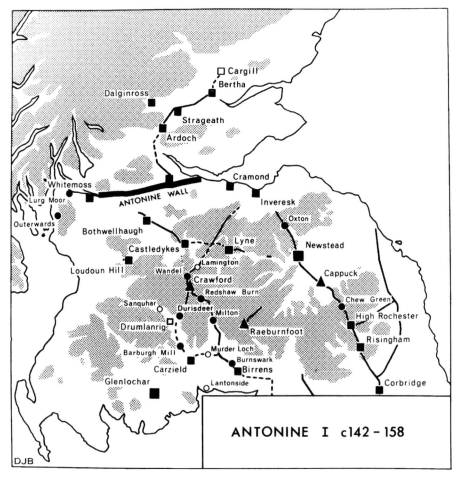

Antonine Scotland. *David John Breeze*

found at Hadrian's Wall, there is no evidence for the Vallum or a comparable structure behind the Wall. However, the ditch in front of the Antonine Wall is substantially larger than the one in front of Hadrian's Wall (to the extent that at Watling Lodge it can accommodate a small house), and it has been suggested in the past, that this may have been influenced by the substantial size of the Vallum further south. Finally, in addition to the forts along the line there were once again forts in advance of the Wall, following the road north past Camelon. So far Antonine occupation has been proved for Ardoch, Strageath and Bertha, and Antonine finds are also known from Dalginross and Cargill, although the latter two appear not to be lying along the road.

This road building is a further feature of Antonine Scotland: the best known example, the Military Road, followed the Antonine Wall, linking the forts and fortlets together. But recent excavations on the road at Innerpeffray just east of Strageath have shown that the road appears to be later than the 63 acre camps, which would suggest that the carefully engineered all-weather road, which included a substantial road cutting and grading in Strageath and Innerpeffray, is more likely to be an Antonine feature than a Flavian one.

In addition to the forts on the Antonine Wall and behind it, a series of new forts were built in Lowland Scotland, including the large fort at Newstead, which re-occupied an earlier Flavian fort site (as did many other sites).

The manpower needed to garrison these forts came from the North of England and Wales. The latter had gradually been deprived of its garrison since the 80s and by the Antonine Period only a handful of military sites remained. The North of England fared little better. The garrisons on Hadrian's Wall were withdrawn as were most of the ones from the Stanegate and Cumbria. South of the Wall, by current understanding, barely a dozen sites remained: Derby, Rocester, Templeborough, Manchester, Ribchester, possibly Low Borough Bridge, Brougham, Watercrook and South Shields, definitely Ambleside and Ravenglass, Maryport, Bowness, Carlisle and Corbridge. The legionary fortresses at Caerleon, Chester and York appear to have stayed in use, but appear to have largely stood empty, their garrisons since the Hadrianic period involved with building Hadrian's Wall and then the Antonine Wall.

Antoninus' reign (138/161) is frequently referred to as the most peaceful period of the Roman Empire, but a reference in Pausanias (who included this as an aside in his Description of Greece (VIII.43.3–4)), mentioned that

'... in Britain... appropriated most of the territory of the Brigantes, because they too had begun a war, invading the Genounian district, which is subject to the Romans'.

Needless to say by now, this source is once again problematic. First of all we still have not identified a Genounian district in Britain (there is one in Raetia), and there are at least two Brigantian tribes in the Roman Empire (one in Britain, one in Raetia on the eastern end of Lake Constance). So Plutarch, who was anything but familiar with Britain or Raetia, may have confused which Brigantes were meant.

Originally this Plutarch reference was connected by Haverfield (1904, 142–4) to an inscription on the Tyne (RIB 1322) mentioning reinforcements travelling between Britain and Germany dating to the governorship of Julius Verus (158), the rebuilding of the fort of Brough-on-Noe under the same governor, a further possible mention of this governor at the outpost fort of Netherby, a passing comment in the SHA mentioning trouble in Britain in 161 (see below) and a coin issue of 154/155 'indicating a victory in Britain' (cited after Breeze 2011, 118). Since the 1970s this Brigantian revolt has received continued criticism, not least as the coin issue in question is a reissue of the Britannia issues of Hadrian; and as we have seen above, both are only available in Britain and do not use the established victory imagery of the Roman Empire, which has led Walker (1988, 290 and 294) to suggest that they merely represent an issue of coins for use in the province of Britain, rather than a coin commemorating any specific historical event. The latest and extremely convincing refutation of any trouble in the Brigantian period came from Breeze in 2011 (pp. 118–119), who also refuted any involvement of this spurious uprising as a contributing factor in the abandonment of the Antonine Wall (or by extension, of a possible intensification of Roman control in the area north of Carlisle in the later part of the second century).

Reassessment of the evidence from the Antonine Wall in the 1990s (Hodgson 1995, 33–42) has shown that the Wall does not have a second period of occupation as once thought and that from 158 onwards, Hadrian's Wall was increasingly brought back into operation (RIB 1389).

For the following few years, both the Antonine Wall and Hadrian's Wall appear to have existed side by side (Breeze 2011, 121), one being gradually run down, while the southern frontier was being put back into operation and possibly in some places finished for the first time. Many of the re-occupied forts both on Hadrian's Wall and in its hinterland have produced inscriptions naming the two governors most involved in this second withdrawal: Virius Lupus and Calpurnius Agricola.

The re-occupation was, however, far from being a restoration of the Hadrian's Wall system of the 130s. Some elements of the system, such as the towers and fortlets along the Cumbrian Coast were not revived. The Vallum was modified by adding further crossings, thus making the Wall area more accessible, and a major change was introduced when Hadrian's Wall acquired its own Military Way linking the forts on the Wall. In addition the Northwest and Northeast saw their hinterland forts either refurbished, or in the case of Dere Street, newly built, providing a chain of large forts along the main routes that could provide a strongly defensive force, but also potentially a substantial force for a sudden move north of the Wall (Breeze 2011, 211). Hodgson (2009, 31 HW) argues also that this is the time that the Hadrian's Wall fort of Brough by Sands (II) finally replaced the earlier detached fort, but it is symptomatic of the gaps in our understanding that the latest report on the fort (published at the same time as Hodgson's overview), is much more restrained in its dating and appears to favour, on the basis of the archaeological evidence, a Hadrianic date for the fort on the Wall (Breeze & Woolliscroft 2009, 77).

Another big change happened at Corbridge, where the earlier fort site was replaced with a civilian site, possibly a planned forum or market centre (which in the event was never finished). The military meanwhile moved to a new irregular walled compound south of the Stanegate, which was to house detachments of *legio VI Victrix* from York and *legio XX Valeria Victrix* from Chester (Bishop and Dore 1988).

As in the Hadrianic Period, the area under Roman control reached far beyond the line of the Wall, with 'outpost' forts (now including Bewcastle and Risingham close to the Wall) stretching at least as far as Newstead in the northeast and Cappuck and Birrens in the northwest. In addition it appears that even further north, occupation around Roman forts such as Castlecary and Inveresk may have continued, although the exact nature of this occupation remains a matter for debate (Leslie 2002, 17–28). We have already seen that at the time the withdrawal from the Antonine Wall began, a number of military sites in the southwest of Scotland appear to have been refurbished. This may have been roughly contemporary to the siege of Burnswark, which appears to have included an Antonine fortlet. The debate on whether this reflects a real or practice siege is still ongoing, with convincing arguments on either side. Certainly, Hodgson (2009, 189) argued in favour of the siege, citing the layer of burning and rebuilding at Birrens in 158, as well as the widespread rebuilding as part of the same reoccupation of the southwest, and proposed the tentative linkage with the Pausanias quote mentioned above; we have already seen that this is strongly refuted by Breeze (2011, 118–119). It is one of the problems of the second century that in the absence of clearly chronologically tied-in historical events, the same quotes can be used for a wide range of different incidents, and so the Pausanias quote is as easily useable for the initial conquest of the Lowlands at the beginning of Antoninus' reign, as for this particular event. Although given the Genounian district in Raetia it may be wiser to use this passage as little as possible.

That there were at least fears of warfare at the time can be deduced by a quote in the SHA dating to the beginning of the reign of Marcus Aurelius (SHA M. Aurel 8,7): 'War was threatening in Britain and the Chatti had invaded Germany and Raetia. Against the Britons Calpurnius Agricola was sent, against the Chatti Aufidius Victorinus.'

Calpurnius Agricola was a governor whose activities in the North of Britain are widely attested through numerous inscriptions: we have already mentioned his involvement in the refurbishment of Hadrian's Wall and its hinterland (examples survive from Ribchester, Hardknott, Corbridge, Vindolanda, Carvoran), which demonstrate that he must have been in Britain in 163. Given that the refurbishments started by 158, it seems at first tempting to suggest that this prolonged building may reflect a period of military build-up in response to some perceived threat. However, few of these forts had seen any maintenance for nearly 25 years, and thus a 5 year programme of refurbishment is hardly excessive.

The next clear reference to warfare in Britain comes from the reign of Commodus (180/192). Xiphilinus, abbreviating Cassius Dio (72.8.1–6) reports as follows that Commodus spent some time fighting in Dacia (modern Romania) 'but the greatest war was the British one. For when the peoples in that island, having crossed the wall, which divides them from the Roman legions, and done a great deal of damage, and cut down a certain general together with the soldiers which he had, Commodus, being alarmed, sent Ulpius Marcellus against them… such a man was Marcellus and he inflicted terrible damage on the barbarians in Britain'.

Diplomas or discharge certificates for Roman auxiliaries date Ulpius Marcellus' presence in Britain to 178, while the conclusion of the British campaign has been linked by Tony Birley (2005, 162–170) with the seventh Imperial acclamation of Commodus of 184 and the issue of coins naming him Britannicus and celebrating *Victoria Britannica* (The British Victory (RIC III, Commodus 451)).

The wall that was crossed by the barbarians, on our current understanding of the withdrawal from the Scotland would have to have been Hadrian's Wall, and Birley argues that the legate killed was not a governor (*legatus pro praetore*), but more likely to be one of the three legionary legates (*legatus legionis*), probably from York.

Identifying this incursion across the Wall archaeologically is a matter of much debate. Hodgson (2009 HW, 31–32) is happy to accept the burnt layers at the forts of Haltonchesters, Rudchester and possibly Corbridge as evidence for this incursion. Birley (2005, 167–8) on the other hand sounds a much more cautious note.

Archaeologically, as we have seen before, burnt layers are exactly that, layers of burning, and only rarely is the evidence good enough to establish if it was caused by deliberate fire-setting or accidental fires. Given the widespread use of combustible materials, accidents were frequent throughout Romano-British history, sometimes leading to widespread damage. On the other hand, three destructions of apparently similar date in close geographical proximity are likely to raise eyebrows. More evidence is clearly needed to resolve the issue.

Possibly contemporary with this trouble are a number of inscriptions from Hadrian's Wall and its hinterland. An altar a few miles northwest of Carlisle was set up 'in thanks for things achieved beyond the Wall' by the Legate of *legio VI Victrix* (RIB 2034), but this may just as easily refer to earlier problems north of the Wall. A prefect in Corbridge set up an altar 'after the slaughter of the Corionototae', which has been interpreted as a possible early reference to the Picts (RIB 1140). A third monument, part of an arch, was set up in Carlisle to commemorate the defeat or slaughter of barbarians (RIB 946).

In addition to this trouble from beyond the Wall, the governor's behaviour appears to have also generated a mutiny according to a fragment of Cassius Dio (72 (73), 9.2a) as the soldiers tried to appoint a legionary legate named Priscus as Emperor, which the latter declined. The SHA (Commodus 8.4) appears to refer to the same episode, when it suggests that Commodus was called by some Britannicus (indicating a victory in Britain), even though the Britons wanted a different Emperor.

The mutinous undercurrent appears to have lasted beyond the governorship of Ulpius Marcellus, as his successor Pertinax (governor

185/187), who would be Emperor in 193, also had to deal with continually insurgent troops (Cass. Dio 72 (73), 9.2a) and 73 (74), 4.1. – SHA Pertinax 3.5–4.1). This suggests that the situation in Britain under Commodus was anything but quiet for a variety of reasons, but once again there is very little detail available to judge the circumstances competently.

The situation appears to have come to a head on 31 December 192, with the murder of Commodus in Rome. As no male heir with suitable qualifications from Marcus Aurelius' or Commodus' line was available, the new Emperor had once again to be found outside the immediate Imperial family, leading as in 69 to multiple contenders, and in this case to a 'year of the five Emperors'. Commodus' immediate successor as Emperor was Pertinax, who lasted only three months, before he was replaced in the city of Rome by Didius Julianus. At the same time the largest armies in the Empire offered their own candidates for the throne; the armies of Illyricum and Pannonia supporting Septimius Severus, the armies of Syria and the Eastern provinces favouring Pescennius Niger, while the British legions cooperating with the German legions finally got their chance of nominating their own candidate; their governor Clodius Albinus.

Unlike in 69 the ensuing civil war took more than a year to resolve. The Roman candidate Didius Julianus was relatively quickly eliminated. Severus at first offered Albinus cooperation (by naming him Caesar). Albinus accepted, leaving Severus free to deal with the Eastern provinces and Pescennius Niger. Only after Niger's death was Severus prepared to attack Albinus, who was eventually defeated on 19 February 197 at the Battle of Lugdunum/Lyon, a battle in which according to the SHA, 150,000 soldiers took part on both sides. These huge numbers are almost definitely inflated in keeping with Roman historiographic tradition. They suggest that British troops were likely to have been used in the battle, but there are no units named in the historical records. As it were, the involvement of Britain as the leading province in an usurpation was going to have repercussions for the province as a whole.

Chapter 11

The Severans and Britain in the Third Century AD

Dividing the province

It is one of the acknowledged 'facts' of Roman history, that Roman senators, who had successfully mounted a coup, attempted to ensure that the same methods could not be used against them by any would-be successors. 193 saw three Roman governors vie for the throne, all of whom used as their power bases the armies of their three legion provinces. It is thus hardly surprising to find that the victors, the Severans, are usually assumed to have been responsible for breaking up these commands into smaller, less dangerous units.

The earliest source for this division is Herodian, a historian of the late second and early third centuries, who has the advantage of being a near contemporary of the events described. Contemporaneity does not necessarily equate to being well informed, however, and Herodian can also be somewhat partial at times. He stated that one of the outcomes of the Battle of Lugdunum (197) was that Severus 'set the affairs in Britain in order and divided the administration in the province into two commands'. There is certainly evidence that there were two British provinces later in the third century. The first was Britannia Superior (which probably refers to its greater proximity to Rome, and certainly does not imply any regional superiority) in the south, which contained the *legio XX Valeria Victrix* (at Chester) and *legio II Adiutrix* (at Caerleon), whilst Britannia Inferior, further north, held *legio VI Victrix* at York. Inferior was governed by a senator of praetorian rank, whilst the southern, more powerful, province remained the preserve of men who had held the Consulate. Nevertheless the early date given by Herodian for the division is contradicted by Cassius Dio, who places it in the reign of Caracalla. There are also inscriptions naming three governors of Severan Britain who all commanded a unified province, as well as one mentioning the legate of one of the southern legions operating north of Hadrian's Wall under Severus. The latter could be explained by sending troops on detached duty to the neighbouring province, but no such convenient explanation exists for the three provincial governors.

Birley (2005, 333–336), following Dio and the epigraphic evidence, makes a good case for the division only occurring under Caracalla, after 213. It may seem surprising in view of the warfare on the northern frontier at this time that close support to Hadrian's Wall was restricted to one legion. Indeed one might have expected Inferior to be the senior, two legion province. It is worth pointing out that the North contained the bulk of the auxiliary forces of Britain, which means that a division which put two legions and the fleet on one side, and a single legion, but with most of the auxiliaries on the other, may actually reflect a fairly even distribution of power in the island. Moreover the fact that two legions now had their bases in separate provinces does not seem to have diminished the presence of some of their members on Hadrian's Wall. The legionary compound at Corbridge continued into the third century, while the fort at Carlisle appears to have been occupied by detachments from *legiones II* and *XX*.

Severan military activity in Britain

There is a surviving fragment of Cassius Dio (75(76), 5.4), which belongs in the immediate aftermath of Severus' Civil War against his final rival Albinus (c. 197/198). As so often with such fragments, it lacks context, but it reads as follows:

> Because the Caledonians did not keep to their promises and had prepared to aid the Maeatae, and because Severus was then devoting himself to the Parthian (or neighbouring) war, Lupus was compelled to buy peace from the Maeatae for a large sum, receiving a few captives.

The events described must have happened a substantial distance north of Hadrian's Wall, as the Maeatae are traditionally associated with the area around Stirling, beyond the (now abandoned) Antonine Wall. This suggests that even at that point, Rome still took considerable interest in affairs in Scotland, a fact underlined by the substantial hoards of Roman coinage of the late second and early third century that have been found there (Hunter 2007, 23–32). The phrasing does, though, suggest that warfare was averted for the moment, although the presence of prisoners suggests that some sort of confrontation with Rome, and perhaps an incursion into Roman territory, had occurred earlier – albeit there is no indication of when this might have happened, or whether anything but the outpost forts north of Hadrian's Wall would have been involved.

Virius Lupus was the first Severan governor of Britain and appears to have governed the whole province. In addition to his attested activities north of Hadrian's Wall, he is also known from three building inscriptions, dateable to 197, from Corbridge (RIB 1163, building unspecified), Ilkley (RIB 637 mentioning the rebuilding of an unknown structure) and Bowes (RIB 730). The latter commemorates the rebuilding of a bath building, which had been destroyed by fire, and there has been a persistent tendency in archaeological literature to suggest that this fire, the rebuilding mentioned in the other inscriptions, and the burning of a barrack at Ravenglass, may be linked to the Maeatae trouble mentioned by Dio. Yet it is hard to see why a tribe from the lower reaches of the Forth, on the east coast, would be responsible for burning a fort on the west coast, and for widely distributed damage between the Stainmore Pass and the still more southerly fort of Ilkley. A bathhouse fire in the central Pennines is surely more easily explained as an accident, rather than the result of enemy action, that even with modern transport lived 4½ hours drive away, and was separated from the forts by Hadrian's Wall.

Septimius Severus (193/211) is one of the most visible Emperors in the epigraphy and archaeology of Roman Britain. During his 14 years in power in Britain, he ordered the rebuilding (or rather finishing) of all three active legionary fortresses in stone (e.g. Ottaway 2004, 75), and substantially rebuilt or refurbished forts all over the north of England. Indeed on Hadrian's Wall his activity was such that early Wall scholars spent considerable time debating whether it was really Severus', rather than Hadrian's Wall.

Much of this building was probably occasioned by the simple fact that forty years after the withdrawal from Antonine Scotland, the fort structures were likely to need 'updating' or, in some cases, complete rebuilding. Such was the case at Risingham, where a gate had collapsed through old age (RIB 1234), and another building inscription from Caernarvon/Segontium (RIB 430 + add), which must predate 209, shows that such activity was not just limited to the Wall. The governor most frequently mentioned in these inscriptions is Alfenius Senecio, who certainly appears on eight, and has been restored on a further three, and thus almost personified the programme. One of these inscriptions (RIB 1337 + add) is not a building inscription, but a dedication to the Victoria of the two Emperors Septimius Severus and his older son Caracalla. But Birley (2005, 191) has pointed out that this may just as likely commemorate the anniversary of the Severan Parthian campaigns, or relate to a war elsewhere, as to a victory in Britain.

There is comparatively little evidence for what was happening north of the Wall during the Severan period. Newstead appears to have been abandoned around 180, but High Rochester, Birrens, Bewcastle and Risingham remained in operation, documenting Rome's continued interest in the area, and it would thus seem much more reasonable to assume, if any trouble was caused by the Maeatae in the aftermath of the Civil War, that it would have occurred in the Scottish Lowlands, in areas under Roman protection through the outposts, but north of Hadrian's Wall and thus more accessible.

In addition to the refurbishments, some forts and installations were clearly new designs. At Vindolanda, the earlier stone fort was demolished and its stone frontage has been found apparently deliberately collapsed into

South Shields fort with granaries. *David John Woolliscroft*

the ditch. Its replacement was built over the Antonine vicus and surrounded on three sides by substantial ditches. The east side, facing the old fort platform, was only defended by a wall, and faced an area of roundhouses arranged in long lines, apparently covering most of the former fort (Birley & Blake 2005, 27–30). This complex is so far unique and its purpose remains debatable. Hodgson's suggestion (2009, 32) that it provided accommodation for levees of civilians from the South, who were involved in the reconstruction of Hadrian's Wall, is one possibility, but it does not explain why the accommodation should take such an unusual form, or be deemed important enough to replace the existing stone fort. South Shields, on the

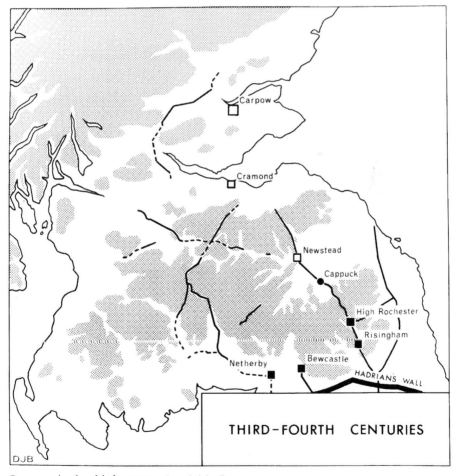

Outposts in the third century. *David John Breeze*

Wall's eastern flank, on the south side of the Tyne mouth, was rebuilt in this period, as a fort plan dominated by numerous granaries, turning it into one of the most striking examples of a supply base in the Roman Empire.

Further north two forts appear to have been built on the East coast: Cramond and Carpow. Carpow was a legionary vexillation fortress serving detachments of both *legio VI Victrix* and *legio II Augusta*. It was located at the apex of the Tay estuary, just below its confluence with the Earn, and close to its lowest crossing point. It is currently the only known Severan

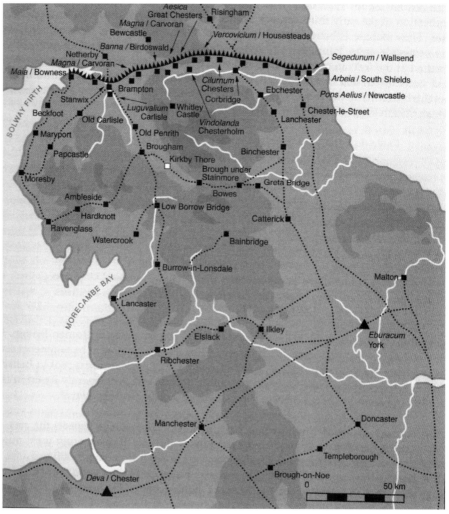

The North of England in the late second and third century. *David J. Breeze*

installation in the area, and its isolation is striking, but Cramond parallels its basic location, this time on the south side of the Forth estuary. The exact date for Carpow is tied up with the reading of its East Gate inscription and will be discussed in further detail below.

Cramond was first built as one of the coastal forts on the eastern flank of the Antonine Wall. The withdrawal from the Wall from 158 onwards does not seem to have involved the fort's demolition and some reduced occupation appears to have continued on the site (Holmes et al. 2003, 153f.), but it was fully reactivated in the Severan period. The date of reoccupation used to be fixed at 208, with reference to the historical sources, but there has recently been a tendency to shift this date back due to the evidence of coins. For example, Holmes (et al. 2003, 155) suggests a possible start date 'in the very early years of the third century'. Like South Shields, Cramond seems to have had a role as a support base, with a considerable provision of workshops and industrial complexes, both internally, in the *praetentura*, and outside the fort, which included evidence for pottery manufacture.

The situation in the south

Roman military installations south of the Pennines became rare during the course of the second century. Apart from the legions and a few large forts left in Wales (e.g. Segontium/Caernarvon), the principal sites were the Cripplegate fort in London (probably designed to house the Governor's bodyguard and any troops passing through) and the fort at Dover. Because of its *classis Britannica* brick stamps, the latter is usually associated with the fleet, and this does seem more likely than the alternative: that it was only built by the navy, but was garrisoned by other troops, given that it has also produced inscriptions recording fleet commanders. It was originally constructed in the early second century and in its rebuilt form lasted to c. 210 (Philp 1981). The *classis Britannica* had been operating in the Channel and along the British coast from the late first century. Its largest base appears to have been on the French side at Boulogne, but in addition to building the fort at Dover, it was also active in Kent and Sussex, and was involved with iron smelting and brick making at sites such as Beaufort Park (built in the late second century and operational until the mid third). A detachment is also recorded on Hadrian's Wall, where its construction skills, along with naval transport, may both have been useful. We know little about the detailed workings of the unit, but in analogy to other fleets, it is usually assumed that it would have served a logistical role (providing transport or at least escorts for supplies, officials and troops moving to and from Britain), as well as monitoring other maritime traffic.

By the late second and early third century, a need seems to have been felt for the military presence along the coast to be increased. The earliest new fort to be identified was at Reculver (Philp 2005, 216), where construction started in the late second century. After a hiatus of several years, it was eventually completed around 211, which matches comparable data from Caister-on-Sea in Norfolk, and our limited evidence from Brancaster. Philp would link these three with Carisbrooke Castle on the Isle of Wight (for which little dating evidence exists), and they may be the beginnings of the coastal defence system, which by the late fourth century had become the so-called 'Saxon Shore'. In origin, though, in view of the dating evidence for Cramond and Carpow, it may be worth discussing whether the original forts were possibly designed as further elements in a supply chain reaching from the iron processing and supply harbours of Kent, to the Hadrian's Wall complex and advanced forts in Scotland, and that they only mutated into a new coastal defence role later, once more costal forts were built over the course of the third century. Once again, more research is clearly needed.

Severus on campaign

Herodian tells us that Septimius Severus had three reasons for coming to campaign in Britain: a) to add a British victory to his other conquests in the East and North b) to get his sons (Caracalla and his younger brother Geta) away from the flesh pots of Rome and c) because the governor had requested help against the barbarians (Herodian III, 14, 1–3). A.R. Birley (2005, 191) points out that the latter is a topos, (a repeated theme that may be rooted in expectation rather than fact). To judge from similar descriptions in Herodian and elsewhere, the chain of logic would run something like this: in Roman eyes it was unjust to start a war without proper cause; this means that it was important to be able to claim that a war was fought in defence of the Empire or its allies. If the governor requested help, this showed that the Emperor was hardly likely to be just fabricating the evidence to justify military action, but was responding to a genuine emergency. In other words, this was a conscientious Emperor fighting a just war. In theory, this would balance the additional motives for waging war in Britain, even though the educational opportunity and self-aggrandizement would not usually be seen solely as acceptable reasons. Nor would a secondary reason given by Dio, that the legions were becoming restless and needed something to keep them occupied (76 (77), 11.1). Herodian, who counted Severus as one of the 'good Emperors', was thus able to provide suitable window dressing for a military adventure.

We have two main accounts for the campaign, as well as a number of other fragments. Cassius Dio, with his now customary disdain for geography and military detail, reports that in the first season Severus pursued the Caledonii and Maeatae, but that the enemy employed guerrilla tactics, luring the Roman army into ambushes and difficult terrain, while not allowing themselves to be engaged in set piece battles. Despite heavy losses (Dio mentions 50,000 dead, which must again be an exaggeration, as it would equate to nearly the entire garrison of Britain at the time), Severus reached the end of the island, where he took astronomical measurements on the length of day, before returning and concluding a treaty with the barbarians. In the second season, Severus responded to a revolt by ordering the soldiers to kill everybody involved. This was apparently carried out, but the Caledonii then joined the revolt of the Maeatae, and Septimius Severus died while preparing for a campaign against both. Again, the account offers little in the way of geographical detail (typical for Dio) and focused instead on the ethnographic peculiarities of the enemy, and on Caracalla's hunger for power and supposed attempts to speed his father's demise.

Herodian's account agrees with Dio's as to the major events, but says that the campaign was fought north of the fortifications that provided the defences of the Empire and adds that Caracalla commanded the second year campaigns, as his father's health had already deteriorated. Beyond the fact of victory, most of the accounts left by the fourth and fifth century historians, Jerome, Orosius, Eutropius and Aurelius Victor, concentrate on Severus' death in Eburacum/York, rather than on the achievements of the campaigns. Orosius (7.17) and Eutropius (8.19) also claim that 'he defended the island with a wall', the latter clearly a reference to the extensive work on Hadrian's Wall conducted in the decade before the Imperial visit. These late sources thus add very little to our understanding of the military operations. Coins issued at the time show Severus riding forth, a standard issue for an Emperor on campaign, and the image of a ship (on one coin accompanied by the legend TRAIECTUM – crossing or transshipment point), which might be taken to suggest that naval operations formed part of the campaign, although it might also just reflect the fact that Britain is an island.

In the past, archaeologists have tended to define the area of operations by means of a series of marching camps, which some publications would project all the way into Moray. More recent work has significantly changed our perception of these camps, however. After extensive excavations at the Kintore example, the 110 acre group, which formed the chain leading to Moray, is now mostly considered to be Flavian, leaving only the 63 acre and 130 acres series, along with the 165 acre camps in the Lowlands, as possible contenders for the Severan campaigns (NB: the groups were defined before metrication and have become a label rather than a strict indicator of size). The 130 acre sites form a close knit series stretching from Ardoch, through most of the Strathmore, and we know that they must at least slightly post-date the 63 acre camps, thanks to Hanson's excavations at Ardoch, where the ditches of an example of each intersect. More recent excavations at Innerpeffray, however, might suggest that the camps were built before the Roman road through the area, and so could be earlier, perhaps Antonine, especially as evidence for a more modern road on this line is currently lacking (Woolliscroft and Hoffmann 2006). Roman temporary camps have always been notoriously difficult to date and, as has been pointed out by Hanson, there has long been a tendency to try to associate them with the two best known campaigns in Scotland: the Flavian and Severan. Yet there were several other occasions in the second, later the third and the fourth centuries where campaigning took the Roman army north of Hadrian's Wall and, as most of the camps still lack dating evidence, it is possible that future work will change our understanding of these structures.

Withdrawal from Scotland
Cassius Dio tells us that after the death of their father, Caracalla and Geta quickly concluded peace with the Caledonians, withdrew from enemy territory and returned to Rome to make sure that their succession as Emperors passed off smoothly. This has usually led to the assumption that a number of forts (including Carpow and Cramond) must have been abandoned at this time. But a fragmentary inscription from the East Gate of the Carpow legionary fortress presents problems. Wright has suggested that it could only have been cut after Geta's death in Rome in 212, suggesting that the base was still under construction then and so remained in use after the end of the Severan campaigns. This has led to the belief that there may have been a continued presence in Scotland, possibly into the 220s or 230s (Bidwell and Speak 1994, 29). More recently, however, John Casey has

pointed out that this same inscription could be restored to refer to Commodus (180/192), giving an earlier start date for Carpow, with interesting historical implications. Moreover, Nick Holmes (2003, 156 with further references) would argue that the coin evidence for both Cramond and Carpow does not support an extended stay beyond 211, and nor have they produced evidence of sufficient post-Severan pottery to suggest continued occupation.

Interestingly the Vindolanda roundhouse settlement was abandoned at about the same time, and Stone Fort II was built on the site (Birley and Blake 2005, 31). Nevertheless some features of the Severan building programme were retained, including the now fully renovated Hadrian's Wall, and the supply base of South Shields, which appears to have continued to function as such into the late third century. But was the abandonment of the new territories necessarily a change of policy by sons keen to abandon their father's goals in favour of a rapid return to Rome? Collingwood and Myres (1937, 160) suggested that the fact that Severus reoccupied very few of the earlier Flavian and Antonine fort sites, despite their lying on his line of advance, implies that he never intended a permanent occupation of Scotland, but only a punitive campaign: 'visiting the wrath of Rome on

Corbridge aerial photograph. *David John Woolliscroft*

enemies of Rome outside their grasp, but not outside their reach'. They would see this as part of the same strategy that brought about the rebuilding/refurbishing of Hadrian's Wall, and thus provided an armoured baseline from which exactly such punitive campaigns could be launched, keeping the area to the north cowed under Rome's political control and the province itself secure. This model, sometimes referred to by Scottish medieval historians as the 'Caracallan' or 'Severan' settlement (Fraser 2009), has been seen as the foundation on which early Medieval Scottish history developed, creating, in effect, an inner/southern zone of close contact with Rome, with a number of outer/northern and western zones beyond, which had much looser connections with the Empire. It is hard to verify this model by archaeological means. Certainly there are differences in what and how much Roman material reached different areas of Scotland, but the data sets are so small, and the historical records so sparse, that it is unlikely that we will ever be able to fully prove or disprove this model. For the moment, therefore, it might be best to leave it as an interesting hypothesis in need of further testing, noting in doing so, that the site of Birnie, in Moray, which should definitely lie in the 'outer zone', contained Severan coin hoards. This suggests at least that the division between inner/southern and outer/ northern regions should not be seen as a simple geographical Lowland/ Highland issue.

After the Severans
With Caracalla's return from Britain, the military history of the, now divided, province once again became an item of little interest to Roman historical writers, and much of it has to be reconstructed archaeologically from excavations in both forts, and increasingly in towns. Over the course of the late second century Romano-British towns had been returning to the idea of defences. Towns that began in the Iron Age, such as Silchester, might have retained original defences in use, while the early *coloniae* such as Lincoln or Gloucester seem to have maintained their pre-existing legionary fortress defences. Indeed some, such as Colchester, actually refortified themselves in the first century in the aftermath of the Boudiccan uprising (as we have seen earlier). From the late second century onwards, however, more and more city defences appear to have been constructed from new. The chronological evidence is too disparate to speak of a centrally guided programme; it seems as likely that the decision was guided by the availability of funds as by any real or suggested threat to each town. After all, city walls,

even in the medieval period, were often as much a status symbol as a serious means of defence. But for whatever reason these sites were defended, the presence of walls added crucially to the military capabilities of the province from the late third century onwards.

Despite the administrative changes, military installations were kept up-to-date in both provinces, as both the numerous inscriptions (set up by or in honour of a series of governors in the early third century) and the substantial archaeological record for sites such as the fortress of Chester attest. But the nature of the army was changing in the third century. Up to this point nominal strengths seem to have remained at 500 or 1,000 for auxiliary units (although it can be argued that, in reality, many of the military units may never have been larger than 700–800), and 5–6,000 for legions. During the course of the third century we see more varied unit types, such as *cunei*, *numeri* and *vexillationes*. *Cunei* seem to be associated with cavalry but, more strikingly, they often consisted of people recruited, or forcefully imported from outside the Roman Empire, such as Frisians from northern Holland and Frisia, or Sarmatians from the Black Sea. *Numeri* and *vexillationes* may have been more generic units formed by combining parts of larger units, or institutionalizing former detachments, although at times on the Continent, the term '*numerus*' came to mean just a military unit of any size. Hadrian's Wall also saw the introduction of new, smaller barracks, which suggests that unit sizes may have shrunk. Certainly by the end of the third century and on into the early fourth, we are probably dealing with substantially smaller units than anything we had seen before, with even legions unlikely to have had more than 1–2,000 men.

The third century also saw the close of a number of our historical sources, in particular Cassius Dio and Herodian who end in the 230s. Moreover, most of the later historians tend to have a much more thematic approach, often focusing on the rise of Christianity as their main topic (e.g. Lactantius, Orosius and Eusebius) Even the later fourth century historian Ammianus Marcellinus (only part of whose work survives anyway), focuses mostly on the Emperors of the period he describes, and shows little interest in events outside the rulers' direct influence. Similar problems are manifest in the Scriptores Historiae Augustae (SHA), which purports to be a collection of Imperial biographies, by a series of different writers, rather than a standard history; but there are serious issues about the origin and validity of much of its material. A number of fourth century historians, such as Eutropius, Jerome and Aurelius Victor seem to use a – now lost – common source for some passages, which scholars refer to as the 'Kaisergeschichte' (Imperial history). But whilst this has left a useful legacy, for example for the reconstruction of Carausius' reign, many of these histories were written long after the events they describe and their sources are even more problematic than those for the first to the early third century.

Older historians often liked to rank the various writers by reliability. But however useful this might appear at first sight, a closer inspection reveals problems, because their reliability is always linked to the quality of the sources they were using for different times and their own motives and preconceptions, so that the same writer can be useful for one period and positively misleading for another. Thus, for example, a historical writer, such as the Anglo-Saxon Bede, may be very trustworthy when writing about the history of Northumberland in the fifty years before he wrote, as he was an eyewitness to at least some of it. Yet his account of the building of Hadrian's Wall is clear nonsense, as he relied on patchy and ill informed sources. Moreover our own understanding of what is or is not trustworthy depends on our ability to corroborate material, which in turn depends on being able to evaluate independent sources. But the closer we get to the end of Roman Britain the rarer such sources become, and while historians may have severe reservations about some accounts, especially Nennius and Gildas, they are often all that we have, so that we lack any means of verifying their data. As a result sources that had long been considered trustworthy, may suddenly become problematic when new source material becomes available (see the discussion of the Notitia Dignitatum below as a striking example). One of the most important sources for the later third century are the speeches in praise of the Emperors (Panegyrics)(Nixon and Rodgers 1995). These are a tour de force of Latin composition, the main aim often being to document the literary excellence of the orator by the use of obscure similes/metaphors, paraphrases and citations, which can be hard to decipher by anybody not part of the literary culture of the time. But they are also, by definition, propaganda, and again, require handling with great care.

The source problem is further exacerbated by a decline in the so-called 'epigraphic habit'. Britain had never been one of the Roman provinces famous for its large number of inscriptions, and during the second century the majority came from military sites in the North. During the third century, however, even this supply tailed off and when we do find a rare late third or fourth century inscription, they are mostly gravestones, of little obvious historical significance. Apart from these few mentions, therefore, late Roman Britain retires almost back into prehistory, which means that we are more and more reliant on the information provided by archaeology. As a result, the publication of a new set of excavations, such as the ones from Reculver discussed above, or a change in the date of a particular type of pottery, has the ability to substantially alter our perception. On the other hand, we have already seen that archaeology is notoriously unable to pinpoint short-term events such as invasions, civil wars or raiding. As a result, it is often silent or ambivalent about just those events we now miss in our waning literary data.

That said, we can produce at least an outline military history for the second half of the third century. By the 260s Britain was once again caught up in the politics of the wider Empire. In the aftermath of the Roman defeat by the Parthians and the capture of the Emperor Valerian in June 260, the Empire began to disintegrate, and several breakaway states formed. In Cologne on the Rhine, the General Postumus killed the son of Valerian's surviving co-Emperor, Gallienus, and proclaimed an independent Gallic Empire. At its greatest extent, this encompassed the Rhine provinces, Gaul, (northern) Spain, Britain and parts of Raetia. Its control in Britain can be identified from four milestones, which name the later Gallic Emperors Victorinus and Tetricus, through inscriptions from Lancaster (dating to 265/266: RIB 605) and Birdoswald (RIB 1883 & 1886), and the large amount of Gallic Empire coinage, together with the near absence of contemporary Central Empire issues.

The Gallic Empire existed for 14 years, but in 274 its last Emperor, Tetricus, surrendered to Aurelian (the central Emperor at the time: ruled 270/275). Unfortunately this reunification was followed by serious invasions of Gaul and Raetia, and it took several years to re-establish order. Britain appears to have decided to look after its own interests at this point and around 280/281 we hear of another Victorinus, this time a general sent to remove a British usurper who had rebelled against the central Emperor (Zosimos I.66.2 and I.68.3 and Zonaras 12.29). Yet despite having returned to central control, there are continued indications of trouble. We hear that two short-lived Emperors, Carinus and Numerian, accepted the victory title '*Britannicus Maximus*' in 283/284 and it is possible that the 'campaign under the North Star', which was celebrated by the court poet at the time, Nemesianus, refers to the same events. After the defeat and death of Carinus in 285, Diocletian (284/305) also accepted the title *Britannicus Maximus*, perhaps due to continued campaigning, but there have also been suggestions that he may have taken it simply as part of the Imperial 'inheritance'. Whatever the case, the record suggests that Britain may have been anything but a quiet backwater militarily, but these events have not yet been recognized archaeologically.

Chapter 12

Carausius and the Early Fourth Century

Barely one year into the reign of Diocletian, another usurpation shook the northwest of the Roman Empire. Carausius had been in command of 'the fleet that formerly protected the Gauls' (Panegyrics Lat. Vet. 8(5) cited after Nixon and Rodgers, 1995). This may well have been the *classis Britannica*, but the scarcity of records might hide other commands that may have been created since then. According to Eutropius (9.21) he was based at Boulogne and charged with pacifying the sea from the Franks and Saxons.

Carausius is recorded to have been Menapian by birth (i.e. from the area of Belgian and French Vlanders) and to have been a pilot or helmsman in his youth (the Latin term can mean both). Immediately before his command in Boulogne he had campaigned with Diocletian's later Caesar Maximian against the Bagaudae in Gaul.

His command in Boulogne was successful, but according to Aurelius Victor and other sources he failed to hand his booty over to the central government and was thus ordered to be executed. Instead he revolted and declared himself Emperor in Britain and the north of Gaul. This scenario is a topos (a prejudice on the basis that usurpers should be considered greedy), and Carausius is not the first Emperor to be tarred with it, as the same story is also told about Postumus twenty years earlier.

Apart from the short entries in the historians (Eutropius and Aurelius Victor), and the references in the Panegyrics, our main understanding of the size and history of the Carausian Empire derives from the study of his coinage, both with regard to the images and legends used, as well as the distribution of the coinage. The conclusions drawn differ between different historians and numismatists, but the general sequence appears clear.

It is frequently assumed that the main power base of the Carausian revolt was the fleet (British or otherwise) and its base at Boulogne, although the appearance of his early coins in northern France could point to a second base, the assumption being that because Constantius laid siege to Boulogne, this must always have been the main base. In addition to any fleet he may have controlled, he seemed to have claimed at the height of his power the support of nine legions or parts thereof, as he commemorated them on his coinage.

It seems that around 289/290 Maximian tried to invade the breakaway Empire and remove Carausius, but failed, a fact that is beautifully circumlocuted in the Panegyrics and commemorated on Carausian coinage by issues with images of ships and *'felicitas'* (good luck) and *'salus imperatoris'* (the wellbeing of the Emperor) as their legend. Furthermore Carausius from this point onwards portrayed himself with Diocletian and Maximian as the third Emperor. The arrangement was clearly one-sided, as neither of the other Emperors returned the gesture, but it is possible that the stand-off in the following year resulted because Maximian did not have the time or manpower to deal with Carausius and problems on the Rhine frontier at the same time.

The situation changed with the appointment of Constantius Chlorus (293/306) as the Caesar and thus as junior Emperor in the West in March 293 (at the same day Galerius (293/311) was made junior Emperor in the East), creating for the first time a college of four Emperors, the Tetrarchy). This meant that Diocletian and Maximian had no intention of accepting Carausius as their colleague and unsurprisingly, soon after the appointment, the attacks on the Carausian Empire were renewed. As a consequence Carausius lost the north of Gaul for good. Constantius proceeded to lay siege against Boulogne and managed to block the harbour exit through the construction of a dam of timber and stone at the mouth of the Liane, leading to the surrender of the base. It seems shortly after this disaster Carausius himself was replaced with Allectus, one of his co-conspirators and officers, but it is symptomatic of our understanding of this period, that we do not know Allectus' rank under Carausius. Aurelius Victor describes him as *'cum ei permissu summae rei praeesset'* (he was in charge of everything with his (i.e. Carausius') permission). This has frequently been interpreted that Allectus may have been the *'rationalis summae rei'* – a very high finance officer in the late Empire, frequently with reference to the abbreviation RSR found in a number of Carausian coins. These have now been shown to refer to a Virgilian quote from the Fourth Eclogue (de la Bédoyère 1998). However, Aurelius does not give the correct title *'rationalis'* and his apparent circumlocution makes too many other interpretations possible.

Having regained control of northern Gaul, and limited Carausius, or rather his successor Allectus, to Britain, it took Constantius another three years to invade Britain itself. The most detailed account of the Constantian campaign both against Boulogne and the Rhine Delta, and the final attack on Britain is provided by the Panegyric of 297 honouring Constantius. While this text provides us with the chance of constructing a narrative for the events leading up to the fall of London, it is worthwhile remembering that Panegyrics are the ultimate praise poems or eulogies, constructed to let both the speaker feel erudite and the Emperor feel flattered. These speeches are clearly not designed to be, in any shape or form, balanced or interested in providing a full picture of what happened. The positive highlights of the campaign are what matters, as chosen by the court of the winning side. Without the chance of verifying the details, we are once again dependent on the account as presented. Critical assessment on what might be covered up may be helpful, but is still just one of several possible scenarios.

The Panegyric stresses the personal involvement of Constantius. It relates the fact that the fleet aimed for the Solent and slipped past the Allectan fleet in thick fog. It also suggests that Allectus, during the final encounter, did not draw up a battleline or make use of any of his considerable preparations. This failure as well as his moral shortcomings consequently (in the mind of the unknown orator) led to his death in battle, where in clear imitation of Tacitus' statement two hundred years earlier, no Roman was killed. Meanwhile a part of the fleet became lost in the mist and found itself in front of London, just in time to kill all the surviving Frankish mercenaries fleeing from the battle, thus saving the city and 'providing a spectacle'. Then 'the necessity of obedience was imposed on many other people who had been accomplices in that criminal conspiracy' (Panegyric VIII, 14, 1ff in Nixon 1995).

Eutropius (IX, 22, 2) and Aurelius Victor (39, 22) suggest that Constantius' praetorian prefect Asclepiodotus may have been in charge of some of the troops, or at least of a detachment of the navy and legions. Asclepiodotus is not mentioned in the Panegyric, as in the context of an Imperial eulogy, it would have been considered a faux pas.

Throughout the account it is never quite made clear where Constantius is. The impression is one of ubiquity, but more than one scholar has suggested that Constantius may have followed after the army and thus it is generally assumed that Asclepiodotus fought the battle against Allectus (Nixon and Rodgers 1995, 136–138).

Constantius is celebrated as an avenger and liberator; Britain's liberation is perceived 'as its restoration to the whole world'. (Panegyric IX, 18,4) Finally, the city of Autun thanked the Emperor for receiving many artisans, with which Britain was amply supplied, for its own reconstruction.

The account is further underlined by the Trier Gold medallion, which celebrates Constantius as REDDITOR LUCIS AETERNAE, the restorer of eternal light. The reverse shows Constantius on horseback approaching a city, whose personification kneels to receive him. LON identifies her as London, and beneath Constantius a galley signifies the accompanying fleet.

Allectus clearly met Constantius' army in battle, but where this was and whether Allectus really was not willing to draw up a battle line should be doubted. The Panegyrist goes to great lengths to present Allectus and his army as barbarians, and barbarians are too wild to do anything but charge wildly against the Roman army. The description that no Roman died is clearly an exaggeration, as the Panegyrist himself admitted. The people on the battlefield were barbarians, or imitating barbarians with their reddish hair and the clothes they wore. That can just mean that the soldiers who fell wore late Roman uniforms, including trousers. But the praise of a victory in a civil war is always problematic, and stressing the foreign character of the opposing side meant the Panegyrist could create a clear 'us' vs 'them' scenario, which is not uncommon in late Roman historiography, and thus offered enough of a distance to remove the bad feeling arising from gloating over your dead fellow citizens.

The actions in London are clearly equally problematic. The Panegyrist claimed that his army killed the barbarian survivors in the town, before they could loot and move out. This sounds harmless and like a welcome rescue, but the barbarian army is the army of Allectus, and therefore the defenders of London, and street fighting in the city of London itself should, therefore, not be ruled out. The latter would also provide an explanation for the phrase 'providing a spectacle', with the invading army portrayed as providing gladiatorial style games at the same time as 'liberating the city'. The latter, a novel way of portraying the situation, was clearly designed to distract from its seriousness by making it appear to the audience like an entertaining game. It can probably be assumed that the residents of London felt very differently about the event.

We do not know what stood behind the phrase 'necessity of obedience'. In other cases of usurpations the winning side was only too willing to execute the leaders of the opposing factions and/or to confiscate their property. That the arrival of Constantius was not all the happiness suggested by the coin issue is made abundantly clear by the reference in the same Panegyric to British artisans arriving in Autun 'to rebuild the city'. If we use the events associated with other usurpations as a parallel, then we have to consider the possibility of mass deportations or even enslavement of the British supporters of Allectus. It is certainly unlikely that Constantius would have found a large volunteer force just waiting to be taken across to Autun in southern France for construction work. The reference to Autun also provides interesting evidence to the extent of Carausius' Empire. Autun in central France clearly thought of itself as loyal to the central government and the Panegyrist clearly saw the provision of craftsmen as a well-deserved boon.

That the opposition were unlikely to have been quite so barbaric as described by the Panegyrics is clear from the Carausian coinage (which ceased to be used shortly after 297). In addition to the standard repertoire of deities lending support to the Emperor and the personification of the core virtues of his reign, Carausian coinage contains frequent allusions to the poetry of Virgil and mention of other Roman institutions such as the Secular Games, thus showing that Carausius was promoting a considerable familiarity with Roman culture including literature and urban Roman traditions.

In addition to the legionary support celebrated on the coins, the armies of Carausius and Allectus were likely to contain foreign (including Frankish) mercenaries, but the same would be true of the army of the Tetrarchs, especially Constantius. The political need for distance between the Roman Emperor Constantius and the 'foreign' usurper Carausius, may have suggested to the Panegyrist that he focus on the foreign mercenaries, as well as Carausius' origin in the borders of the Empire to discredit his claim as a 'Roman' ruler.

The Saxon Shore

In 1961 White proposed that the Saxon Shore was in its origin Carausian. Numerous excavations on the coastal sites in the south and west of Britain have since then proved that the history of the coastal defences is more complicated than this statement suggested.

In its origin the modern concept of the Saxon Shore goes back to a command of the *Litus Saxonicum* listed in the pages of the Notitia Dignitatum (which is highly problematic as a source: see appendix), to which nine forts were assigned:

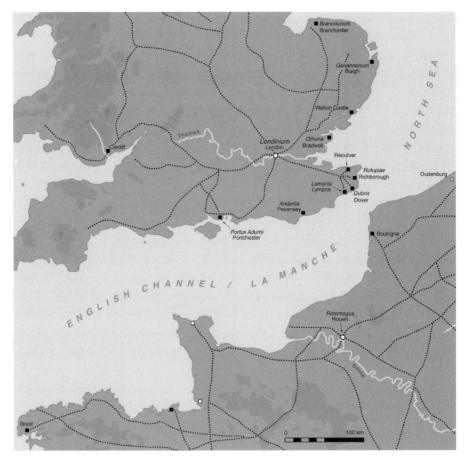

The Saxon Shore. *Frontiers of the Roman Empire project / RGZM / David John Breeze*

Branodunum / Brancaster, Gariannonum / Burgh Castle, Othona / Bradwell, Regulbium / Reculver, Rutupiae / Richborough, Dubris / Dover, Lemanis / Lympne, Anderita / Pevensey, and Portus Adurni / Portchester.

Published excavation reports have shown that these forts were not built as a unified scheme, but piecemeal over a considerable period of time. Of those listed Brancaster and Reculver can now be shown archaeologically to have been started before or at the end of the second century; thus at the time of the Carausian revolt they would have been in existence for nearly 100 years.

Richborough, at the opposite end of the Wantsum Channel from Reculver, appears to have started in 275; a similar date is now assigned to

Pevensey (Fulford 1995). Lympne has produced early third century pottery, but most of the pottery and coins date to the period 270/348, suggesting that this may have been the heyday of the fort. Therefore all four may actually predate the Carausian usurpation.

By contrast extensive metal-detecting surveys at Burgh Castle produced a coin list whose earliest significant coin losses do not begin before the 320s, and which would thus suggest that its construction post dated Constantius' re-conquest and indeed the accession of his son Constantine in 306 (Davies 2009, 219). The southernmost fort in the sequence, Portchester is the only one where coin finds suggest a start date in the late third century, perhaps even in the course of the reign of Carausius.

On the other hand, even in the area covered by these forts, there are other structures, which are clearly designed to be coastal forts and are designed to the same construction techniques with thick walls and the (subsequent?) protruding towers. These additional forts include Walton Castle (now eroded), Caister-on-Sea, as well as Reedham in Norfolk (Davies 2009, 221) and possibly Carisbrooke Castle on the Isle of Wight (underlying the medieval castle), a candidate proposed by Brian Philp (2005) on the basis of the overall similarity of shape to Reculver and Brancaster. Of these Caister-on-Sea, across

Burrow Walls, Workington. *David John Woolliscroft*

the bay from Burgh Castle, was constructed in the early third century, and remained in use until c. 370.

Even beyond the Saxon Shore area, shore defences in the form of large forts close to coastal inlets, and natural harbours and beaching sites, can be found by the early fourth century in other parts of Britain, including Burrow Walls, as well as Cardiff, Holyhead, Lancaster and Moresby in the west (White 2007, 55–59), suggesting a growing interest in protecting the harbours and possible shipping routes around the island. Distribution maps of Late Roman pottery and other finds clearly document the importance of maritime shipping for the supply of the army, but also the civilians of the third century and later. Similar coastal defences are also found along the opposing side of the Channel, documenting that the protection these forts afforded was seen as a universal need in the north-western provinces, and was not specific to Britain or the southeast of the island.

So what did Carausius do along the coast? His ability to hold his British powerbase for nearly ten years against the rest of the Roman Empire suggests that he was very lucky (in picking a period where the Roman Empire was facing pressure from numerous other enemies), although he is usually also credited with being a great strategist and tactician, although admittedly in adulatory biographies. It is thus hardly surprising to find him credited with the creation of the Saxon Shore command by modern scholars, despite the lack of any supporting literary evidence. It is also clear from Casey's coin diagrams, that most of the shore forts were in use in the Carausian period. Unfortunately, archaeology is not able to provide evidence for the interpretative jump from 'in use' to 'used as a single strategic unit'. We thus are simply unable to answer the basic and most important question of when this command was created, what size it was or what it was meant to achieve. Its creator may have been Carausius, if we assume that he regrouped existing forts together for a new purpose, or it may not have been him. What we do know, however, is that by the time he came to power, Britain was provided with several forts close to harbours and coasts. Whether they were used as coastal defences, which would suggest that they were envisaging their role as a defence of the hinterland from sea-borne raiders, or whether they served as naval bases, in which case they might have seen their role primarily as protecting the shipping lanes around Britain, or as a combination of both, needs to be further studied. Preliminary studies at Pevensey and Richborough suggest that the answers might vary from fort to fort.

Roman Britain after Carausius

After the takeover, Constantius Chlorus remained in Britain. For how long is not known. Tony Birley (2005, 397–8) points out that it was likely to have taken some time to replace Allectus' administrative structure and implement the changes necessary to integrate the provinces within the reformed structures of the Tetrarchy, but this could have been done by delegating, in a similar manner to Claudius' appointment of Aulus Plautius.

In the aftermath of the reintegration of the Empire, Britain became exposed to the reforms of Diocletian and Constantine. These reforms, which in many areas created or at least codified the changes that made the difference between the early Roman Empire and the Late Empire, affected most areas of daily life. Instead of two provinces under direct rule from Rome, Britain was now faced with a two-tier administration, the higher, the diocese of Britain was further subdivided into four provinces: Prima, Secunda, Flavia Caesariensis and Maxima Caesariensis (the latter two clearly named after Constantius' victory titles and family name). These four were administered by *praeses* or later *consulares*, who while in charge of the day-to-day running of the provinces, only had very limited control of the military. That came under the sole administration of military officers, *comites* (sg. *comes*) and *duces* (sg. *dux*), whose commands did not have to coincide with the boundaries of the civilian provinces. The boundaries of these military commands or the provincial boundaries within Britain are subject to numerous reconstructions, all equally based on very slim evidence. Nor is it likely that these boundaries remained static over the next 120 years. New military commands may have been created or others amalgamated, without leaving any traces in the archaeological record. Only at the very end of Roman Britain do we have a potential source for the disposition of some of the army and the administration in the form of the Notitia Dignitatum, although this has recently been questioned (see appendix).

The reforms also affected the structure of the army units. We have already seen that there is evidence for a decrease in unit size during the course of the third century and the creation of smaller *vexillationes* that operated for long stretches away from their parent unit, often in more mobile parts of the army, which would become the field army of the later Emperors (the *comitatenses*, literally: the companion army). A large number of these changes had gradually evolved, but were now made permanent. Many of the surviving units remained at their bases with more defensive duties and were eventually referred to as *limitanei* (literally: the border troops).

The sources often imply that this field army may have been of higher quality than the stationary troops. At least in some cases this can probably be put down to inter-corps rivalry, similar to the cordial comments passed today about members of the army by navy and air force personnel, and vice versa. But service as an officer in the *comitatensian* units appears to have provided better chances of promotion, as it was easier to attract the attention of the Emperor and his commanders; while service on the frontiers may have gone unnoticed by anybody but the neighbourhood and the local commander. Curiously, while there is a fairly decent understanding of the accommodation of the *limitanei* in their late Roman forts, so far it has proved difficult to identify the barracks or winter quarters of the field army anywhere in Britain.

Typically changes in accommodation can be seen in the whole province; the most striking (if only due to the scale involved) is the fortress of Chester in the early fourth century. There is continued evidence for the maintenance and substantial rebuilding of many of its main buildings, such as the baths and the *principia*. The barracks provision, however, appears to be reduced, with the barrack buildings in Deanery Field going out of use with the dismantlement of the structures, while in the neighbouring Abbey Green site, the accommodation survived well into the fourth century (Hoffmann 2002). The results are large open areas inside the Roman fortress. Similarly reduced accommodation areas can be identified in many forts and fortresses in active use, which survive into the fourth century. Michael Gechter (2001) has recently argued, on the basis of similar evidence in Bonn fortress, that these open spaces may have been used as protected campsites for the field army. While this argument is tempting, it is hard to prove. Elsewhere the finds of military equipment in walled civilian towns are associated with billeting of the field army, but other scenarios, such as the rise of the *buccellarii*, the armed body guards of the wealthy, cannot be ruled out.

In the auxiliary forts, new smaller types of barracks, first seen in the third century, continued to be built. Outside the civilian *vici*, which up to now were considered as constant companions to Roman forts, seem to vanish from the late third century onwards. By the beginning of the fourth century, *vici* were a rarity in the north of England, with Malton the striking exception. It used to be thought that the civilians used the open spaces inside the forts as their new residences, but with the recognition of 'chalets' as regular barracks instead of family accommodation, Bidwell and Hodgson (2009, 34) have recently argued that the reduced garrisons and the disappearance of the *vici* may be linked, suggesting that the reduced numbers inside the fort removed the economic viability of the civilian settlements outside it. However, this economic argument is problematic: historic evidence for the abandonment of villages in other periods suggests that economic viability is only ever one reason why a site is abandoned; frequently single houses survived, when the rest of a village may have gone elsewhere. Also, the abandonment of *vici* appears to be independent of the size of fort. If the reduced numbers were to blame, we would expect the larger forts to be able to continue to maintain smaller *vici*, while the smaller forts lose theirs. However, the loss of the civilian settlements can affect forts of all sizes, including the large fort of Pevensey, which was originally built next to a civilian settlement of second and third century date of considerable size.

After Constantius

In 305, after the resignation of Diocletian and Maximian, and his promotion to senior Augustus, Constantius Chlorus returned to Britain. The main source material for his presence in the island is the Panegyric for his son Constantine in 310 (Panegyrics Lat. vet 7(6)). The text's flowery language reduced Constantius' presence in Britain to a need to move closer to the stars at the end of his life, and to provide York with the opportunity to be the place of Constantine's inauguration in 306, and thus the first step to Constantine's route to becoming the first sole ruler of the Roman Empire in a generation.

The contrived suggestion of the Panegyrist that dying and making room for his son was Constantius' only achievement in Britain is contradicted by Constantius' coinage which proclaims him in 305 'Britannicus Maximus'. The title is shared with his son Constantine, who joined his father in Britain in 305, early enough to get involved in the campaigning. This suggests that in a similar manner to other Emperors (especially Septimius Severus), Constantius may have come to Britain to provide his son with the chance of gaining experience in warfare at Constantius' side, and thus establish him in the eyes of the army as the heir designate. If so, then the ploy worked. The army appointed Constantine Emperor immediately after the death of his father and remained his staunchest supporter in the years to come (Barnes 1981, 71).

If we know little about the events of 305/306, there is even less to say about further possible visits of Constantine between 307 and 311/312, and in 313/314 or 314/315. The evidence for all of these are a series of coins struck in London proclaiming the ADVENTUS AUG and two passages in Eusebius (VC 1.8.2 and 1.25.2), which describe Constantine as returning to Britain to wage war and possibly to gather troops for his campaign against Maxentius. The visits in 313/314 or 314/315 appear to have resulted in Constantine being called Britannicus Maximus (again). Four Imperial visits in 10 years would suggest serious problems in the province, especially in view of the precarious relationships with Constantine's colleagues Severus, Maxentius, Severus II, Galerius and later Licinius in Italy and a volatile situation on the Rhine frontier. A campaign in Britain always carried the risk of the inability to return if more serious trouble erupted along the eastern and southern borders, but again there is little beyond the coins and the fleeting references in Eusebius to tell us about the situation.

Archaeologically, we see the abandonment of the outpost forts of Hadrian's Wall by 312 (Casey and Savage 1980). The continued mentioning of the Picti in the Roman sources, as well as finds of Roman silver, including the late Roman Traprain Treasure suggest that the abandonment of these advanced posts did not mean that Rome had lost all interest in the lands north of the Wall; but it may signify a change of policy, with the importance in how the northern neighbours were 'engaged with Rome' shifting from military presence to payment of money (one assumes for continued good behaviour). Elsewhere, the late third and early fourth century generally appear to have seen another phase of rebuilding in the North of England, covering both Hadrian's Wall, as well as some hinterland forts such as Chester-le-Street and Old Penrith, and a major refurbishment of Chester fortress (Mason 2005, 69–81).

In c. 325 Constantine closed the mint in London. This probably happened as part of the general reorganization of Constantine's part of the Empire, and would be of little significance for a military history of Britain, were it not for the fact that we now lose the ADVENTUS coinage as an indicator of Imperial visits to Britain. We are thus even more dependent on the slim literary sources for our understanding of events in the province.

The next Imperial visit recorded was by Constantine's son, Constans in 343. Our sources are Ammianus Marcellinus who refers back to a part of the Histories that is now lost, as well as passages in the speeches of the late Roman orators Libanius and Firmicus Maternus: the two agree that the most noteworthy item was that Constans crossed the Channel in mid-winter, and Libanius (who lived in the eastern part of the Empire) added that it was not caused by any military emergency. However, Ammianus' corresponding reference suggested that Constans was active at the northern frontier and that he may have come to the aid of people in Britain. In addition coin issues claimed a victory around this time.

Seven years later Britain became part of the Imperium of Magnentius, a usurper, who had been declared Emperor in Autun in January 350; his direct opponent, Constantine's son Constans, was killed shortly after, leaving Magnentius in charge of the Western Empire. Constantius II, brother of Constans and Emperor in the eastern part of the Empire managed to defeat Magnentius at Mursa a year later, but Magnentius held on to power in the West until his eventual defeat in 353.

Battles between Emperors in the fourth century tended to be costly in manpower, even more so, if they involved the *comitatenses* of both the Western and Eastern Empire. In the past it has become a stock-in-trade theory amongst historians to link the two facts, and claim that usurpations resulted in the army of Britain being depleted in preparation for these battles, and – if the battle was lost – that the soldiers never returned. There is little evidence to support these claims, but there is as little evidence that Britain remained exempt from the repercussions of these recurring bouts of Roman self-destruction.

Ammianus Marcellinus is, however, explicit that Britain did suffer in the aftermath of the fall of Magnentius in 353. The winning Emperor had sent Paulus, nicknamed Catena (the Chain), to 'clean up' in Britain. The episode is reported only by Ammianus Marcellinus (14.5.6), and remains thus unconfirmed. According to Ammianus' account, Paulus, a *notarius* (a high civilian official) at the court of Constantius II was sent to Britain to apprehend some military persons associated with Magnentius. Upon arrival, he appears to have started a witch-hunt. When the highest civilian official in Britain, the *vicarius* Martinus could not stop Paulus, he attempted to kill him, but in the event failed and subsequently Martinus committed suicide.

The next historical event known is equally difficult to understand: Constantinian coins overstruck with the legend DOMNO CARAUSIUS CES may refer to another usurpation by another Carausius in the late 350s. This so-called Carausius II is not mentioned in the admittedly scanty historical record, and thus it is impossible to decide whether the coins are forgeries (especially in view of the misspellings) or perhaps the only witness to another problem in the province in the middle of the fourth century (Birley 2005, 420).

In the winter of 360, Julian, the cousin and brother-in-law of Constantius II, revolted against his cousin in Paris. Shortly before these events, Ammianus Marcellinus (20.1.1–3) reported that either the Scotti or Attacotti (the text is corrupted at this point, but both would refer to originally Irish tribes) and the Picts harassed the area close to the frontier. Instead of coming to Britain himself, as apparently his uncle Constans had done, Julian sent his *magister militum* Lupicinus to deal with the problem. Again we hear about a winter crossing, but the problem was apparently quickly resolved as Lupicinus was back in Gaul in the spring after the declaration. There is more than a hint in the surviving account that he may have been sent to Britain mainly to have him out of the way during the usurpation, rather than to solve a military problem. Ammianus mentioned previous disaster befalling Britain, but again the account is too short to make any sense of what may have happened.

After Constantius II in 361, Julian united the Empire under his sole rule (something last seen in the 330s), but on 26 June 363 Julian died during fighting in Parthia: with him and his successor and distant cousin Jovian (363/364), the Constantinian dynasty came to an end: Valentinian (364/375), commander of one of the Imperial bodyguards, became Emperor, and quickly divided the Empire with his brother Valens (364/378), who took over the Eastern half. This led to a militarily successful period in the West for the next 11 years, frequently associated with large-scale defensive building and vigorous campaigning on the Rhine and Danube.

The period is also a watershed for Britain. The early fourth century has been described by some as the 'Golden Age of Britain', with many of the villas seeing their largest expansion, and the development of the large distribution networks for pottery, which can be taken as an indicator of comparative safety for large-scale transport. This is also, for many towns, the period where their buildings see their final expansion phase, although as noted above, in the North, this goes hand in hand with the loss of the civilian *vici* around many forts.

Chapter 13

The Barbarian Conspiracy and the End of Roman Britain

A s we have seen, the scant historical accounts suggest that by the 360s military trouble had been building in Britain for some time, and the geography of the island means that this was most likely to have come either from invasion threats/raiding along the coast (with Ireland the most likely candidate) or along the northern frontier, with the Picts and possibly the Scotti or Attacotti mentioned as the enemies.

The Picti appear to have been the successors to the Caledonii and the Maeatae of the earlier period. The term 'Picti' became the name for a Roman perception of the situation around the frontier: that by the late third century, there was a marked difference between the British inside the province (exposed to Roman goods and Roman laws) and the British outside, the Picti, who were, from the name given to them, stereotyped as being in some way 'painted'. Late Antiquity favours these new group names for the emerging enemies, which for the most part consist of a number of tribes. In most cases, they do not appear to represent any recognition of an early state, just a vaguely similar kind of enemy: thus Franci attack in Lower Germany across the frontier and often close to water, the Saxones are the German pirates who live beyond the Franci, Alamanni are a problem of Upper Germany and appear to be associated with the hill country on the east of the Rhine, while the Picti are the British tribes north of the border. In the case of the Picts we lack the necessary detail, but the better source situation on the Rhine clearly demonstrates that within these large '*nationes*', several kingdoms and chains of command could exist side by side; they were thus at best acting as opportunistic short-lived federations, not as large early states.

The other tribes usually associated with trouble in Britain, the Scotti and Attacotti are in origin firmly locatable in Ireland. Since the nineteenth century there have been researchers suggesting that increasingly the Scotti may have represented Irish settlers in western Scotland. Archaeological and historical research in the last twenty years has now changed this picture markedly. It stresses that there is little or no break in the archaeological culture in the west of Scotland during the Iron Age, as would be expected from a wave of newcomers settling in the area. On the other hand, the foundation myths of the Dalriada or Gaels, as presented by Gildas, Bede and numerous other sources, have been shown to owe much more to the political realities of the sixth and seventh centuries, than to authentically transmitted oral history (Fraser 2009, 144–149). We are thus even in the last decades of Rome's rule in Britain unable to pinpoint the exact location of Rome's enemies.

By 367, whatever threat had been building up along the British frontier erupted into open warfare. According to Ammianus Marcellinus (27.8.1–2), who is once again the main source for events, the Emperor Valentinian heard on his way from Amiens to Trier about a Barbarian Conspiracy that had left Britain helpless. Two of the military commanders, Nectaridus, the *comes* of an unspecified coastal tract (which may well be the same as the Saxon Shore discussed above, although this is just one possibility), and a *dux* Fullofaudes, had been killed or caught in an ambush (and thus presumably also killed, but not taken prisoners as the translation sometimes appears). We have too little understanding of the military structure of Britain at the time to make a well-informed guess as to what or whom Fullofaudes was commanding, but the term in general signifies one of the highest ranking officers in the provincial armies.

For a province to lose two such high-ranking officers at the same time, suggests a serious incursion or even multiple incursions.

Valentinian's response was to send in quick succession a series of senior officers from the court to assess and remedy the situation. The first, Severus, was *Comes Domesticorum*, a position that amongst others entailed command of the Imperial bodyguards. But he must have been recalled quite quickly only to be replaced by the higher-ranking *magister equitum* Jovinus, whose post involved command of all the cavalry in the central field army. Jovinus may have spent the summer in Britain. Ammianus mentions that both men were trying to find an army to deal with the situation, which suggests that we are dealing here with more than a set of quick raids.

Before the end of the campaigning season (so presumably by the end of August) Jovinus was replaced with the lower ranking, but better equipped *dux* Theodosius, a *comes rei militaris*, sometimes also referred to as Theodosius the Elder. His role in the pacification of Britain is given an unusually large amount of space by Ammianus Marcellinus, and most scholars agree that this was because Theodosius' son eventually became the Emperor Theodosius the Great (379/395) and, perhaps more importantly, was the reigning Emperor at the time Ammianus was writing: thus by praising the father he may have intended to compliment the son.

In addition to the account in the Histories, there are also brief mentions of Theodosius' campaign in the later historians Jerome, Jordanes (probably copying Jerome) and Zosimus, as well as numerous very florid mentions in the Panegyrics to his Imperial son Theodosius, and his grandson the Emperor Honorius. The latter reference suggests that the campaigns might have reached as far as Ireland, the Orkneys and even Thule, and that they involved warfare on land and sea. It is very tempting to reduce these very poetic contributions to flattery or necessary stylistic metaphors. On the other hand, they provide one of the few geographical clues as to the location of the trouble, while Ammianus appears to restrict himself to the less than helpful 'north of London', a geographical pointer that tells us more about the unfamiliarity of the historian with the geography in Britain than about any real location. We are thus once again left without a map to assess the scale of the problem or a means to evaluate the tactics employed by the general. It is, however, striking that the literature of the time suddenly abounds with references to the Orcades (Orkney Islands), to the extent as we have already seen, that the contemporary historians credit Claudius with receiving the surrender of the king of the Orkneys.

Ammianus' account (27.8.3–9 and 28.3.1–2) covered the latter part of 367 and 368 with Theodosius crossing from Boulogne to Richborough, bringing with him four units from the field army: the *Batavi*, *Heruli*, *Jovii* and *Victores*. The army progressed towards London. Here Theodosius split it into detachments and pursued and captured the raiders and their booty.

For the next part of his campaign Theodosius needed more troops and thus offered deserters immunity and recalled soldiers on leave. At the same time, he requested a new *vicarius* for the *diocesis* (a *vicarius* would have been the predominantly civilian governor for the island as a whole, but it is not said what happened to the old one) and a new *dux* (Dulcitius), presumably as replacement for Fullofaudes.

Having raised a sufficiently strong force, Theodosius set out from London. His next actions are described in the generic phrases that are frequently used for the topos of general relief operations: 'he brought great assistance to the defeated and confused Britons', he 'chose locations for ambushes', 'he did not ask anything of the soldiers that he was not willing to do himself' and thus 'routed and put to flight' the enemy, 'he restored cities and forts that had suffered damage'. This suggests a successful campaign, but the phrases are commonplace and it is impossible to find out what happened in detail.

In addition to pacifying the enemy, Theodosius also had to deal with an incipient usurpation, which had been started by an exile called Valentinus. The language at this point is extremely partisan, as is to be expected from an account that attempts to portray Theodosius in the best possible light. Valentinus was apparently hatching a nefarious plot and hated Theodosius, who was the only one who could deal with him, which is why Valentinus was defeated and handed over to *dux* Dulcitius for execution. Theodosius was now able to prove his excellent character and military ability by forbidding any further investigations into the supporters of this usurpation. In this he behaves in the exact opposite manner to Paulus Catena earlier; and while Theodosius by behaving this way conforms to the ideal of a perfect Emperor (another topos), that was not his position and it is debatable whether this would not have exceeded his competences, had it really happened this way.

Ammianus' account closes with a review of Theodosius' long-term achievements: cities restored, forts garrisoned, frontiers protected with watch posts and defence works, and the restored province was now renamed in honour of the Emperor and his family (and clearly not after the usurper mentioned earlier): Valentia. He also did away with the '*areani*', a group of people whose task it had been to 'range backwards and forwards over wide areas and to report to our generals threatening behaviour among the neighbouring people'. Apparently in connection with the conspiracy these 'spies', appear to have turned double agents and handed vital information over to the enemy. Theodosius' command came to an end about a year after he had taken office and he was recalled to the Imperial court, where he succeeded Jovinus as *magister equitum*.

The trouble with Ammianus' account is not only its general vagueness, but also the fact that the original manuscript has numerous problems, with gaps and unintelligible text. As Ammianus also tends to refer back to his accounts of earlier events, we are in some cases, such as with the *areani*, left with problems of understanding what was really going on. Thus modern researchers commonly assume that the *areani* operated north of Hadrian's

Wall, where a number of the outpost forts are known to have held scouting units, with one called *castra exploratorum* (the Fort of the Scouts). But this would not provide information on the situation of the Scotti and Attacotti, who most academics think of as settling in Ireland at the time. Are we seeing in fact a seaborne force or an early loose network of undercover agents? The suggestions are numerous, but without Ammianus' description of what happened under Constans, we are unlikely to move beyond pure surmise.

The episode of Theodosius' campaign against the usurper might actually also hide a story behind the story. The account, as it stands, allows Theodosius to claim all the credit for the pacification of the province. However, modern specialists in late Roman politics have noted some time ago, that third and fourth century usurpations are not only fuelled by the need of the usurper to become the Emperor of the Roman Empire, but appear sometimes to have arisen in response to a local crisis in the province and the unwillingness or (increasingly) the inability of the Emperor to respond to this problem. The latter was possibly a contributing factor in the creation of the Gallic Empire, and very likely in the later British usurpations (such as Carausius but also Constantine III), as well as a number of usurpations in the Balkans and the East (e.g. Odenathus). Amongst the many possible readings of this passage of Ammianus', it cannot be ruled out that Valentinus' usurpation was a local response within Britain to the Barbarian Conspiracy and the rather convoluted sequence of fact-finding missions and possibly undermanned response teams. However, as we only have the pro-Theodosian accounts, our hypothesis has to remain exactly that for the moment.

A further problem is the scale of the operations. Ammianus' account is willing to credit Theodosius with wide-ranging reforms and rebuilding; and in the past numerous burnt layers and refurbishment phases, including a whole phase on Hadrian's Wall, have been claimed to show the results of this campaign. A better understanding of the pottery sequence, as well as further excavation, now leaves us with very little evidence for any of this rebuilding and construction. Even the Yorkshire coast towers, long associated with this campaign, are now seen to be about 15 years later and more likely to be associated with Magnus Maximus (see below).

This leaves the fourth century historian with the question: how much of the historical account can be trusted? Is the account, as presented, as exaggerated as the Panegyrics, or are archaeologists just looking in the wrong place? We have seen in earlier chapters, that evidence for warfare itself can be hard to identify in the archaeological record and the Barbarian Conspiracy is no exception. In fact, because of the vagueness of the account, we cannot even be sure which parts of the province were affected. Hadrian's Wall appears to show remarkably little damage at the period in question; so did the Picts circumnavigate the Wall, only to strike at the softer, richer targets further south? If so, it would be good to have a better understanding of the coastal defences around Britain at the time, but while we have a series of forts that could have served as such, there are still long stretches of open coast, plus, especially on the coast of North Yorkshire and County Durham, too much erosion to get a reliable picture of the system, if coastal defence at the time was indeed designed as a single system. Are we correct in reading *comes tractus maritimae* as a synonym for the Saxon Shore command, or should we reconsider an old suggestion that this was more likely to refer to another coastal command in the West (after all it was the Scotti who were involved in the conspiracy)? Any position chosen is likely to have serious effects on the resulting view of the province in the later fourth century, but as so often before, the amount of evidence allows for multiple valid scenarios, but not for a definitive decision as to which one is right.

Valentia

The direct aftermath of Theodosius' activities in Britain in 367/368 was 'the recovery of the part of the province that had fallen to the enemy', which was reconstituted as Valentia (Amm. Marc. 28.3.7). This term Valentia is also used by the Notitia Dignitatum and Polemius Silvius (who also knows of a sixth province 'Orcades', whose existence is a matter of contention between scholars, some of whom prefer to see it as an interpolation, based on it being mentioned in Eutropius).

A lot of ink has been spilled about the exact meaning and position of the province, and suggestions range from a separate province north of the Wall, to it being a new name for the whole diocese of Britannia, to it replacing the name of one of the old provinces or being split from any of the four pre-existing provinces south of the Wall. As the total evidence consists of no more than this reference to its creation and two other brief mentions, it is impossible to progress further than to admit that given our problems with the location of the four original Constantinian provinces there are just too many unknowns to come to any definitive conclusion, unless further evidence (perhaps in the form of an inscription) is discovered.

Magnus Maximus

There is now a hiatus of 14 years before Britain is mentioned again in the late Roman sources. In 383 one of the British military commanders, Magnus Maximus was declared Emperor by his troops. Very little is known about him, except that two years later he defeated and supplanted Valentinian's son, the Emperor Gratian (367/383) and remained in power until 388, when he was captured and killed by Theodosius the Great, who might possibly have been a distant relative.

The Gallic Chronicle of 452, a fifth century Gallic source, reports for the year after his accession, that Magnus Maximus defeated energetically the invading Scots and Picts, suggesting that half a generation after the Theodosian campaigns, there were new attacks on the British province.

In addition, his bid for power might have led to the loss of troops from Britain. At least one unit the *(pedites) Seguntienses* (presumably originally from Segontium/Carnarvon, but other places with similar names exist in the Roman Empire, most famously Saguntum in Spain) is listed in the Notitia Dignitatum as stationed in Illyricum. Older histories of Britain blame Magnus Maximus for a serious depletion of troops, thus weakening the frontier and allowing further raiding. As under Magnentius, this claim, while possible, cannot be substantiated. One single unit is hardly a significant weakening, especially as it is quite possible that it may have formed part of a troop exchange, as there are numerous examples in the Notitia of troops from the Continent stationed in Britain, such as the *militum Turnacensium* in Lympne, which would presumably originally have come from Tournai in northern Gaul. These patterns of raising troops in one area and stationing them elsewhere was after all a tradition that dated back to the beginnings of the Roman Empire under Augustus.

A feature that has been recently ascribed to Magnus Maximus is the construction of the Yorkshire Coast towers. This series of coastal installations are commonly agreed to be the last system of military installations to have been constructed in Roman Britain. The system, as currently known, consists of six small military installations at Huntcliff, possibly Whitby, Goldsborough, Ravenscar, Scarborough and Filey. All of the surviving sites resemble the *burgi* found elsewhere in the Western Roman Empire. A large ditch surrounds a perimeter wall with a single entrance and four slightly projecting corner towers. The sites are about 30 x 30 metres. In the centre is a thick-walled tower measuring 15 x 15 metres, which has internal supports, suggesting that it was able to support a building of considerable height (possibly as high as 20m). The Ravenscar inscription (RIB 721) gives us the Latin name for these structures: *turris et castrum* (tower and fort); on the Continent they are commonly referred to as *burgi*.

Most of the Continental *burgi* were built by Valentinian I (364/375), which has led us to ascribe them to rebuilding in the aftermath of the Barbarian Conspiracy. The coin profile from the installations would, however, fit better with a date under Magnus Maximus. The find, profiles from these towers, especially Filey, suggest that they stayed in use to the end of Roman Britain or beyond.

At the very end of the fourth century, Britain's military establishment once again received attention from the central court. Two laudatory speeches by Claudian praising Stilicho, the *magister militum* of Honorius (393/423) appear to refer to his taking some 'protective measures'. Birley (2005, 452f.) argues that this may have taken place after the review of the Rhine frontier in 398, but admits that the references are vague, and it should not be ruled out that Claudian was indulging in a literary flourish, reviewing all the military threats of the northern frontier to portray the *magister militum*, so to speak, as the 'very model of a modern major general'.

Six years later, in 406, the situation in Britain appears to have significantly deteriorated. The various sources give several reasons, '*stasis*', i.e. mutiny of the soldiers being the most common. Olympiodorus of Thebes (a fifth century historian), and following him, his slightly younger colleagues Zosimus and Sozomen, suggest that following the invasion of Gaul in 406, the troops in Britain were afraid that they would be next.

Consequently, they put up three usurpers in quick succession: Marcus, quickly replaced by Gratianus, and finally Constantine III. The chronology of these actions and how they relate to events elsewhere in the Empire is contested and various time frames have been proposed, but the general sequence, it appears, is largely accepted. Unlike his two predecessors, after having been proclaimed Emperor, Constantine III moved his army rapidly over to the Continent. While he prepared for the battle against the Italian court and field army, the Gallic Chronicle of 452 reports that Britain suffered yet another invasion, this time by the Saxons. As a result, in 409 the British decided that as not even the Emperor they had appointed was dealing with their problems (see the notes on the motivation behind usurpations above), they would revolt against Roman rule. They expelled the remaining officials and, according to Zosimos (6.5.2–6.1) 'took up arms, braving danger for their own independence, freed the cities from the barbarians threatening them.'

Constantine III's usurpation would eventually last until 411, but as the officials being removed would have to have been Constantine's own appointees, Zosimos de facto suggests that Britain may have declared independence from the usurper, rather than the central court. In 410 Honorius, while coordinating the defence of Italy against Alaric (who would shortly sack the city of Rome), wrote a letter suggesting that the recipients should look to their own defence. The recipients are named as 'Brettania', which is clearly out of context, and as the above passage shows, Britain was screened from the central Empire by Constantine's usurpation in Gaul and Spain, and thus hard, if not impossible to reach. There has been for at least thirty years a vibrant debate as to what exact mistake Zosimos was likely to have made to reach this particular sequence of events (such as mistaking Brettania for Brettia/Bruttium in Southern Italy or confusing Bononia/Bologna in Italy with Bononia/Boulogne in France and thus thinking that he was talking about a completely different area): all parties are able to agree that the letter is clearly a mistake (see Birley 2005, 461f. for a summary of the arguments). In addition to this debate, there is also a continuing suggestion that Zosimos really meant what he said and that Honorius did take time out in Ravenna to deal with far away problems, while Rome was about to burn.

So what did the end of Roman Britain actually mean? It is debatable, in fact, whether the change of government had that much impact, at least at first. To judge from the decline in the use of coinage we must conclude that large numbers of settlements had stopped receiving new coinage after the 390s, while some sites managed to access new coin supplies until 406/408, but few if any after this date. This did not, however, mean the end of coin use everywhere. There are very late coins and silver ingots from Richborough, as well as fifth century coins known from a few (mostly eastern) parts of Britain including Hoxne, Patching, Eye, Good Easter and the coin hoard from Heddon-on-the-Wall and Great Whittington near Hadrian's Wall, which ends with a coin of 406/408 (Collins 2008). It is not clear when these late hoards were accumulated. As Casey (1993, 69–80) suggests, late Roman high quality coinage was not available to the Anglo-Saxons when they arrived, but in some areas, such as the North of England, this did not happen until the late fifth/mid sixth century, some three to five generations after '410 AD'. Destruction deposits at Filey and finds of multiple skeletons or skulls in the wells of Huntcliff and Goldsborough suggest that the inhabitants met a violent end, but the exact point when this happened remains unclear.

The defences of forts such as Vindolanda and Malton continued to be updated in the second half of the fourth century, and in the fifth, a very large ditch was dug at the southeast gate of Malton. At Vindolanda, fifth century evidence inside the fort has been accumulating over the last decade and adds to the long known Brigomaglus stone. At Birdoswald occupation continued into the sixth century in the form of timber halls on the site of the former granaries, whilst at South Shields the West Gate and *principia* show evidence of continued use into the sixth century. Occupation continued elsewhere in Britain in cities such as Silchester, at forts like Richborough, and at various rural settlements, whilst Richard Reece has argued in the Richborough report the latest coinage may have continued to circulate for quite some time after issue (Reece 1968, 200–217). But with the lack of new coinage, it is harder to construct closely dateable pottery sequences, and it seems that as the more expensive parts of Roman culture were becoming more valuable, they became all the less likely to be lost. The result is a long period after 408 where life in Roman Britain may have continued without much in the way of cataclysmic change, but also without any clearly dateable objects that allow us to distinguish this period from what went before, and so date continued

Birdoswald – evidence for continued fifth century occupation was first identified over the granaries in the centre. *David John Woolliscroft*

usage of sites, including Birdoswald or Richborough, or for that matter to date the violent end of sites like Filey. That said, there are signs that military structures survive into this late period all over the country: Chester's Fortress Baths (Mason 2005, 81f.), Richborough, Birdoswald, Vindolanda, South Shields, Segontium, York – the list is substantial. What is less clear is whether these structures continued to function as military installations or if they were increasingly turning into fortified civilian sites, or even whether such distinctions continued to have much meaning.

There did continue to be an army in Britain, or at least men who bore arms (White 2007, 195–201). Were they Roman? It is hard to say. As we have seen, the Romans had long been recruiting troops from beyond the Roman Empire and stationing them in Britain. Over time (in fact several generations) these troops had blended into the general culture of the Roman army. This blending was, however, not a one way process, but increasingly the Roman army acquired more trappings of the Germanic or other troops they were hiring, with the result that the troops paid by Allectus may indeed have been considered to be barbarian by those Romans who considered themselves 'of the old stock'. At the very least, they were markedly different from the army of the early second century. It is worth remembering, though, that Constantius' army would have probably looked just as 'barbaric' as the same processes affected the army on the Continent. By the end of the Roman Empire, Germanic mercenary troops and regular soldiers, who were second or third generation descendants of Germanic immigrants, were everywhere, and Germans were fighting on both sides. The *dux* Fullofaudes, who was caught in an ambush in the Barbarian Conspiracy had a Germanic name, so did Fraomarius, tribune of an Alamannic unit stationed in Britain in the later fourth century. It is likely that some of the Germanic mercenaries stationed in British forts would have had their families with them. If we can believe Gildas, in the end Roman Britain fell because the successor kingdoms lost control of the mercenaries they hired. What would change after 409 was the increasing number of these troops who would start operating for more localized commanders (such as the Tyranni mentioned by Gildas) or eventually for themselves, with their leaders becoming ever less officers in the Roman tradition, and ever more medieval warlords.

By 409 the Britons decided to become independent from Rome and the central government was no longer in a position to prevent them. This did not mean that there was an exodus of Roman born citizens to the Continent (much of which was overrun by other Germans at the time), any more than that the entire army of the island sailed away to defend the Imperial heartland, as it was once fashionable to claim. But it would probably have meant that British tax revenues were now spent directly on their own home needs (including military expenses), instead of being sent to Rome or at least given to an official sent from Rome. The end of the military history of Roman Britain in this scenario was thus a tax revolt, not the defeat of the Roman army. That would come later, and is usually considered to be part of the early medieval history of Britain.

Appendix I

Orosius on the Conquest of Britain under Claudius

Josephus, Jewish War 3,4 9
(Translation J. Manley)
Vespasian has added to the Empire by force of arms Britannia, although till then it had been a hidden land, and hence he provided for Nero's father, Claudius, a triumph that cost him no personal sweat.

Orosius 7,5.9–10
Claudius quarto imperii sui anno, cupiens utilem reipublicae ostentare se principem, bellum ubique et uictoriam undecumque quaesiuit. itaque expeditionem in Britanniam mouit, quae excitata in tumultum propter non redhibitos transfugas uidebatur: transuectus in insulam est, quam neque ante Iulium Caesarem neque post eum quisquam adire ausus fuerat, 10 ibique – ut uerbis Suetoni Tranquilli loquar – sine ullo proelio ac sanguine intra paucissimos dies plurimam insulae partem in deditionem recepit. Orcadas etiam insulas ultra Britanniam in Oceano positas Romano adiecit imperio ac sexto quam profectus erat mense Romam rediit.

(Orosius, Historiae adversos paganos, ed. C. Zangemeister 1889)
(Translation B. Hoffmann)

In the fourth year of the reign Claudius had the intention to prove himself to the state as a useful Emperor… Therefore he invaded Britain, which was apparently in unrest, because the refugees had not been returned. There was a crossing onto the island, which nobody either before or after Julius Caesar had dared to approach. There – in the words of Suetonius Tranquillinus – without a battle and bloodshed, he accepted in the shortest span of days the surrender of the larger part of the island. He even added the islands of the

Orkneys which lie beyond Britain in the Ocean to the Roman rule and returned to Rome in the sixth month after his departure.

Eutropius 7, 13, 3–4
(Translation J.S. Watson)

He made war upon Britain, which no Roman since Julius Caesar had visited; and, having reduced it through the agency of Cn. Sentius and A. Plautius, illustrious and noble men (a.k.a. senators), he celebrated a magnificient triumph. Certain islands also, called the Orcades, situated in the Ocean, beyond Britain, he added to the Roman Empire, and gave his son the name of Britannicus.

Appendix II

Notitia Dignitatum

R eaders of the above history will have noticed the near absence of discussion of the Notitia Dignitatum (ND). The ND is a document that was found originally bound together with a number of other texts all pertaining to Roman government and the army, and usually referred to as the Codex Spirensis. The ND itself purports to be a list of all positions in the administration of the Roman Empire towards its end, but assessments as to when exactly it was compiled differ: with dates ranging from 395 to the 430s, depending on the area covered in each chapter and whether the text was updated or left unchanged. For a long time, the British section of the Notitia has been seen as a document showing the disposition of troops close to the end of Roman Britain. A mention in the ND suggested that a fort remained in use until late in the sequence, and for much of the island, including the Saxon Shore, it is our only evidence for the military structure of the late Roman provinces. The proposed dates of composition thus focus around 408 (when it would represent the situation of the Roman army at the very end of Roman rule). But even if other suggestions are taken into account, for example that the system represents the situation in 395, and may have been updated until the 430s in places, there are difficulties in matching it with the archaeological record. There are a number of forts in the north that clearly remained in use to the end of Roman Britain, which are not listed by the ND, and the reverse is also true. Hodgson (2009, Northern Britain 28) has recently compiled a list of such problems in the North of England, showing that Ribchester and Housesteads are listed in the ND, but have archaeology that suggests they were abandoned well before 395, while Manchester and Lancaster remained in use, but are not listed. In addition it has long since been noted that the ND omitted any mention of Wales, something that is sometimes explained away as the loss of a page. But such problems are not restricted to Britain; they form a general failing of the document.

Kulikowski (2000) has recently argued that rather than portraying an actual state of play, the ND might have been a document created as a memorandum or wish-list of the government in Ravenna, an image of what a restored Empire might look like, drawing on old records, but not laying claim to current accuracy. If this were the case, it would fit well with another document in the Codex Spirensis, the '*de re militari*', substantial parts of which appear to consist of great ideas that ought to be implemented at some point in the future. Kulikowski's argument will no doubt be bemoaned by many, as it robs Late Roman archaeology of a heretofore useful source, but it would certainly go a long way towards explaining the numerous problems of the text. For the moment it might be safest to suggest that if a site is documented in the ND, it may have existed at some point in the fourth century, but it may be well worth checking against the archaeology whether the information can be deemed accurate.

Bibliography

Aldhouse-Green, M. (2006). *Boudica Britannia: Rebel, War-leader and Queen*. Harlow, New York, Pearson.

Atkinson, M. and Preston, M. J. (1998). "The Late Iron Age and Roman settlement at Elms Farm, Heybridge, Essex, excavations 1993–5: an interim report." *Britannia* 29: 85–110.

Scriptores Historiae Augustae (2000). Historia Augusta. *Loeb Classical Library*. D. Magie. Cambridge, Mass., Harvard University Press.

Aurelius Victor (1994). De Caesaribus. Translated with an introduction and commentary by H. W. Bird. Liverpool, Liverpool University Press.

Balsdon, J. P. D. (1934). *The Emperor Gaius (Caligula)*. Westport, Connecticut, Greenwood Press.

Barnes, T. D. (1981). Constantine and Eusebius. Cambridge and London, Harvard University Press.

Barrett, A. A. (1989). *Caligula. The Corruption of Power*. London, Guild Publishing.

Barrett, A. A. (1990). "Chronological Errors in Dio's Account of the Claudian Invasion." *Britannia* 11: 31–33.

Barrett, A. A. (1991). "Claudius' British Victory Arch in Rome." *Britannia* 22: 1–21.

Barrett, A. A. (1998). "The Date of Claudius' British Campaign and the Mint of Alexandria." *Classical Quarterly* 48(2): 574–577.

Barrett, J. C., Freeman, P. W. M. et al. (2000). *Cadbury Castle, Somerset. The Later prehistoric and early historic archaeology*. London.

Bates, S. (2000). "Excavations at Quidney Farm, Saham Toney, Norfolk 1995." *Britannia* 31: 201–238.

Bidwell, P. (1999). *Hadrian's Wall 1989–1999*. Kendal, Titus Wilson & Son Ltd.

Bidwell, P. (2005). "The systems of obstacles on Hadrian's Wall, their extent, date and purpose." *Arbeia Journal* 8: 53–76.

Bidwell, P. (2008). *Understanding Hadrian's Wall. Papers from a conference held at South Shields, 3–5 November, 2006, to mark the publication of the 14th edition of the Handbook to the Roman Wall*. Kendal, Arbeia Society.

Bidwell, P. and Hodgson, N. (2009). *The Roman Army in Northern England*. Newcastle, Arbeia Society.

Bidwell, P. and Speak, S. (1994). *Excavations at South Shields Roman Fort.* Newcastle on Tyne Society of Antiquaries of Newcastle on Tyne with Tyne and Wear Museums.

Bird, D. G. (2000). "The Claudian Invasion campaign reconsidered." *Oxford Journal of Archaeology* 19(1): 91–104.

Bird, D. (2004). *Roman Surrey.* Stroud, Tempus.

Birley, A. and Blake, J. (2005). *Vindolanda Excavations 2003–2004.* Bardon Mill, Vindolanda Trust.

Birley, A. R. (1981). *The Fasti of Roman Britain.* Oxford, Clarendon Press.

Birley, A. R. (1997). *Hadrian the Restless Emperor.* London and New York, Routledge.

Birley, A. R. (1998). "A new Tombstone from Vindolanda." *Britannia* 29: 299–306.

Birley, A. R. (2005). *The Roman Government of Britain.* Oxford, Oxford University Press.

Birley, E. (1951). "The Brigantian problem and the first Roman contact with Scotland." *Transactions of the Dumfriesshire and Galloway Natural History and Antiquarian Society* 29: 46–65.

Birley, E. (1976). *Roman Britain and the Roman Army. Collected Papers.* Kendal, Titus Wilson & Son Ltd.

Bishop, M. C. and Dore, J. N. (1988). *Corbridge. Excavations of the Roman fort and town, 1947–80.* London, HBMCE.

Black, E. W. (1998). "'How many rivers to cross'." *Britannia* 29: 306–307.

Black, E. W. (2000). "Sentius Saturninus and the Roman Invasions of Britain." *Britannia* 31: 1–10.

Branigan, K. and Niblett, R. (no year). *The Roman Chilterns.* Chesham, Chess Valley Archaeological Society.

Braund, D. (1996). *Ruling Roman Britain: Kings, Queens, Governors and Emperors from Julius Caesar to Agricola.* London and New York, Routledge.

Breeze, D. J. (2003). "Warfare in Britain and the Building of Hadrian's Wall." *Archaeologia Aeliana. Fifth Series* 32: 13–16.

Breeze, D. J. (2006). *The Antonine Wall.* Edinburgh, John Donald.

Breeze, D. J. (2006). *Roman Scotland: Frontier Country.* London, Batsford/ Historic Scotland.

Breeze, D. J. (2011), The Roman Military Occupation of Northern England. Transactions Cumberland and Westmoreland Antiquarian and Archaeological Society. 3rd series. 11, 113–136.

Breeze, D. J. (2011b). The Frontiers of Imperial Rome. Barnsley, Pen & Sword.

Breeze, D. J. and Woolliscroft, D. J. (2009). *Excavation and Survey at Roman Burgh-by-Sands.* Kendal, Cumberland and Westmorland Antiquarian and Archaeological Society.

Brodersen, K. (1998). *Das römische Britannien. Spuren seiner Geschichte.* Darmstadt, Wissenschaftliche Buchgesellschaft.

Bushe-Fox, J.P. (1913), The use of Samian pottery in dating the early Roman occupation of the north of Britain. Archaeologia 64, 296–317.

Bushe-Fox, J. P. (1932). *Third Report on the Excavations at the Roman fort of Richborough.* London Society of Antiquaries.

Bushe-Fox, J. P. (1949). *Fourth Report on the Excavations at the Roman Fort of Richborough*. London, Society of Antiquaries.

Caesar, J. De Bello Gallico. *Loeb Classical Library*. Cambridge, Mass. and London, Harvard University Press.

Casey, P. J. (1987). "The coinage of Alexandria and the chronology of Hadrian." *Melanges Bastien*: 65–72.

Casey, P. J. (1993). The end of garrisons on Hadrian's Wall: an historico-environmental model. *The Later Roman Empire Today*,. D. Clark, M. Roxan and J. J. Wilkes. London, University College of London: 69–80.

Casey, P. J. (1994). *Carausius and Allectus: The British Usurpers*. London, Batsford.

Casey, P. J. and M. Savage (1980). "The coins from the excavations at High Rochester in 1852 and 1855." *Archaeologia Aeliana. Fifth Series* 8: 75–89.

Cassius Dio (1932). Roman History vol. VIII: Book Epitome of LXI-LXX. *Loeb Classical Library*. E. Cary. Cambridge, Mass, Harvard University Press.

Cassius Dio (1982). Roman History: Books LVI-LX. *Loeb Classical Library*. E. Cary. Cambridge, Mass., Harvard University Press.

Cassius Dio (1982). Roman History: Books LXI-LXX. *Loeb Classical Library*. E. Cary. Cambridge, Mass., Harvard University Press.

Clarke, K. (2001). "An island Nation: Re-reading Tacitus' Agricola." *Journal of Roman Studies* 91: 94–112.

Collingwood, R. G. and Myres, J. N. L. (2.1937). *Roman Britain and the English Settlements*. Oxford, Clarendon.

Collins, R. (2008). "The Latest Roman Coin from Hadrian's Wall: A Small Fifth-century Purse Group." *Britannia* 39: 256–261.

Cooper, N. J. and Buckley, R. (2003). New Light on Roman Leicester (Ratae Corieltauvorum). *The Archaeology of Roman towns*. P. Wilson. Oxford, Oxbow: 31–44.

Creighton, J. (2006). *Britannia. The creation of a Roman province*. London and New York, Routledge.

Crow, J. G. (1991). "A Review of current research on the Turrets and Curtain of Hadrian's Wall." *Britannia* 22: 51–65.

Crummy, P. (1997). *City of Victory: The Story of Colchester – Britain's first Roman town*. Colchester Archaeological Trust.

Crummy, P. (2003). Colchester's Roman town wall. *The Archaeology of Roman Towns*. P. Wilson. Oxford, Oxbow: 44–52.

Crummy, P., Benfield, S., et al. (2007). *Stanway: An Elite burial site at Camulodunum*. London, Society for the Promotion of Roman Studies.

Cunliffe, B., Ed. (1968). *Fifth Report on the Excavations at the Roman Fort at Richborough*. London, Society of Antiquaries.

Cunliffe, B. (1971). *Fishbourne: A Roman Palace and its Garden*. London, Thames and Hudson.

Cunliffe, B. (1995). *Iron Age Britain*. London, English Heritage.

Cunliffe, B. (2008). *Europe between the Oceans. 9000BC–AD1000*. New Haven and London, Yale University Press.

Daniels, C. M. and Harbottle, B. (1980). "A new inscription of Julia Domna from Newcastle." *Archaeologia Aeliana. Fifth Series* 8: 65–75.

Davies, J. (2009). *The Land of Boudica: Prehistoric and Roman Norfolk*. Oxford, Oxbow.

Davies, J. and Robinson, B. (2009). *Boudica: Her Life, Times and Legacy*. Cromer, Poppyland Publishing.

Davies, J. L. and Jones, R. H. (2006). *Roman Camps in Wales and the Marches*. Cardiff, University of Wales Press.

de la Bédoyère, G. (1998). "Carausius and the Marks RSR and INPCDA" in *Numismatic Chronicle* 158: 79–88.

Demandt, A., Engemann, J. (2006). Imperator Caesar Flavius Constantinus . Konstantin der Grosse . Trier, Konstantin-Ausstellungsgesellschaft.

Dobat, E. (2009). The Gask 'system' in Perthshire: the first artificial frontier line of the Roman Empire? *First Contact. Rome and Northern Britain. Tayside and Fife Archaeological Committee Monograph 7*. D. J. Breeze, L. M. Thoms and D. W. Hall. Perth, Tayside and Fife Archaeological Committee: 39–48.

Feldherr, A. (2009). *The Cambridge Companion to the Roman Historians*, Cambridge, Cambridge University Press.

Fraser, J. E. (2009). *From Caledonia to Pictland. Scotland to 795*. Edinburgh, Edinburgh University Press.

Frere, S. and Fulford, M. (2001). "The Roman Invasion of Britain of AD 43." *Britannia* 32: 45–55.

Frere, S. S. (3.1987). *Britannia. A History of Roman Britain*. London, Pimlico.

Frere, S. S. (2000). "M.Maenius Agrippa, the expeditio Britannica and Maryport." *Britannia* 31: 23–29.

Fronto, M. C. (1963). The correspondence of Marcus Cornelius Fronto with Marcus Aurelius Antoninus, Lucius Verus, Antoninus Pius and Various Friends. *Loeb Classical Library*. Cambridge, Mass., Harvard University Press.

Fuentes, N. (1983). "Boudicca re-visited." *London Archaeologist* 4(12): 311–317.

Fulford, M. and Timby, J. (2000). *Late Iron Age and Roman Silchester. Excavations on the Site of the Forum Basilica 1977, 1980–86*. London, Society for the Promotion of Roman Studies.

Fulford, M. and Tyers, I. (1995). "The date of Pevensey and the defence of an 'Imperium Britanniarum'." *Antiquity* 69(266): 1009–1014.

Gechter, M. (2001). Das römische Bonn – ein historischer Ueberblick. *Geschichte der Stadt Bonn in vier Bänden. I. Bonn von der Vorgeschichte biz zum Ende der Römerzeit*. M. Van Rey. Bonn, Stadtarchiv: 35–180.

Gibson, D. and Lucas, G. (2002). "Pre-Flavian kilns at Greenhouse Farm and the Social Context of early Roman pottery production in Cambridgeshire." *Britannia* 33: 95–129.

Gillam, J. P. (1953). "Calpurnius Agricola and the Northern Frontier." *Transactions of the Architectural and Archaeological Society of Durham and Northumberland* 10(4): 359–375.

Goldsworthy, A. (2006). *Caesar*. London, Weidenfeld & Nicolson.

Grainge, G. (2002). *The Roman Channel Crossing of A.D. 43*. Oxford, Tempus Reparatum.

Grainge, G. (2005). *The Roman Invasions of Britain*. Stroud, Tempus.

Grainger, J.D. (2003). Nerva and the Roman Succession Crisis of 96–98 AD. London and New York, Routledge.

Grasby, R. D. and Tomlin, R. S. O. (2002). "The Sepulchral Monument of the procurator C. Julius Classicianus." *Britannia* 33: 43–76.

Haensch, R. (1997). *Capita Provinciarum. Statthaltersitze und Provinzialverwaltung in der roemischen Kaiserzeit*. Mainz, Philipp von Zabern.

Halsall, M. (2000). Pre-Hadrianic Legionary dispositions in Britain. *Roman Fortress and their Legions*. R. J. Brewer. London, Society of Antiquaries: 51–67.

Hanson, W. S. (1978). "Roman Campaigns North of the Forth-Clyde Isthmus: the Evidence of the Temporary Camps." *Proceedings of the Society of Antiquaries of Scotland* 109: 140–150.

Hanson, W. S. (1987). *Agricola and the Conquest of the North*. London, Batsford.

Hanson, W. S. (2007). *Elginhaugh: A Flavian fort and its Annexe*. London.

Hanson, W. S. (2009). The fort at Elginhaugh and its implications for Agricola's role in the conquest of Scotland. *First Contact. Rome and Northern Britain. Tayside and Fife Archaeological Committee Monograph 7*. D. J. Breeze, L. M. Thoms and D. W. Hall. Perth, Tayside and Fife Archaeological Committee: 49–59.

Hanson, W. S. and Campbell, D. B. (1986). "The Brigantes: from Clientage to Conquest." *Britannia* 17: 73–91.

Hartley, E., Hawkes, J., Henig, M. and Mee, F. (2006). Constantine the Great. York's Roman Emperor. York Museums and Gallery Trust.

Hartgroves, S. and Smith, J. (2008). "A Second Roman fort is confirmed in Cornwall." *Britannia* 39: 237–239.

Haselgrove, C., Fitts, R., Turnbull, P. (1991). Stanwick, North Yorkshire, Part 1: recent research and archaeological investigations. Archaeological Journal 147, 1–15.

Haselgrove, C., Armit, I., et al. (2001). *Understanding the British Iron Age: An Agenda for Action*. Salisbury, Wessex Archaeology.

Haverfield, F. (1904). "Discovery of Roman inscriptions etc, at Newcastle." *Archaeologia Aeliana. Second Series* 25: 142–144.

Henig, M. (2004). A house divided: the study of Roman art and the art of Roman Britain. *Archaeology and Ancient History: Breaking Down the Boundaries*. E. W. Sauer. New York and London, Routledge: 134–151.

Herodian (1970). Herodian in Two Volumes. *Loeb Classical Library*. C. R. Whittaker. Cambridge, Mass., Harvard University Press.

Hind, J. G. F. (1989). "The Invasion of Britain in AD 43 – An Alternative Strategy for Aulus Plautius." *Britannia* 20: 1–21.

Hind, J. G. F. (2007). "A.Plautius' campaign in Britain: an alternative reading of the narrative in Cassius Dio (60.19.5–21.2)." *Britannia* 38: 93–107.

Hingley, R. (2005). "Freedom fighter – or tale for Romans?" *British Archaeology* (83): 40–41.

Hobley, A. S. (1989). "The Numismatic Evidence for the Post-Agricolan Abandonment of the Roman Frontier in Northern Scotland." *Britannia* 20: 69–75.

Hodgson, N. (2000). "The Stanegate: a frontier rehabilitated." *Britannia* 31: 11–22.

Hodgson, N. (2009). The abandonment of Antonine Scotland: its date and causes. *The Army and Frontiers of Rome*. W. S. Hanson. Portsmouth, Rhode Island, Journal of Roman Archaeology: 185–193.

Hodgson, N. (1995). Were there two Antonine occupations of Scotland? Britannia 26, 29–49.

Hodgson, N. (2009). *Hadrians Wall 1999–2009*. Kendal, Titus Wilson & Son Ltd.

Hodgson, N. (2009). *Roman Scotland*. Newcastle upon Tyne, Tyne and Wear Museums.

Hoffmann, B. (2002). 'Where have all the Soldiers gone? Some thoughts on the Presence and Absence of Soldiers in Fourth Century Chester. *Deva Victrix: Thirty years of Research on Roman Chester.* P. Carrington (ed.). Chester, Chester Archaeological Society: 79–88.

Hoffmann, B. (2004). Tacitus, Agricola and the role of literature in the archaeology of the first century AD. *Archaeology and Ancient History: Breaking Down the Boundaries.* E. W. Sauer. New York and London, Routledge: 151–167.

Hoffmann, B. (2009). Cardean: the changing face of a Flavian fort in Scotland. *First Contact. Rome and Northern Britain. Tayside and Fife Archaeological Committee Monograph 7.* D. J. Breeze, L. M. Thoms and D. W. Hall. Perth, Tayside and Fife Archaeological Committee: 29–32.

Holmes, N., Collard, M., et al. (2003). *Excavations of Roman Sites at Cramond, Edinburgh.* Edinburgh.

Howarth, N. (2008). *Cartimandua. Queen of the Brigantes.* Stroud, The History Press.

Howe, F. and Lakin, D. (2004), Roman and medieval Cripplegate, City of London. Archaeological excavations 1992–8. MoLAS Monograph 21. London, Museum of London.

Hunter, F. (2007). *Beyond the edge of the empire – Caledonians, Picts and Romans.* Rosemarkie, Groam House.

Ireland, S. (2008). *Roman Britain. A Sourcebook.* London & New York, Routledge.

Jarrett, M. G. (1964). "Early Roman Campaigns in Wales." *The Archaeological Journal* 121: 23–39.

Jarrett, M. G. (1976). "An Unnecessary War." *Britannia* 7: 145–152.

Johnson, S. (1976). *The Roman forts of the Saxon Shore* London, English Heritage.

Jones, B. and Mattingly, D. (1990). *An Atlas of Roman Britain.* London, Blackwell.

Jones, G. D. B. and Reynolds, P. (1987). A probable Roman supply depot at Llansantffraid-ym-Mechain (Powys), *Manchester Archaeological Bulletin,* 2, 21–6.

Jones, G. D. B. and Woolliscroft, D. J. (2001). *Hadrian's Wall from the Air.* Stroud Tempus.

Jones, M. J. (2002). *Roman Lincoln. Conquest, Colony & Capital.* Stroud, Tempus.

Jones, M. J. (2003). Water through Roman Lincoln. *The Archaeology of Roman Towns.* P. Wilson. Oxford, Oxbow: 111–128.

Jones, R. H. (2009). Chasing the army: the problems of dating temporary camps. *First Contact. Rome and Northern Britain. Tayside and Fife Archaeological Committee Monograph 7.* D. J. Breeze, L. M. Thoms and D. W. Hall. Perth, Tayside and Fife Archaeological Committee: 21–28.

Jones, R. H. (2009). Recent work on Roman camps in Scotland. *Roman Scotland.* N. Hodgson. Newcastle upon Tyne, Tyne and Wear Museums.

Justin, C. Nepos, et al. (1910). (literally translated, with notes and a general Index by the Rev. John Selby Watson). J. S. Watson. London, G. Bell and Sons.

Karl, R. (2004). Celtoscepticiscm: a convenient excuse for ignoring non-archaeological evidence? *Archaeology and Ancient History: Breaking Down the Boundaries*. E. W. Sauer. New York and London, Routledge: 185–200.

Kaye, S. (2010). "Can Computerised Terrain Analysis Find Boudica's Last Battlefield?" *British Archaeology* 114(Sept-Oct).

Kemmers, F. (2006). "Coins, Countermarks and Caligula. The Connection between the auxiliary forts in the Lower Rhine delta and the invasion of Britain." *Hadrianic Society Bulletin, n.s.* 1: 5–11.

Kienast, D. (1990). *Römische Kaisertabelle*. Darmstadt, Wissenschaftliche Buchgesellschaft.

Kulikowski, M. (2000). "The "Notitia Dignitatum" as a Historical Source." *Historia: Zeitschrift fuer Alte Geschichte* 49(3): 358–377.

Laurence, R. (2004). The uneasy dialogue between ancient history and archaeology. *Archaeology and Ancient History: Breaking Down the Boundaries*. E. W. Sauer. New York and London, Routledge: 99–114.

Leslie, A. (2002). "The Roman fort at Inveresk". In Bishop, M. C. (ed.). *Roman Inveresk: Past, Present and Future*. Duns, The Armatura Press. 17–28.

Levick, B. (1990). *Claudius*. Batsford, London.

Lewin, T. (1862). *The invasions of Britain by Julius Caesar (2nd edition)*. London, Longman, Green, Longman & Roberts.

Lyne, M. (2009). *Excavations at Pevensey Castle, 1936 and 1964*. Oxford, Tempus Reparatum.

Manley, J. and D. Rudkin (2003). *Facing the Palace: Excavations in Front of the Roman Palace at Fishbourne*. Lewes, Sussex Archaeological Society.

Mason, D. J. P. (2000). *The Elliptical Building: An image of the Roman world*. Chester, Chester City Council.

Mason, D. J. P. (2001). *Roman Chester. City of Eagles*. Stroud, Tempus.

Mason, D. J. P. (2003). *Roman Britain and the Roman Navy*. Stroud, Tempus.

Mason, D. J. P. (2005). *Excavations at Chester: The Roman Fortress Baths, Excavation and recording 1732–1998*. Chester, Chester City Council.

Matthews, K. J. (1999). The Iron Age of North-West England and Irish Sea Trade. *Northern Exposure: interpretative devolution and the Iron Ages in Britain*. B. Bevan. Leicester, School of Archaeological Studies. 4: 173–197.

Mattingly, D. (2006). *An Imperial Possession*. London, Penguin.

Maxfield, V. A. (1989). *The Saxon Shore. A Handbook*. Exeter, Exeter Dept of Archaeology and History.

Maxwell, G.S. (1991). Springboards for Invasion: Marching-camp concentrations and coastal installations in Roman Scotland. *Roman Frontier Studies 1989: Proceedings of the XVth International Congress of Roman Frontier Studies*. Maxfield, V.A. and Dobson, M.J. University of Exeter. 111–113.

McWhirr, A. (1970). "The Early Military History of the Roman East Midlands." *Transactions of the Leicestershire Archaeological and Historical Society* 45: 1–19.

Meier, C. (1995). *Caesar*. London, BCA.

Mellor, R. (1993). *Tacitus*. London and New York, Routledge.

Mellor, R. (1999). *The Roman Historians*. London and New York, Routledge.

Millar, F. (2.1999). *A study of Cassius Dio*. Oxford, University Press.

Millett, M. (1990). *The Romanization of Britain*. Cambridge, Cambridge University Press.

Millett, M. and Wilmott, T. (2003). Rethinking Richborough. *The Archaeology of Roman towns*. P. Wilson. Oxford, Oxbow: 184–194.

Niblett, R. (2001). *Verulamium. The Roman city of St.Albans*. Stroud, Tempus.

Nixon, C. E. V. and Rodgers, B. S. (1995). In Praise of Later Roman Emperors. the Panegyrici Latini. Introduction, Translation and Historical Commentary. Berkeley, University of California Press.

Ogilvie, R. M. and Richmond, I. (1967). *Cornelii Taciti, De Vita Agricolae*. Oxford, Clarendon Press.

Orosius,   Historiarum   adversum   paganos   libri   VII   ex   recogn. C. Zangemeister.Teubner, 1889.

Ottaway, P. (2004). *Roman York*. Stroud, Tempus.

Philp, B. (1981). *The Excavation of the Roman forts of the Classis Britannica at Dover, 1970–1977*. Dover, Kent Archaeological Unit.

Philp, B. (2005). *The Excavations of the Roman fort at Reculver, Kent*. Canterbury, Kent Archaeological Society.

Polak, M., Kloosterman, R. P. J., et al. (2004). *Alphen aan den Rijn – Albaniana 2001–2002*. Nijmegen.

Poulter, J. (1998). "The date of the Stanegate and a hypothesis about the manner and timing of the construction of Roman roads in Britain." *Archaeologia Aeliana. Fifth Series* 26: 49–56.

Reece, R. (1968). Summary of the Roman coins from Richborough. *Fifth Report on the excavations of the Roman fort at Richborough, Kent*. B. W. Cunliffe. Oxford, Society of Antiquaries: 200–217.

Rice Holmes, T. (1907). *Ancient Britain and the Invasion of Julius Caesar*. Oxford, Clarendon Press.

Richmond, I. A. (2.1963). *Roman Britain*. Harmondsworth, Penguin.

Richmond, I.A. and McIntyre, J (1939), The Agricolan fort at Fendoch. Proceedings of the Society of Antiquaries of Scotland 73, 110–154.

Ritterling, E. von. (1924). Legio. *Pauly's Realencyclopädie der classischen Altertumswissenschaft* 12, 1: 1186–1837.

Russell, M. (2006). "Nero to the south. Hero to the North." *British Archaeology* 89: 42–47.

Russell, M. (2009). *Bloodline. The Celtic kings of Roman Britain*. Stroud, Amberley.

Salway, P. (1981). *Roman Britain*. Oxford, Clarendon Press.

Sauer, E. (2001). "Alchester Roman Fortress." *Current Archaeology* (173): 189–191.

Sauer, E. (2005). "Alchester: In search of Vespasian." *Current Archaeology* (196): 168–176.

Sauer, E. W. (2002). "The Roman Invasion of Britain (AD 43) in Imperial Perspective: a response to Frere and Fulford." *Oxford Journal of Archaeology* 21(4): 333–363.

Sauer, E. W. (2004). *Archaeology and Ancient History: Breaking Down the Boundaries*. New York and London, Routledge.

Sharples, N. (1991). *Maiden Castle*. London, English Heritage.

Shotter, D. (2009). When did the Romans invade Scotland? *First Contact. Rome and Northern Britain. Tayside and Fife Archaeological Committee Monograph 7.* D. J. Breeze, L. M. Thoms and D. W. Hall. Perth, Tayside and Fife Archaeological Committee: 15–21.

St. Joseph (1951), Air reconnaissance in North Britain. Journal of Roman Studies 41, 52–65.

Statius (1955). Silvae – Thebaid I-IV. *Loeb Classical Library*. J. H. Mozley. Cambridge, Massachusetts, Harvard University Press.

Suetonius (1980). The Twelve Caesars. An illustrated edition. Harmondsworth, Penguin.

Suetonius Tranquillinus (1997). Lives of the Caesars II. *Loeb Classical Library*. Boston, Mass., Harvard University Press.

Syme, R. (1963). *Tacitus*. Oxford, Clarendon Press.

Tacitus (1937). *The Annals. Books XIII-XVI. Loeb Classical Library*. Cambridge, Mass. & London, Harvard University Press.

Tacitus (1999). Agricola.Germany. *Oxford World Classics*. A. R. Birley. Oxford, Oxford University Press.

Tacitus, P. C. (1984). Historiae. *Sammlung Tusculum*. J. Borst, H. Hross and H. Borst. Muenchen und Zuerich, Artemis.

Tacitus, P. C. (1985). *Saemtliche Werke*. W. Boetticher and A. Schaefer. Stuttgart, Fackelverlag.

Todd, M. (2007). "Roman military occupation at Hembury (Devon)." *Britannia* 38: 107–125.

Waite, J. (2007). *Boudica's Last Stand*. Stroud, Tempus.

Walker, D. R. (1988). Roman coins from the Sacred Spring in Bath. *The Temple of Sulis Minerva at Bath, II: Finds from the Sacred Spring*. ed. B. Cunliffe. Oxford: 281–338.

Wallace-Hadrill, A. (1983). *Suetonius: the scholar and his Caesars*. Duckworth.

Webster, G. (1960). "The Roman Military advance under Ostorius Scapula." *The Archaeological Journal* 115: 49–98.

Webster, G. (1978). Boudicca. London, Batsford.

Webster, G. (1980). *The Roman Invasion of Britain*. London, Batsford

Webster, G. (1981). *Rome against Caratacus. The Roman campaigns in Britain AD 48–58*. London, Batsford.

Webster, G., (ed.). (1988). *Fortress into City. The consolidation of Roman Britain*. London, Batsford.

Webster, G. and Chadderton, J. (2002). *The Legionary Fortress at Wroxeter*. London, English Heritage.

Webster, G. and Dudley, D. R. (1965). *The Roman Conquest of Britain*. London, Pan Books.

Welfare, H. and Swan, V. (1995). *Roman Camps in England. The Field Archaeology*. London, HMSO.

Wheeler, R. E. M. (1954). The Stanwick Fortifications: North Riding of Yorkshire. London, Society of Antiquaries.

White, D.A. (1961). *Litus Saxonicum*. Madison, Wisconsin.

White, R. (2007). *Britannia Prima. Britain's last Province*. Stroud, Tempus.

Wilson, P., Ed. (2003). *The Archaeology of Roman Towns*. Oxford, Oxbow.

Wilson, P. (2009). Holding the line? The Humber frontier and the expansion into Yorkshire reconsidered. *First Contact. Rome and Northern Britain. Tayside and Fife Archaeological Committee Monograph 7*. D. J. Breeze, L. M. Thoms and D. W. Hall. Perth, Tayside and Fife Archaeological Committee. pp.8–14.

Wolfson, S. (2008). *Tacitus, Thule and Caledonia. The achievements of Agricola's navy in their true perspective*. Oxford, Tempus Reparatum.

Woolliscroft, D. (2009). 79 AD and all that: when did the Romans reach Perthshire? *First Contact. Rome and Northern Britain. Tayside and Fife Archaeological Committee Monograph 7*. D. J. Breeze, L. M. Thoms and D. W. Hall. Perth, Tayside and Fife Archaeological Committee: 33–38.

Woolliscroft, D. J. (2001). *Roman Military Signalling*. Stroud Tempus.

Woolliscroft, D. J. (2002). *The Roman Frontier on the Gask Ridge, Perth and Kinross*. Oxford, Tempus Reparatum.

Woolliscroft, D. J. and Hoffmann, B. (2006). *Rome's First Frontier. The Flavian Occupation of Northern Scotland*. Stroud, Tempus.

Zonaras, (2009) The History of Zonaras: From Alexander Severus to the Death of Theodosius the Great. Transl. Banchich, T. and Lane, E. London, Routledge.

Zosimus (1814), New History. London, Green and Chaplin.

Index